Adaptation or Expiration in Family Firms

Adaptation or Expiration in Family Firms

Organizational Flexibility in Emerging Economies

Andrés Hatum

IAE Business School
Austral University
Argentina

Edward Elgar

Cheltenham, UK • Northampton, MA, USA

Published by
Edward Elgar Publishing Limited
Glensanda House
Montpellier Parade
Cheltenham
Glos GL50 1UA
UK

Edward Elgar Publishing, Inc.
William Pratt House
9 Dewey Court
Northampton
Massachusetts 01060
USA

A catalogue record for this book
is available from the British Library

Library of Congress Control Number: 2006940755

ISBN 978 1 84542 834 1

Printed and bound in Great Britain by MPG Books Ltd, Bodmin, Cornwall

Contents

Abbreviations

FDI	foreign direct investment
GDP	gross domestic product
HR	human resource
ISI	import substituting industrialization
IT	information technology
M&A	merger and acquisition
NBE	national business environment
OTC	over-the-counter medicines
SME	small and medium size enterprise

Acknowledgements

Several people made this investigation possible. First of all, I would like to thank Professor Andrew M. Pettigrew. His patience, dedication and motivation could never be given adequate recognition. The meaning of the Spanish word 'maestro' would best illustrate the way in which Andrew has guided me throughout this journey. Without Andrew's guidance this research would not have achieved the depth it attained.

My particular gratitude to Adriana Urquía and Santiago García Belmonte for their help in opening the doors of the companies and make it possible to collect the information needed to achieve the depth of research that was needed.

I would also like to thank IAE Business School, the institution to which I have a real feeling of belonging and commitment.

During this journey I made many friends whom I would like to thank. I offer my gratitude to Anupama Mohan, Sotirios Paroutis, Lud Marquez, Paul Norris and the Spark family. Santiago, Hugo and Ezequiel, my beloved friends from Argentina, were always there to help me and boost my morale. Thanks to them and their families. Javier Quintanilla played a fundamental role, not only in helping me to settle down in a different culture, but also for the beginning of a friendship for life.

Again, to Ethna and Andrew Pettigrew, but now as friends and part of my family. Without them this journey would have been impossible. Their constant affection and support were the pillars of strength that my family and myself needed to be able to finish this research. They not only replaced our families in Argentina, but became our family and friends in England forever.

My brother Damián, my mother Hayat and my father Imad deserve the warmest gratitude possible, their affection was indispensable during these four years in England. Finally, without the love and unconditional support of my wife and my son this journey would neither have been possible nor worthwhile. I dedicate this book to Gabriela, Nicolás and Sofía.

Foreword

This is a pioneering study of organizational flexibility in the emerging economy of Argentina. It seems odd to characterize an economy which in the early part of the twentieth century was the sixth wealthiest in the world as emergent. But successively throughout the twentieth century Argentina has politically and economically lost its way and its wealth. In the period 1975–1990, just before the events detailed in this book, the Argentinian economy contracted by 17 per cent, and inflation peaked in 1989 at nearly 5000 per cent. Furthermore, exports had fallen from 3 per cent of the world total earlier in the twentieth century to 0.3 per cent in 1990 (Gerchunoff and Llach, 1998).

Political turmoil also affected the country over the period 1975–1990. A coup d'état in 1976 ended the troubled democratic government of Isabel Perón. A military junta governed the country until 1983. Democracy was restored, but in 1989 the government of Dr Alfonsin resigned, unable to tackle the financial crisis.

In 1989, the new government, led by Dr Menem, started a process of far-reaching changes in the economy. In the course of five years (1989–1994), the country went from being a tightly regulated and protected economy to an open one allowing free competition. The economic plan, which affected virtually every aspect of the economy, was based on three pillars of reform: monetary, fiscal and trade, and regulatory reforms.

The effects of these reforms were as dramatic at the level of the economy as they were at the level of firm competitiveness. Inflation was slashed from its peak of 5000 per cent in 1989 to 0.7 per cent in 1997. Wholesale privatizations dramatically increased government revenues and reduced government expenditures. De-regulation quickly exposed protected Argentinian firms to previously unknown competitiveness pressures and a process of concentration was accelerated by a wave of acquisitions of indigenous Argentinian firms by foreign-owned multinationals. It was in this punishing and liberating context that Andrés Hatum's study of organizational flexibility was born.

But what are the central questions of this book and in what sense is Andrés Hatum's study a pioneering piece of management research, the impact of which extends way beyond the troubled shores of Argentina at the end of the twentieth century?

Andrés Hatum's book is founded on the central assumption that the competitive performance of firms is an innovation contest where the bureaucratic and inflexible cannot survive or flourish. He sees the routes of enhanced performance resting on the development of sets of organizational and managerial capabilities which will deliver higher levels of organizational flexibility. His research was guided by three broad questions.

1. Do some firms display more flexibility than others in similar competitive circumstances?
2. Why are some firms able to create and exploit more flexibility?
3. How over time do such firms build and utilize the set of organizational and managerial capabilities, which allow them to be more agile and responsive?

He offers an analysis based on four case studies from a population of large Argentinian family-owned businesses in two industries: pharmaceuticals and edible oil. The case studies – two in each section – are polar types: one highly flexible firm and another less flexible firm. Both industries experienced unprecedented levels of competitive pressures in the 1990s and some of these firms adapted to that pressure much more quickly and adroitly than others. But what were the determinants of such organizational flexibility?

Andrés offers a theoretically rich and diverse analysis of the determinants of organizational flexibility. He draws upon the contextual and longitudinal work on change developed at Warwick Business School by Pettigrew (1985); Pettigrew and Whipp (1991); Pettigrew *et al.* (1992) and Pettigrew *et al.* (2003); the literature on organizational innovativeness of Damanpour (1991); Van de Ven *et al.* (1999) and others; the neo-institutional research of Greenwood and Hinings (1996) and Ang and Cummings (1997); and the novel work on organizational flexibility of Volberda (1999). He combines deductive theoretical development from the above literatures plus astute inductive analysis from his empirical findings to develop a five factor interdependent model of the determinants of organizational flexibility. Drawing upon a compendium of quantitative and qualitative time series data, he is able to convincingly demonstrate that a combination of heterogeneity of the firm dominant coalition, and apposite balance of centralization and formalization decision making, low macro-culture embeddedness, developed mechanisms of environmental scanning and a strong organizational identity all contributed to firm responsiveness.

His first determinant was the extent of heterogeneity of the top management coalition. His data show that the more highly flexible firms in his sample had a much more heterogeneous top management coalition than their less flexible comparatives and that this heterogeneity provided the kind of diversity of experience, views and mindsets which delivered greater cognitive width and capacity for action. The more flexible firms also managed more effectively to combine strategic centralization with operational autonomy and decentralization. Furthermore, the more flexible firms instituted more explicit formalization of decision making so that they could best monitor the greater autonomy of operational decision making they allowed.

More flexible firms also made themselves less institutionally embedded in their sectors than their less flexible comparators. This greater detachment from the established policies and practices, indeed conventional wisdom, of their sector peers gave the more flexible firms greater capacity for independent thought and action. This 'disembeddedness' of the flexible firms was also aided by and through greater capabilities to obtain superior information about their environments. Andrés refers here to capabilities of environmental scanning and demonstrates that his more flexible firms created and used greater variety of formal and informal structures for environmental scanning and combined these mechanisms with greater external openness and cognitive diversity than was evident in the less flexible firms.

Andrés's fifth determinant of organizational flexibility connects organizational identity with an understanding of how flexible firms adapt. He is able to show how and why the possession of a strong sense of identity, rooted in a sustainable set of values which favour change, innovation and risk taking, contributed to organizational adaptation. Paradoxically, a strong sense of identity thereby gave the more flexible companies the organizational anchor they needed to be able to move forwards and change (Hatum and Pettigrew, 2006).

The empirical findings of this study are a valuable addition to existing work on the adaptation of firms to competitive pressure. Crucially, however, Andrés Hatum's findings are a corrective to existing work on firm responsiveness which has been largely carried out in large non-family owned businesses in developed economies. He is able to show that research on the link between centralization and formalization and firm responsiveness in developed economies is not transferable to the rather different context of the emergent economy of Argentina. He is also able to demonstrate that the national business environment of Argentina, as represented in and through the influences of the State, financial and other institutions and managerial culture, all contributed to shape the particular response patterns of his set of Argentinian firms.

Finally and crucially, Andrés's book is a rare study of the adaptation and the flexibility of family firms. Existing literature on the behaviour and performance of family firms has thus far developed somewhat in isolation from the main currents of management research. Drawing as he does on core elements of the literature from organization theory and strategic management, Andrés Hatum brings the behaviour of family firms centre stage in the theory and practice of organizational flexibility and change.

Andrés Hatum's book on organizational flexibility is indeed a pioneering contribution to knowledge of the adaptation of family firms in emergent economies. In combining cross-levels of analysis of firm, sector and national business environment he gives a unique picture of the contextual forces driving change. Through his detailed time series analysis of managerial action, he is able to expose and explain the mixture of context and action which accounts for variation in organizational flexibility over time. This is a notable contribution which others can build on for years to come.

Andrew M. Pettigrew
School of Management
University of Bath

July 2006
Brilley, Hertfordshire

1. Introduction

> In the old days in science, the universe was fairly simple. Nearly every science museum has a huge, old model of the solar system in which all the movements of the planets are represented with clockwork gears. Then we realized that reality was much more complex. All motion was relative. The universe is a system in dynamic motion and flux with all motion being determined by the forces of inertia, complex gravitational interactions of heavenly bodies and even unseen gaseous clouds, random collisions, millions of asteroids, and the overall movement of galaxies toward the outer boundaries of the universe. (D'Aveni, 1994: xiii)

D'Aveni goes on to draw an analogy between our increasing perception of the complexity of the universe and the complexity of the business world. Business has entered a new reality, one that is more complex and dynamic, in which timely adaptation is critical for a firm's survival. Since the 1990s the new business context has been characterized by macro-environmental changes, changes in the way firms are organized, and changes in management style.

The macro-environmental changes affecting businesses have been shaped by an acceleration of change in the economic, social, technological and political worlds. March (1995) underlines four factors that have brought volatility and uncertainty into the environment in which firms operate: global linkages (that is, the business networks that cause global interdependencies to multiply and national boundaries to fade); information technology (which affects the possibilities for coordinating and controlling organizations); knowledge-based competition (that is, the use of knowledge as a primary source of competitive advantage); and political uncertainty (that is, the loss of autonomy of the national state through a general loss of control over boundaries).

All these factors have caused competition to intensify, product life cycles to shorten and technological innovation to increase. Hypercompetition, D'Aveni (1994) states, best describes the process by which the business environment accelerates. He indicates that the choice is clear for managers: either to stand still and allow constant change to wash over them, trying to resist the environmental changes, or actively to adapt to the environment and take advantage of its opportunities. In a dynamic world, D'Aveni (1994: 356) points out, only dynamic firms and those that can adapt rapidly to hypercompetitive environments, will survive.

Over the last decade, management literature has heralded the importance of new forms of organizing to confront uncertain and hypercompetitive environments. Theories regarding ideal types of organization have proliferated in an attempt to find ways that firms can adapt rapidly under high levels of competition. Goranson (1999: 65) suggests the concept of agile and virtual enterprise, understanding by virtual organization 'aggregations of smaller units that come together and act as though they were a larger, long-lived enterprise'. Such an organization has the advantage of being highly responsive.

Hedlund (1994) introduced the N-form in which different elements of an ideal organization are highlighted, namely lateral rather than vertical communication, temporary constellations of people and units rather than permanent structures, and heterarchy instead of hierarchy, among others. Heldlund's N-form is less futuristic but still more an ideal than a realization.

The latest empirical attempt to understand the ways firms organize themselves to adapt to competitive contexts comes from Pettigrew and Fenton (2000) and Pettigrew *et al.* (2003). Instead of focusing on ideal ways of organizing, Pettigrew and Fenton (2000) have stressed how firms organize themselves and what the indicators are. The conclusion of their European survey is that the most adaptable and innovative firms have combined changes in structure (that is, more decentralization, delayering and project forms of organization), changes in processes (that is, horizontal communication, investments in information technology and new human resource practices), and, changes in their boundaries (that is, downscoping, outsourcing and more strategic alliances).

Finally, the changing environment of the 1990s has also brought challenges in terms of the way firms are managed if they want to adapt successfully. These challenges have been signalled in management literature as a need for environmental sensing and sense-making (Pettigrew and Whipp, 1991), a managerial culture favouring change (Newman and Nollen, 1998), a broad knowledge base and variety of managerial expertise (Grant, 1996), and the development of high-order learning (Teece *et al.*, 1997).

Behind such claims of environmental, organizational and managerial changes lies a new interest in the dynamics of adaptation and in particular in a firm's flexibility as a way of adjusting under conditions of uncertainty (Volberda, 1999; Child, 2005). Amongst those who champion the new dynamic view of the firm, there is a belief that managers are unable to influence their rapidly changing environment (Astley and Van de Ven, 1983). Hence, they urge the adoption of flexible structures and systems which react to change automatically. This is a highly deterministic view – the actions of the manager being limited merely to making adjustments to the structure and systems. Others (Child, 1972, 1997; D'Aveni, 1994) suggest a more proactive role for the manager in which he/she does have the ability to influence the environment in which the firm operates.

In spite of the recognition of the importance of a firm's adaptation and flexibility, much of writing on adaptation concentrates on short-term strategic and organizational adaptations (Lewin *et al.*, 1999). Moreover, research into adaptation still involves using cross-sectional research designs combined with the static metaphors of contingency thinking to analyse the fit between firm and environment. The inadequacies of this tradition are now well recognized by an emergent approach in the field of adaptation that seeks more dynamic explanations (Lewin and Volberda, 1999). This emergent approach has encouraged researchers to identify the best ways for firms to adapt rapidly to ever changing realities (Dreyer and Grønhaug, 2004; Volberda, 1999). Lewin *et al.* (1999) applaud research which utilizes historical and longitudinal data to reveal the chains of causality that help to make up a more dynamic theory of adaptation and discover the essence of the adaptation process. Our research into determinants of organizational flexibility comes at a time when a more dynamic approach to the study of organizational adaptation under conditions of environmental uncertainty is badly needed.

This book takes up the challenge of exploring the dynamics of organizational adaptation under the conditions of environmental volatility that prevailed in Argentina over the period 1989–1999. In particular, we focus our attention on the determinants of organizational flexibility that made it possible for some firms to adapt rapidly in uncertain contexts. The empirical focus of the research is the study of the transformation process in four family-owned firms – two of which are considered flexible and two less flexible in two different industries: pharmaceuticals (an industry in the process of deregulation) and edible oils (a deregulated industry).

Family firms are the majority of businesses in several countries. In Latin and Central America, 65 per cent of companies are family-owned on average (IFERA, 2003). Poza (1995) indicates that in Latin America, the percentage of family businesses among the privately-owned companies varies between 80 per cent and 98 per cent. Although these are only estimates, they clearly indicate that family businesses constitute an overall majority of Latin American economies.

The existing family business literature has not directly tackled the issue of adaptation or flexibility. Even the most often acknowledged studies in the field of family businesses and change have been more preoccupied with the family side than the context surrounding the firm (Aronoff and Ward, 1997; Gersick *et al.*, 1997; Ward, 1987). The existent studies have been acontextual and ahistorical, always focusing on the firm's lifecycle and the transitional stages of the family firm but forgetting about the context in which the firm is embedded. Neither explorative nor longitudinal studies of the context have been produced in order to understand how firms adapt under rapidly changing environments and what capabilities are needed to do so (what we term 'determinants of organizational flexibility').

Our analysis draws upon longitudinal data collected from the firms by means of interviews, archive material and statistical data. Using an innovative analysis, we combine coding analysis from interview transcripts, statistical analysis and the use of original display charts, to show the determinants of organizational flexibility as a set of organizational capabilities that enabled some firms to adapt rapidly in the changing and highly competitive business environment that prevailed in Argentina in the 1990s.

OUTLINE OF THIS BOOK

Chapter 2 has a double focus. First, it presents views on a firm's adaptation. Second, it introduces views on inertia in organizations as a force that prevents them from adapting. The approaches analysed are: contingency theory and strategic choice theory (to explain a firm's adaptation) and population ecology and elements of strategic management theory (to explain the causes of inertia in organizations). While these theories allow us to understand why and how firms adapt, they do not analyse those factors that allow a firm to adapt quickly under conditions of environmental turmoil. We describe how three alternative literatures – flexibility (Volberda, 1999), innovation, and institutional embeddedness (Greenwood and Hinings, 1996) – can be used to build a more precise approach towards adaptation under conditions of environmental turmoil. We then use the concept of organizational flexibility to refer to the organizational and managerial capabilities that firms need to enable them to adapt quickly following environmental shifts. This literature review also raised several issues about what determines whether an organization is flexible, and from this exploration of the determinants of flexibility we state the three main questions of this book:

- Do some firms display more flexibility than others in competitive circumstances?
- Why are some firms able to display more flexibility?
- How do they do it?

In Chapter 3 we begin our multilevel analysis by examining the national business environment (NBE) in which firms were embedded over the period of analysis. Three main elements of the NBE were examined in order to understand how the NBE has affected the competitiveness of the industries and companies over time. The three elements considered in our analysis were the role of the state; the financial institutions; and the role of the national culture.

The results of our four comparative case studies are described in Chapters 4 to 8. Chapters 4 to 7 outline significant strategic and organizational transformation within the four case studies. Chapter 8 compares the four family-owned firms and describes factors our analysis identified as determining organizational flexibility – namely the heterogeneity of the dominant coalition, the levels of centralization and formalization of the decision-making process; the low level of macroculture embeddedness; environmental scanning and the strong organizational identity found in the flexible firms. Each determinant was operationalized and analysed according to a series of methods identified in the empirical literature relating to the different fields.

Chapter 9 concludes this book. Having summarized our findings we discuss the contributions made by this research in the field of family businesses and in particular organizational adaptation and flexibility. We also comment on the limitations of our investigation and suggest areas for future research to address these limitations and to utilize further the methodology we have developed in this research.

An Appendix is also included in which the methodology adopted for our empirical research is described. While our focus is the firm level of analysis, a dual phase research strategy was used: the sectoral level and firm level of analysis.

2. Adaptation, innovation and the flexible organization

INTRODUCTION

The business literature on organizational change is replete with prescriptions regarding the management and design organizations require to confront highly competitive and changeable environments. Such characteristics include decentralization of decision-making, flatter structures, risk-taking attitudes, empowerment and innovations of different sorts.

In spite of all the business literature offering these signposts for flexibility, there is little theory on the determinants of organizational flexibility. However, it is necessary to develop such a theory in order to understand how organizations can adapt rapidly to the sudden environmental and market changes that occur in volatile contexts (D'Aveni, 1994).

The chapter is divided into six sections. After this brief introduction, the second section sets out to understand how and why firms adapt. In particular we are interested in the environmental pressures exerted on firms, and organizational and managerial processes influencing their adaptation. Inertial approaches are used as an explanation of those factors that may prevent organizations from adapting.

In the third to fifth sections we describe how three alternative literatures can be used to build a more precise understanding of how organizations adapt under conditions of environmental turmoil. This combined approach includes literature on the determinants of organizational flexibility, organizational innovativeness and institutional embeddedness. The third and fourth sections deal with both determinants of organizational flexibility and determinants of organizational innovativeness as related and sometimes overlapping concepts. The research on institutional embeddedness in the fifth section sheds light on the strategic and organizational constraints environmental pressures impose and seeks to explain variation in how firms respond to a given set of institutional pressures. The sixth section states the patterns of adaptiveness from which the determinants of organizational flexibility are derived. In the final section we underline a set of researchable questions to guide the analysis.

ADAPTATION AND INERTIA IN ORGANIZATIONS

Many writers have characterized today's business environment as 'hyper-competitive' (D'Aveni, 1994; Volberda, 1996, 1999, Lewin and Volberda, 2003), 'high velocity' (Brown and Eisenhardt, 1997), or shaped by 'jolts' (Meyer *et al.*, 1990). In emerging economies, such as Argentina, these environmental features have been exacerbated by a sudden opening up of the markets to free competition. In these circumstances, rapid adaptive organizational processes are essential to a firm's survival and success (D'Aveni, 1994).

From a social science point of view, organizational adaptation is 'the ability of an organisation to change itself, or the way in which it behaves, in order to survive in the face of external changes which were not predicted in any precise way when the organisation was designed' (Tomlinson, 1976: 533). This definition confirms March's assertion that adaptation is essential to survival: those companies that do not adapt 'seem destined to expire' (March, 1995).

However, adaptation views of organization development have been contested. In an attempt to distinguish between the different debates within organizational theories, Astley and Van de Ven (1983) argue that one of these debates is about the adaptation/selection dichotomy. Even though the adaptation approach is widely accepted in strategy and organization theory (Lewin and Volberda, 1999, 2003), some theories emphasize the idea of selection, retention, or inertia (Hannan and Freeman, 1977 and 1984; DiMaggio and Powell, 1983).

Those favouring the inertia approach – such as the ecological perspective – stress environmental selection rather than 'selection of the environment' (Child, 1997: 45). For them, organizations are swept along by environmental pressures. These approaches highlight tensions between the possibilities an organization has for adaptation and change, preservation and inertia.

So what makes it possible for organizations to adapt rapidly to environmental changes? How can organizations learn to adapt to volatile conditions? Concepts such as the flexible firm (Volberda, 1999), the innovative firm (Pettigrew and Fenton, 2000), the adaptive firm (Haeckel, 1999), the chaordic enterprise (van Eijnatten and Putnik, 2004) or the agile firm (Goldman *et al.*, 1995) were coined as a way of explaining the organizational capabilities needed in organizations to allow them to adjust to the ever-changing environment.

This book draws heavily on the concept of organizational flexibility for two reasons: first, because of its appropriateness to understanding unpredictable and uncertain contexts such as the Argentinian one (Dreyer and

Grønhaug, 2004; D'Aveni, 1994); second, the concept of organizational flexibility also sheds light on the enhanced capabilities organizations under environmental turmoil develop to enable them to adapt quickly and undertake great transformations (Volberda, 1999; Bahrami, 1992).

So, why and how can organizations adapt? In particular, what are the contextual, managerial, and organizational challenges organizations have to meet so that they can adapt? What role do environmental forces play in a firm's adaptation? And does the organization and its top management have an active or reactive role in the adaptation process? By asking two final questions we aim to understand those factors preventing firms from adapting: Why are organizations inert? and, do inertial forces stem from environmental forces or from within the organization? In our analysis of the adaptation and inertia approaches, we focus on three main issues (that is, role of outer context, organization and top management team) that will help us to determine why and how adaptation is possible and identify the forces that may prevent organizations from adapting. We leave aside one important question, however: what are the capabilities needed by organizations to enable them to adapt? This question, however, will be addressed later in the analysis as we discuss the importance of a firm's flexibility in adapting in rapidly changing environments.

We therefore use key organizational frameworks to understand the possibilities organizations have for adaptation and the inertial forces that might prevent them from doing so. Following traditional studies in the field of organizational adaptation and inertia (Lewin *et al.*, 1999; Lewin and Volberda, 1999, 2003; Lewin and Koza, 2001) we note four organizational perspectives in which the role of the context, organization and management feature as key elements in understanding a firm's adaptation process. These perspectives are: contingency theory, strategic choice theory, population ecology theory, and elements of strategic management theory. Work on organizational renewal and the neo-institutional theory, both of which are clearly relevant to this theme, were deliberately excluded at this stage. These streams of research, however, are picked up later in the book. In the following pages we briefly describe key organizational frameworks and the dominant themes of these frameworks as they relate to adaptation or inertia.

Organizational Adaptiveness

How can firms adapt? And what is the role of organizational flexibility in a firm's adaptation? The answer is highly dependent on one's conceptions of the environment and perspective on the organization–environment relationship. In this section, two theories dealing with the organization-environment relation are considered: contingency theory and strategic choice theory. These theories may clarify the extent to which the environment affects the possibilities a firm has of adapting and being flexible.

The old contingency approach was based on the assumption that organizations adjust their aims and shape in order to suit themselves to market and other environmental characteristics (Astley and Van de Ven, 1983). Burns and Stalker (1961: 21) pointed out: 'Very often, the environment of the person or organisation is itself changing, so that even to maintain the same degree of fitness for survival, people and institutions may have to change their ways.' The consequence of the contingency approach for a firm's adaptation is that the firm should achieve a fit with the changing and competitive environment through 'appropriate organisational form' (Lewin and Volberda, 1999: 522).

On the basis of their qualitative research, Burns and Stalker (1961) identified organizational forms which they characterized as mechanistic and organic. They postulated that the more variable and unpredictable the environment is, the more flexible the organizational structure and process must be to enable the firm to adapt rapidly. According to this perspective, organizational flexibility is considered to be the reactive capacity of organizations to confront turbulent environments (Volberda, 1999).

Burns and Stalker (1961) and Woodward (1965) also emphasize that an organization's successful adaptation to the environment depends on the ability of top management to interpret the conditions facing the firm in an appropriate manner and to adopt relevant courses of action. The role of the top team then is to be reactive and their most important task is to be in tune with the environment (Singh *et al.*, 1986).

Contingency theory is useful in identifying the importance of environmental pressure in organizational life and in balancing out more subjective approaches towards organizational adaptation. In emerging markets in which environmental turmoil is frequent it is essential to appreciate the role exerted by the environment in triggering internal changes.

However, the most important shortcoming of contingency theory is that it fails to explain internal organizational factors that may influence adaptive processes – that is, social and cultural aspects, and leadership factors among others (Pettigrew *et al.*, 1992). It also fails to understand the role of the management in organizations and their ability to influence decision making and exert strategic choice (Child, 1972). It was the combination of external and internal factors (that is, environmental pressures, organization and top management team roles) that defined the determinants of organizational flexibility we introduce later in Chapter 8.

Some organizational scholars have become increasingly disenchanted with the mechanical and deterministic conception of the organization–environment relationship as described by contingency theory. Its strong deterministic bias largely ignores the important variable of managerial choice. It was Child (1972) who most explicitly argued for a less rigid view of the interaction between organizations and their environment. He called for a more voluntaristic or 'strategic choice' approach to organization–environment relations.

The strategic choice perspective suggests that proactive adaptability and loose coupling between organizations and environments allows structural variation and renders organizations less vulnerable to homogenizing forces exerted by the environment. Child and several others (Khandwalla, 1977; Hrebiniak and Joyce, 1985) have argued that organizations are not always passive recipients of environmental influence but also have the power to reshape the environment. Organizational flexibility is thus necessary to enable a firm to make rapid and viable choices (Child, 1997, 2005) and to enact environments (Weick, 1979). Organizational flexibility will not, however, be a reactive capacity (as it is in contingency theory) but a proactive one (Volberda, 1999).

The strategic choice approach then drew attention to the active role of those who have the power to make decisions. However, new approaches within the theory (Child, 1997; Hrebiniak and Joyce, 1985) argue that organizational adaptation is the result of the interdependence of and interaction between strategic choice and environment. Both agency and environment are necessary for a satisfactory explanation of organizational adaptation.

In this research we view the adaptation process as a dynamic one in which, for any given organization, elements or variables related to managerial choice and environmental influence coexist. Thus we avoid the deterministic and voluntaristic extremes provided by some organizational approaches. Change, then, is the outcome of environmental context and managerial action. Here, we view organizational flexibility as the interplay between outer and inner organizational contexts, in which managerial and environmental factors are interrelated (Pettigrew, 1985, 1990; Lewin and Koza, 2001). Such a view of organizational flexibility allows us to appreciate more holistically how organizations adapt quickly in conditions of environmental turmoil.

So far, we have been analysing how and why firms adapt. We have established the importance of the interrelation between environmental pressures and managerial choice, thereby avoiding extreme and incomplete explanations of adaptation. However, there are many factors that may restrict the ability organizations have to adapt to environmental changes and take advantage of opportunities the environment offers. But what are the factors that may hinder an organization's ability to adapt? Do those factors stem mainly from the firm's outer context or can inertia be found in the inner context of the organization? Organizational inertia is offered as an explanation as to how and why firms are prevented from adapting.

Organizational Inertia

Many authors have argued that organizations are fundamentally inert and therefore constrained in their ability to respond to environmental change (Hannan and Freeman, 1977; Miller and Friesen, 1980). In other words, organizations may be limited in their ability to recognize and act upon opportunities despite the fact that those opportunities are present in their industry.

Early organizational theory researchers recognized some of the negative consequences of bureaucracy (Blau, 1956; March and Simon, 1958). Stinchcombe (1965) suggested that firms tend to become institutionalized and that the basic structure of organizations remains relatively stable over time. More recently, organization theorists have argued that major stimuli are required for organizations to undergo periods of revolution, and therefore organizations are, by nature, sluggish in their ability to respond to environmental change (Miller and Friesen, 1980).

However, population ecology writers have taken a more extreme stance on the subject of organizational inertia. Organizational ecology has developed in response to the reactive adaptation bias generated by contingency theory. It considers the dynamic processes affecting the development of organizational populations over time and, in contrast to the prevailing adaptive perspective, focuses on selection as the main mechanism of adaptation and change. According to this perspective, adaptation and change is severely constrained and most organizations flounder helplessly in the grip of environmental forces (Carroll, 1988).

Hannan and Freeman's (1984) seminal paper presents a model of structural inertia. They argue that inertial properties in organizations are so strong that timely adaptation to environmental change is impossible. When levels of inertia are high, adaptive behaviour is more difficult and the environment selects out those organizations that do not fit (Hannan and Freeman, 1984; Delacroix and Swaminathan, 1991). For the population ecology approach environmental selection replaces internal adaptation. As the environment is relentlessly efficient in weeding out any organization that does not fit, the role of managers is therefore insignificant (Hannan and Freeman, 1977, 1984).

In population ecology theory, there is no place for flexibility; rather, population ecology emphasizes the anti-flexibility of organizations and their slowness in responding to changing environmental opportunities and threats. In this view, organizations are rarely able to engage in transformations.

Latterly some population ecology theorists, however, have admitted structural change of units. In his study of strategic business exit in Intel Corporation, Burgelman (1994) argued that it was not corporate strategy but the internal selection environment that caused a shift from memory chips to the more profitable microprocessor business. Burgelman found that the context set by top management had strong selective effects on the strategic actions of the firm. Similarly, Noda and Bower (1996) try to explain how selection processes operate within organizations. They reveal how the initial internal constraints in two different companies – BellSouth and US West – shaped the firms' very different strategies in cellular telephony over the period 1984–1990.

While some researchers in the field of population ecology have thus admitted structural change, the general fatalistic tendency of population ecology exposes it to more fundamental criticism. Its underlying theories represent a view of individual-organization interactions that are grounded in the assumption that the human role in organizations is essentially passive.

The early ecologist approach also failed to explain several relations and organizational aspects. This approach could not explain situations in which the environment had been altered (that is, regulated environments like the pharmaceutical industry in this research). Moreover, while theories of structural inertia can explain variation in change across large populations of organizations, they provide less insight into variation in change within organizations. Their tendency to take inertial forces for granted has led population ecologists to overlook the process by which individual firms adapt to environmental changes by renewing their organizations to confront different contextual realities in a competitive way. Nor could it explain how radical change and innovation can occur. The transformation stories of Sidus and AGD in Chapters 5 and 7 of this book are proof of the inability of population ecology theory to understand the way firms can undertake profound changes and avoid inertial forces stemming from the environment.

While the population ecology perspective has emphasized the ruthless role of the environment as a key factor in understanding inertia in organizations, elements of the strategic management literature have placed considerable importance on internal sources of inertia.

Miller and Chen (1994) point out that competitive inertia reflects the number of market changes a company makes to attract customers and overcome competitors' practices. Inertia would be high when, compared with competitors, firms make few changes in competitive practices. In their analysis of 32 US domestic airlines, Miller and Chen (1994) found the sources of competitive inertia in the managers' willingness to act.

Like Miller and Chen (1994), Sull (1999a, 1999b) tries to determine what the internal sources of inertia in organizations are. Studying the process of adaptation in Firestone and Laura Ashley, Sull (1999a, 1999b) mentions four factors that may cause companies to fail to adapt appropriately in the event of environmental shifts: strategic frames, processes, relationships, and values. Each of these factors can restrict adaptation. Strategic frames or mental models can act as blinkers and make it difficult to assess competitors, customers and business strategies. Processes may become routines, thus impeding effective responses (as in the case of Firestone and radial technology). Relationships (that is, with customers and suppliers) may fetter the company, thereby limiting flexibility. Finally, the company's set of beliefs may harden into dogma, thereby precluding other business possibilities. Elements of the strategic management literature thus widen our understanding of the problems the less flexible firms may have when they try to adapt. In Chapter 8 we discuss the different managerial and organizational factors that may have caused the sluggish response of the less flexible firms in conditions of environmental pressure.

Concluding Remarks

The review of adaptation and inertial theories has stressed different challenges organizations have to meet to be able to adapt and those factors that may deter them from doing so. Some perspectives (population ecology, contingency theory) emphasize the constraining influence of contextual forces; others (strategic choice) recognize the opportunities for human agency. Each of these perspectives helps to understand a particular aspect of how organizations develop 'fitness' within a given context, but they do not explain how organizations survive in endogenously dynamic environments and how they cope with unknown future states. In the perspectives analysed, nothing is said about what organizational capabilities are needed to adapt and avoid inertial traps. What are the enhanced capabilities organizations need to cope with higher levels of disorder? Is it possible for some organizations to learn to adapt to more volatile conditions?

By organizational capabilities we mean the 'unique internal management processes and intangible resources, which are less visible and less easily copied [and which] have come to be seen as potential sustainable sources of advantage' (Galbraith, 1994: 2). Capabilities are developed by organizations as they grow in size and scope (Galbraith, 1994).

Firms that are careful about the capabilities they develop relative to the environment in which they operate can transform and adapt quickly to very dynamic markets (Eisenhardt and Martin, 2000; Raff, 2000; Helfat, 1997, 2000; Huygens *et al.*, 2001). However, under extreme competitive pressure, very persistent or long-standing core capabilities that do not incorporate new competences and skills may evolve into core rigidities (Rosenbloom, 2000; Leonard-Barton, 1992), thereby impeding organizational adaptation. Organizational flexibility is the concept used in this research to refer to those capabilities that allow organizations to adapt rapidly under conditions of environmental turmoil.

But what determines whether an organization is more or less flexible? The following section deals in particular with the determinants of organizational flexibility. Innovativeness is not rejected. On the contrary, as Quinn (1985), Volberda (1999) and Georgsdottir and Getz (2004) suggest, organizational flexibility is an inclusive concept that encompasses the idea of innovation. Thus, organisational flexibility is a necessary condition for innovation. But what makes a firm more innovative or flexible? The lack of precision and blurred boundaries between these two concepts warrants a discussion of the similarities and differences between organizational flexibility and organizational innovativeness.

Institutional theory is introduced as a complementary theory because it emphasizes the role of mimetic behaviour in explaining patterns of adaptation, innovation and change among firms in an industry (Dacin *et al.*, 2002) thus shedding light on both the capacity for action and inertial forces of companies in an industry (Greenwood and Hinings, 1996). Institutional theory also spells out the capabilities firms need in order to overcome isomorphic pressures arising from the environment (Greenwood *et al.*, 2002).

Finally, issues affecting organizational flexibility in family firms are tackled. Considering the particular organizational features of family firms, it is convenient to point out and understand the main internal challenges family-owned firms have to go through to be able to achieve organizational flexibility.

RESEARCH ON DETERMINANTS OF ORGANIZATIONAL FLEXIBILITY

What is organizational flexibility? What does being a flexible firm imply? How do we know if we are in the presence of a flexible organization?

Bahrami (1992: 34) indicates that organizational flexibility varies according to the situational context and attributes this variation to the polymorphous nature of the concept of flexibility. Thus, the precise meaning of flexibility is dependent on the focus of the research. Thus, it is possible to talk about manufacturing flexibility (Anand and Ward, 2004), numerical flexibility, functional flexibility (Atkinson and Meager, 1986), flexible information systems (Golden and Powell, 2000), flexible automation (Adler, 1988) and a flexible workforce (Dastmalchian, 2001).

The polymorphous nature of the concept of flexibility indicated by Bahrami (1992) led us to expect difficulties in finding an accurate definition. However, there have been some attempts to bring conceptual clarity into the field of organizational flexibility.

The most relevant work on organizational flexibility has been done by Volberda (1999: 100). In his book he defines organizational flexibility as 'the degree to which an organization has a variety of managerial capabilities and the speed at which they can be activated, to increase the control capacity of management and improve the controllability of the organization.' Through this definition Volberda articulates one of his core arguments: the flexible organization needs to balance the conflicting demands of stability (namely control) and dynamism. While many organizational scholars present flexibility and stability as opposite ends of a continuum (Boynton and Victor, 1991), Volberda argues that flexibility and stability are two sides of the same coin, in that flexibility without stability results in organizational chaos.

While Volberda's definition is revealing in terms of the role of management and the need for rapid reaction to achieve flexibility in organizations, he does not consider organizational capabilities that may boost or hamper the attainment of flexibility. For Volberda, organizational flexibility is comprised of two components: managerial task (that is, 'the creation or promotion of capabilities for situations that generate unexpected disturbance') and organizational design (that is, structure of the organization) (see Volberda, 1999: 100, 101). However, Volberda's concept of flexibility does not identify other organizational factors that are not related to the design of the firm such as those we have considered in our research (that is, organizational identity or the role of organizational embeddedness in the firms' institutional macroculture).

A more comprehensive definition of organizational flexibility is given by Teece *et al.* (1997). The American literature has tended to use the concept of dynamic capabilities to refer to flexibility (Teece *et al.*, 1997; Rosenbloom, 2000; Tushman and Smith, 2001). In their theoretical framework, which is based on dynamic capabilities as enablers of adaptation and change in a rapidly changing environment, Teece *et al.* (1997: 516) define dynamic capabilities as 'the firm's ability to integrate, build, and reconfigure internal and external competences to address rapidly changing environments'. More concretely, Teece *et al.* (1997) indicates that dynamic capabilities should be able to enhance technological, organizational, and managerial processes inside the firm to enable it to organize more effectively. Teece *et al.* (1997: 521) also state that firms that have honed and perfected these capabilities are referred to as 'high-flex'.

Daniel and Wilson (2003) pointed out that dynamic capabilities are necessary for business transformation. Others, such as Ching and Hsu (2006), have demonstrated the importance of dynamic capabilities for strategic management of business in a dynamic changing environment that requires organizations to be flexible and to adapt to continuous change.

In this book we use the concept of organizational flexibility in a way similar to that proposed by Teece *et al.* (1997), considering organizational flexibility as a repertoire of organizational and managerial capabilities that allow organizations to adapt quickly under conditions of environmental change. We must now consider the organizational and managerial capabilities mentioned in the literature that allow organizations to be flexible.

Organizational Flexibility as an Organizational Task

For many authors, the ability of an organization to achieve organizational flexibility depends on the design adequacy of organizational variables, such as technology, structure and culture (Zammuto and O'Connor, 1992; Volberda, 1999). Organizational structure, however, is the main focus of the organizational flexibility writers (Volberda, 1999; Englehardt and Simmons, 2002). The design of the organizational structure encompasses not only the actual distribution of responsibilities in an organization, but also the planning and control systems set up in the companies, the process of decision making and coordination (Zammuto and O'Connor, 1992; Volberda, 1999).

The theoretical literature on organizational flexibility stresses the importance of multidimensional design (that is, units that can be easily added and subtracted) (Ackoff, 1977), lateral organization (that is, in terms of coordination across functions and businesses) (Galbraith, 1994), innovative structure (that is, a structure that allows the rapid shift of product composition and decentralization of decision making) (Krijnen, 1979), virtual organizations (that is, organizations that exist within a space not bound by legal and physical structures) (Child, 2005) and an organizational design aligned with market needs, the nature of competitors, and the industry (Overholt, 1997).

From an empirical point of view, many other writers have suggested networking forms of organizing (in Liebeskind *et al.* (1996); Birkinshaw, 2000), flat structures (in Rosenbloom's (2000) analysis of the process of transformation in NCR), and collaboration partnerships (in Bahrami (1992) and Bahrami and Evans' (1995) study of organizational flexibility in the hi-tech sector in Silicon Valley). These empirical studies provide evidence of how a flexible design allows companies to become front-line organizations that deal with problems rapidly by reducing the lag between strategy and operation.

One of the problems associated with the foregoing research is that it does not examine how the suggested designs can be implemented in organizations.

The authors do not attempt to clarify whether 'a flexible design' is suitable for every company or whether it should apply to those organizations competing in industries with fast product cycles (that is, information technology). This book undertakes an examination of the changes in the organizational design of the firms under study from an empirical point of view, and thereby complements the existent theoretical studies.

Besides organizational design, other organizational factors are also mentioned as influencing organizational flexibility. For example, Volberda (1999) considers that culture plays an important role in promoting flexibility. He distinguishes between conservative and innovative culture: an innovative culture (the culture required to encourage flexibility) will be heterogeneous, with a delegative leadership style and managers with an attitude that favours improvization rather than routine. It will also tolerate ambiguity and autonomy.

Delegation and autonomy are not new ideas in the literature however. Overholt (1997) examines the organizational archetypes needed under conditions of environmental change and severe competition. He points out that flexibility may be achieved through highly autonomous and decentralized organizations. These firms are process-based with fewer layers and high levels of permeability of boundaries.

In his study of organizational flexibility in companies in Silicon Valley, Bahrami (1992) provides evidence of how the most flexible firms accommodate opposing tendencies such as centralization and decentralization. The companies described as flexible by Bahrami are centralized in terms of their strategic direction with a lot of autonomy for managers to run the business. The case of a telecommunication corporation illustrates these ideas. The corporation has very small and decentralized units with a great deal of autonomy. However, centralization of strategic decisions was a key element for coordination and cooperation between units.

In flexible organizations not only are levels of centralization of decision making low, but there is also a low number of formalization processes. Again Volberda (1996, 1999) and Ng and Dastmalchian (2001) indicates that organizations with the potential to be highly flexible have low levels of standardization (that is, specification of the contents and result of the work), and low levels of formalization (that is, job descriptions, work instructions and general rules).

Such flexible organizational factors – decentralization and formalization of decision making – will provide great leeway for managers to assume more responsibilities in the firms and to move quickly, thereby achieving fast responsive capacity. The managerial role in achieving organizational flexibility will be the subject of the analysis of the following subsection.

Organizational Flexibility as a Managerial Task

This subsection concentrates on two main questions: what are the managerial features of flexible firms? And what kind of flexible capabilities are needed to respond and adapt to sudden environmental shifts?

From a manufacturing perspective, Adler (1988) states that technological flexibility requires managerial flexibility. He highlights the new content of these managerial capabilities as attitudinal, that is taking responsibility for the whole process; cognitive, meaning the process of identifying and solving problems; and, lastly, systemic interdependence, which is reflected in inter-functional cooperation and teamwork.

Volberda (1999) and Combe and Greenley (2004) assert the importance of a broad knowledge base and a variety of managerial expertise in devising appropriate responses. The heterogeneity of backgrounds and experiences needed in a flexible firm is related to the need to face competitive environments. Boynton and Victor (1991) show how a company like Corning, which had managers with a broad knowledge base deriving from a variety of expertise, was able to develop capabilities in order to introduce new products and seize market opportunities.

Diverse managerial expertise may encourage the organization to recognize the need for change. This was studied empirically by Calori *et al.* (2000) while analysing the process of change in Novotel. Novotel increased its management team from eight to 18 employees and in so doing broadened the kinds of experience in the management team. The new management team complemented each other in terms of different cognitive styles, thus bringing new strategic options, innovation and creativity to the company.

Heterogeneity and broad managerial mindsets foster the ability to create and support ideas. Bahrami (1992) points out how the cosmopolitan mindset at Apple Computers has led to different cultural assumptions and premises being incorporated. Volberda (1999) indicates that management must have the ability to identify, experiment and explore new fields and ideas rather than exploiting existing routines. Experimentation, for Volberda, can be achieved by having heterogeneous managers with broad managerial mindsets. Volberda illustrates differences in heterogeneity and managerial mindsets in two electronic firms: Sharp and Texas Instruments (TI). While Sharp was able to develop dynamic capabilities in the electronic calculator industry, TI failed because its limited managerial mindsets caused it to focus exclusively on the semiconductor market.

The literature on organizational flexibility makes a number of predictions about the factors determining the flexibility of an organization. Each company's flexibility will be determined by a variety of organizational and individual factors. At the organizational level, an adequate 'flexible' organizational design and low levels of centralization and formalization of decision making were mentioned. In addition, the literature has suggested that at the top management level, heterogeneity of the managerial team and a broad knowledge base are required to build a flexible organization.

The perspectives analysed so far have limitations. Most of the literature reviewed in this section is theoretical and little empirical research has been done in organizational settings. Take, for example, the most comprehensive research in the field by Volberda. As Volberda (1999: 264) admits, his analysis of the flexible firm 'is to some extent speculative, based on a limited number of observations'. There has been little empirical verification of the concepts Volberda presents. Our analysis of the determinants of organizational flexibility is thus an attempt to link both theory and practice in a field in which empirical analysis is scarce.

Many questions regarding the content and process of being flexible remain unanswered. Volberda, for example, suggests that organizational flexibility is an emergent process triggered by highly competitive environments. As such, he focuses on describing the way firms react using some 'flexible capabilities' rather than trying to understand what causes them to be flexible and the way those determinants have been built up over time. Furthermore, can organizational flexibility be built as an intended process instead of just an emergent one? The intentionality of the process of being flexible opens up a series of questions that have not been tackled directly: is the building of organizational flexibility a long-term process? What are its antecedents and origins? What antecedents are necessary or sufficient? We have filled this void in the literature by analysing the determinants of a firm's flexibility and have empirically demonstrated the importance of flexibility as an intended process in the firms.

RESEARCH ON DETERMINANTS OF ORGANIZATIONAL INNOVATIVENESS

> A variety of innovations are essential for our economic health. In the corporate environment that has been emerging since the 1960s, business must be innovative, learning to operate in an unfamiliar context and within new constraints stemming from worldwide trends, changes in the labor force, the ups and downs of government regulations, and technological development. (Kanter, 1983: 22)

Kanter's statement shows an awareness of the importance of the study of the determinants of innovativeness as another means of understanding how organizations adapt to their ever-changing context.

However, before examining the determinants of a firm's innovativeness, it is important to achieve clarity regarding the conceptual basis of innovation.

In the literature there are multiple definitions of the content and scope of innovation. This book adopts a broad approach to understanding innovation, considering product, processes and services among all the innovative activities companies can engage in (Van de Ven and Poole, 1995; Pettigrew and Fenton, 2000).

But what determines whether a firm is innovative? The determinants most frequently researched in the literature on organizational innovativeness can be divided into two different levels: the organizational level and the top management team level (Wolfe, 1994; Slappender, 1996).

The Influence of the Characteristics of the Top Management Team

Much of the literature on innovation stresses the impact of the characteristics of the top management team on an organization's innovativeness. This view of innovation assumes that certain individuals have personal qualities that predispose them to innovative behaviour (Slappender, 1996).

Hage and Dewar (1973) empirically compared the concept of elite values and structural factors in 16 health and welfare organizations. They argued that the diversity of occupations in an organization led to more ideas about what needed to be done in the organization and also facilitated adoption of innovations. This variety also implied a variety of contacts outside the organization in which the professionals were working.

Robertson and Wind (1983) gathered together both the diversity of managerial experience and the contacts managers have with people outside the firm or industry under the name of 'cosmopolitanism,' or the 'cosmopolitan mindset.' Their empirical analysis of more than a hundred hospitals reveal that innovativeness is higher in those hospitals in which professionals (that is, the physicians) have a cosmopolitan orientation. Diversity among top managers may provide the external linkage needed to bring new ideas into the organization.

Diversity in the top team can also bring administrative innovations into the organization (pertaining to organizational structure, administrative processes and human resources) rather than only technical innovations (referring to products, services and technology used in the company).

Finally, some writers assert that the diversity of experience and mental models that will foster innovativeness in an organization will be supported by the managers' tenure in the job or company and their educational background. In that respect, some have argued that new managers with different perspectives, new ideas and less commitment to the organization are thus more receptive to innovation and change than those with longer tenure in the companies. Kimberly and Evanisko (1981), in their study of innovation in hospitals, show evidence of how the personal traits of managers (that is, tenure, cosmopolitanism, educational level) are significant predictors of both technological and administrative innovation.

The concepts of diversity of backgrounds and cosmopolitanism highlight the importance of the internal heterogeneity of the management team. This heterogeneity might boost the setting up of networks outside the organization (Robertson and Wind, 1983), the possibility of introducing new ideas into the organization (Pettigrew, 1972), and the creation or diffusion of both technical and/or administrative innovations (Daft, 1978).

Criticism of the perspective focusing on the traits of the top team and their influence on a firm's innovativeness stems from the fact that it tends to focus its analysis on the innovative actions of the organizational participants, thus leaving aside important organizational and contextual characteristics (Slappender, 1996). In our research we need to look at the way these concepts are operationalized in family firms: do the firms analysed in this study have a degree of diversity that grants them internal heterogeneity? How did the family firms in our research balance out the need for diversity among the top team and the critical role played by family members in the direction of the companies? The literature has not yet addressed these questions.

The Influence of Organizational Characteristics on Innovativeness

The most frequently investigated organizational determinants of innovativeness include the degrees of centralization and formalization of the decision-making process. There is a general consensus among theorists in the field of organizational innovativeness that higher degrees of centralization and formalization influence innovation in a negative way because together they concentrate decision making, hindering the ability of members of the organization to participate in and be committed to organizational.

Thompson (1965) tries to explain the rigidity of the centralized organization by using the Weberian concept of the 'bureaucratic' organization. In this kind of organization, each member receives orders from a superior. Internal distribution of power and status are relevant goals. The bureaucratic organization is characterized by efficiency but low innovative capacity.

Hage and Dewar (1973) and Hage (1999) justify the idea of the negative relation between innovation and centralization by arguing that when power is concentrated in only a few people, there are fewer opportunities for creation and innovation since those who have power prefer to maintain the status quo.

Bringing together earlier empirical work that takes an organizational level view, Damanpour (1991) indicates a negative relationship between innovativeness and the degrees of formalization and centralization. However, Damanpour also argues that the implementation stage of the innovation process requires a higher degree of formalization and centralization than the initiation phase.

The process view of innovativeness (Van de Ven *et al.*, 1999) stresses that at any time an organization is likely to be in the process of adopting several innovations, each at a different stage of generation and implementation. The innovativeness of an organization, therefore, will depend on its ability to address the different requirements of each phase of adoption simultaneously. Hence, while low levels of formalization and centralization of decision making may increase innovativeness in the creation phase, there will be a point at which the relaxation of control will disrupt implementation.

The literature on organizational innovativeness thus identifies a number of patterns of adaptiveness. Innovativeness in a firm will be determined by a variety of organizational and individual factors, which include the characteristics and diversity of the firm's top management team and the degree of centralization and formalization of decision making.

Context is central to our understanding of organizational innovativeness. With the exception of some processual writers (Whipp and Clark, 1986; Clark, 1995; Van de Ven *et al.*, 1999) the research examined so far tends to look into organizational and managerial features without taking into consideration the importance of a firm's embeddedness in the sector and national business environment. The sector, industry and national systems of innovation do, however, influence the process of innovation in an organization (Tidd *et al.*, 1997).

Institutional influence comes into play when levels of uncertainty and unpredictability increase (Webb and Pettigrew, 1999). In the face of uncertainty, mimetic behaviour and institutional embeddedness would protect companies from turmoil (DiMaggio and Powell, 1983; Abrahamson and Formbrun, 1994). Questions arise as to how companies in volatile contexts – as in the Argentinian case – can adapt rapidly without being caught by inertial forces. A consideration of the so-called neo-institutional theory and, in particular, the degree of embeddedness in the macroculture domain will lead to an appreciation of the influence of institutional pressures on the process of adaptation.

INSTITUTIONAL EMBEDDEDNESS

In the literature on organizational innovativeness and flexibility, the debate concentrates on the ways organizations adapt and what determines organizational adaptability (Volberda, 1999; Kessler and Chakrabarti, 1996). In institutional theory, however, the debate is split between those writers that stress the explanation of similarities (that is, isomorphism and stability in a population of organizations), and those that consider the institutional approach as the basis for a theory of continuity and change (Greenwood and Hinings, 1996). In this section we shall concentrate on the latter. We also explore the mechanisms needed by companies to overcome environmental pressure and how this affects new business initiatives and strategic decisions taken by firms.

Institutional theory explains adaptation as a homogenization process by which firms within a sector will become increasingly alike over time. The process of homogenization in a sector is called isomorphism by DiMaggio and Powell (1983: 149): 'Isomorphism is a constraining process that forces one unit in a population to resemble other units that face the same set of environmental conditions.'

One of the consequences of the process of homogenization is that it tends to increase the organization's levels of inertia and also increases the similarity of member organizations' strategic profiles (DiMaggio and Powell, 1983). Hence this line of institutional argument suggests that it is very difficult to find firms that are applying a different strategic pattern or doing things in a very different way from other businesses in the same sector.

Abrahamson and Fombrun (1994: 729) go further by stating that

insularity and sluggishness result because homogeneity of beliefs within an interorganizational macroculture encourages member firms' managers to interpret environment in similar ways, to identify similar issues as strategic, and so to adopt similar competitive positions.

Therefore, in assessing the adaptation process of an organization in an industry it is important to address the issue of what determines the threshold level at which institutional pressures are overcome and the company can adopt new initiatives or strategies that differ from the rest of the actors in the industry. The threshold level will be determined then by the degree of embeddedness in the dominant macroculture or institutional field (Webb and Pettigrew, 1999). Institutional embeddedness may encourage companies to copy other successful organizations within the same institutional settings (Haveman, 1993; Renzulli, 2005). The zones of manoeuvre available for firms are severely constrained by institutions (Scott, 1987).

DiMaggio and Powell (1983) and Abrahamson and Fombrun (1994) suggest that embeddedness is determined by a range of factors which include the degree of connectedness of an organization to its institutional field (for example participating in trade or professional associations, facilitating and sharing information) and the perceived similarities to other members of the sector (for example similarity of education and career background of key decision makers).

Cognitive mechanisms are also said to influence embeddedness. The concern in this literature is how frameworks of meaning affect individual and corporate actors as they interpret and make sense of their worlds (Dacin *et al.*, 1999, 2002; Zilber, 2002). Dutton and Dukerich's (1991) work on the Port Authority of New York sheds light on the embeddedness of that organization in terms of cognitive mechanisms. They found that the attitudes and actions of both administrators and employees of the Authority were the outcome of moral and emotional concerns.

Thus far, our discussion has highlighted the importance of embeddedness and the inertial forces that embeddedness brings to the organization. But firms may simply not conform to institutional pressures (Ang and Cummings, 1997; Westphal and Zajac, 2001). So, how can they avoid becoming deeply embedded in their industry macroculture? Do organizations exhibit different processes of change in response to a pressing institutional context? What are the mechanisms of disembeddedness, or de-institutionalization? More recent literature in this area has tried to answer these questions by taking a different approach towards embeddedness and the organization's ability to overcome institutional pressures. Oliver (1991, 1992) and Greenwood and Hinings (1996) introduce a less deterministic perspective to the institutional literature by recognizing the critical role of managerial action (see also Hargadon and Douglas, 2001).

Oliver (1991, 1992) introduces the notion of dissipation and de-institutionalization as a way of explaining the gradual deterioration in the acceptance and use of a particular institutionalized practice. For Oliver, characteristics of the institutional field interact with the internal features of an organization. The outcome of this interaction is the possibility of breaking down institutionalized practices and replacing them with new ones.

Greenwood and Hinings (1996), on the other hand, introduce a framework for understanding adaptation and change in which exogenous factors (such as market context and institutional context) are tied up with endogenous dynamics (for example interest, values, power dependencies and capacity for action). If there are competing mindsets or values and a fluctuating balance of power among the dominant coalition, the endogenous dynamics are enablers of change. Diversity among the top team – deriving from different professional experience and backgrounds, and even the appointment of a new CEO stimulates the flow of new ideas in the organization. These mechanisms mean that an organization is less tied down by prevailing archetypes (Greenwood and Hinings, 1988), less likely to accept environmental pressure and more likely to challenge the outer context (Westphal and Zajac, 2001).

Zondra and Hinings (1998) develop a taxonomy of organizations in order to understand how they respond to violations of institutional norms.

In that taxonomy, they argue that 'renegade' organizations are those organizations operating outside institutional norms. Renegades have organizational diversity, are willing to take risks and respond to exogenous change with – if necessary – fundamental reorientations. Renegades avoid complying with institutional pressures.

The neo-institutional perspective adopted by Oliver (1991, 1992) and Greenwood and Hinings (1996) provides some insight into adaptation processes. This newer approach in institutional theory opens up the discussion of a firm's capacity for action, that is 'the ability to manage the transition process from one template to another' (Greenwood and Hinings, 1996: 1039). This capacity for action means that change, adaptation and innovative behaviour are possible, and avoids the rather deterministic perspective of earlier approaches in institutional theory in which organizations were passive recipients of environmental pressure (DiMaggio and Powell, 1983). Thus, organizations can challenge the environment in which they are embedded by introducing new practices and strategies.

ISSUES AFFECTING ORGANIZATIONAL FLEXIBILITY OF FAMILY FIRMS

Family businesses face very particular challenges in their attempt to achieve organizational flexibility. These challenges arise at different stages in the life of a family firm. Ward (1987) point outs that over these stages (for example the founding stage, and second generation tenure, among others) family firms need to learn to delegate authority (that is, decentralizing operational and strategic decisions), cope with transitional stages, and professionalize the company by bringing in new managerial skills from outside the company (that is, non-family members). Family companies that are not able to meet these challenges stagnate, and thus their ability to adapt to new market conditions is impaired (Ward, 1987: 33).

Broadly speaking, the factors mentioned by Ward (1987) as affecting the development of organizational flexibility within family-owned firms fall into three categories. These categories are: the life cycle of the family firm and the role of the founder; the control systems and professionalization of the management team; and finally, ownership issues.

Life Cycle of the Family Firm: the Role of the Founder

Many organizational writers have emphasized the relationship between a firm's history and its current capabilities. Teece *et al.* (1997) and Rosenbloom (2000) recognize that the development of organizational capabilities is strongly related to the history of the firm (the 'path dependencies' for Teece *et al.*, 1997). Thus, a firm's previous choices shed some light on its current organizational capabilities. Similarly, Raff (2000), studying the transformation of two book retailers in the USA, states that the founders' vision and values influence what the companies become and the capabilities they can develop. These writers consider history to be one of the factors contributing to the development of organizational capability.

Based on his longitudinal study of the birth and early development of a medical school, Kimberly (1979) underlines the problems that the organization had to confront during the different stages of its development. Being influenced by its founder's ideals of innovativeness, Kimberly shows how this imprint constituted a significant constraint for the organization's subsequent choices. He also points out the tensions between the innovativeness of the early phases and the institutionalization and formalization that occur at later stages in the organization's development.

In his empirical study in a British boarding school, Pettigrew (1979) also explores the critical role of the founder of an organization (in this case the founder of the boarding school) in creating organizational culture and set of beliefs. The founders, 'entrepreneurs' in Pettigrew's words, give energy, purpose and commitment to the organization they are creating (Pettigrew, 1979: 580).

Kimberly's (1979) and Pettigrew's (1979) findings are particularly revealing of the role of the founder and the imprint that is left on the organization. In family firms it is particularly important to understand the role of the founder in determining the company's set of beliefs and how this value system can help the firm to confront the demands of new organizational stages. The fact that our sample contains family firms at different life stages (the second and third generations of family leadership) also illustrates the process of how the family firms in this study move from one stage to the next (that is, through the succession process) and how they cope with the requirements for institutionalization (that is, more formal mechanisms and professionalization). These issues are addressed in the following subsection.

Control Systems and Professionalization of the Management Team in Family Firms

Control systems also evolve throughout the life cycle of a family firm. In the first tenure of the company – the founder or entrepreneurial experience – control tends to be informal, with little planning and coordination. Decision making, on the other hand, is highly centralized in the founders. Moores and Mula (2000) show empirical evidence in Australian family firms to suggest that at successive stages of life, family firms tend to formalize mechanisms of control and decentralize decision making. This happens because after the founder's tenure, the different family branches need to keep abreast of company issues, and accordingly control and formalization must increase. On the other hand, the size and scope of some businesses and the increasing professionalization of the firm make decentralization a necessary process.

How professionalization is handled in family firms can often determine whether or not the firm will continue to grow and thrive. There are a number of reasons why a family firm might want to professionalize its current management team. Dyer Jr (1996) states that one reason for bringing non-family managers into the company is because there is sometimes a lack of management talent within the family. A second reason Dyer stresses is that professionalizing the management is a way to change the norms and values of the firm.

Ward (1987) highlights the fact that a family firm's health might suffer if, in the middle or late stages of its organizational development, it does not learn to professionalize, delegate authority and establish formal management systems. Success in business, states Ward (1987), hinges on the development of new management processes according to the different stages of the company's life.

Ownership Issues

The structure and distribution of ownership – who owns how much of what kind of stock – can have profound effects on the governance and growth of the firm. Ward (1987) proposes a progression of ownership from founder to sibling partnership, and finally to the family dynasty. Gersick *et al.* (1997) introduce an ownership developmental dimension with three stages: controlling owner, sibling partnership and cousin consortium. What the different classifications show, however, is simply how ownership becomes increasingly diluted from a single majority owner (that is, the founder stage for Ward or the controlling owner for Gersick *et al.*) to a few or several owners.

The possibilities for growth are linked with the ownership structure of the family business. In successive generations of family members, as Haynes *et al.* (1999) underline, family firms intermingle business and family resources. However, relying on a firm's profits and family savings may restrict a company's growth. Family firms, as Mahérault's (2000) empirical study on family firms' finance shows, prefer not to open the company up to the public because they are afraid that the dilution of equity structure will diminish family power. The result of this process for family firms is a crisis of identity (Mahérault, 2000).

PATTERNS OF ADAPTIVENESS DERIVED FROM THE LITERATURE REVIEW

Our review of the literature on organizational flexibility, organizational innovativeness and institutional embeddedness offers insight into the determinants of organizational flexibility. This combined approach was needed to provide depth and scope in the study of adaptation under conditions of environmental turmoil. Table 2.1 is a composite table that shows patterns of adaptiveness derived from the literature review.

The common patterns identified in Table 2.1 inform the choice of determinants of organizational flexibility in this study. Our literature review and empirical evidence have identified five determinants of organizational flexibility. Three of them are drawn deductively from the literatures on organizational flexibility, innovativeness and institutional theory (see Table 2.1). These determinants are: low macroculture embeddedness; heterogeneity of the dominant coalition; and low degree of centralization and formalization of decision making. In addition, we are going to explore two further determinants that have emerged inductively from our empirical findings. These are environmental scanning and a strong organizational identity.

The neo-institutional approach developed by Greenwood and Hinings (1996) and Oliver (1991, 1992) allows us to see how low macroculture embeddedness is needed to avoid mimetic and inertial forces exerted by the institutional domain. Organizations that are more peripheral and thus less embedded in an institutional context are less committed to prevailing practices and more ready to develop new ones.

The literature on organizational flexibility and innovation, on the other hand, makes two predictions: first, that heterogeneity in the dominant coalition (for example through diverse backgrounds and experience) will enable different cognitive frameworks to emerge, helping companies navigate turbulent times and cope with change and uncertainty; and second, the low degree of centralization and formalization of decision making (for example through more autonomy and flat structures) are needed to adapt quickly to environmental changes.

Environmental scanning and a strong organizational identity emerged inductively and are elaborated in two different bodies of literature that will be analysed in Chapter 8. It will be necessary to examine the empirical results of this research, however, in order to understand the extent to which the latter two determinants are significant in explaining organizational flexibility.

The competitive landscape faced by firms throughout the 1990s has become more uncertain (D'Aveni, 1994). In such a hyperturbulent or hypercompetitive environment, traditional approaches to adaptation have failed because of their assumptions of stability (Brown and Eisenhardt, 1997;

Table 2.1 *Patterns of adaptiveness in the literature review on organisational flexibility, innovativeness and institutional theory*

Patterns of adaptiveness	Sources in the literature
At the sector/industry level Low level of embeddedness in the dominant macroculture	*Institutional theory literature*: DiMaggio and Powell (1983); Oliver (1991, 1992); Abrahamson and Fombrun (1994); Greenwood and Hinings (1996); Ang and Cummings (1997); Fox-Wolfgramm *et al.* (1998); Zondra and Hinings (1998); Webb and Pettigrew (1999); Hargadon and Douglas (2001); Renzulli (2005)

At the organizational level
Decentralization of decision
   making (through autonomy
   of decision making and a
   flexible organisational design)
Low level of formalization of
   decision making
	Literature on organizational flexibility:
	   Krijnen (1979); Overholt (1997); Bahrami (1992); Galbraith (1994); Bahrami and Evans (1995); Volberda (1996, 1997, 1999); Birkinshaw (2000); Englehardt and Simmons (2002)
	Literature on organizational innovativeness:
	   Normann (1971); Zaltman *et al.* (1973); Kanter (1983); Nicholson *et al.* (1990); Damanpour (1991, 1992)

At the top managerial level of
   the firm
Heterogeneity of the dominant
   coalition (for example
   diversity of backgrounds
   and experience and
   cosmopolitan mindset)
	Literature on organizational flexibility:
	   Adler (1988); Bahrami (1992); Volberda (1996, 1997, 1999); Heijltjes (2000); Calori *et al.* (2000); Combe and Greenley (2004)
	Literature on organizational innovativeness:
	   Moch and Morse (1977); Hage and Dewar (1973); Daft (1978); Kimberly and Evanisko (1981); Rogers (1983); Damanpour (1991, 1996)
	Institutional Theory Literature: Oliver (1991, 1992); Greenwood and Hinings (1996); Zondra and Hinings (1998); Fox-Wolfgramm *et al.* (1998)

Lewin *et al.*, 1999). In our literature review we have seen how new concepts have emerged that reflect this highly dynamic situation (that is, our combined approach to determinants of organizational flexibility, innovativeness and institutional embeddedness).

As we have seen in this chapter, research on adaptation has been dichotomized by polar positions postulating either environmental determinism or managerial choice. Neither position is realistic and therefore cannot help to understand adaptation in a dynamic reality. We have, therefore, stated how organizational flexibility is needed to adapt to rapidly changing environments. In particular, we have identified a possible set of determinants of organizational flexibility as the capabilities firms need to adapt under conditions of uncertainty. It is this theme that will form the basis of our empirical research. This leads to the first research question:

- Do some firms display more flexibility than others in similar competitive circumstances?

By asking this question we aim to understand the adaptive capability of organizations in a rapidly changing environment. Flexible firms will be those that cope with acceleration of change in the business environment. Competitive changes force firms to move more quickly and boldly and to experiment with new strategies and new ways of organizing. There is a sense in the management literature that these experiments characterize the rise of a flexible firm, which leads to our second and third questions:

- Why are some firms able to display more flexibility?
- And how they do it?

If firms are consistently adapting to environmental pressures and leap-frogging industry boundaries, this would suggest that a set of determinants of organizational flexibility is influencing their behaviour. Throughout the literature review we have mentioned the importance of three elements as factors affecting how and why firms adapt. These elements are: the institutional pressures firms have to bear, and the managerial capabilities and organizational arrangements needed to confront quickly changing environments and achieve flexibility.

3.   Argentinian business environment

INTRODUCTION

Studies of organization have often omitted the importance of national differences as shapers of the organizational action of firms (Whittington and Mayer, 2000; Pettigrew *et al.*, 2001). Clark (2000: 8) argues that this may have happened due to the fact that many organizational theorists are located in the USA and therefore tend to consider the context of their findings (that is the American context) as 'an undiscussed background' and consequently universalize them. National and regional specificities are, however, becoming increasingly acknowledged as factors affecting the ways in which firms in emerging economies respond to competitive pressures (Pettigrew *et al.*, 2001; Hoskisson *et al.*, 2000). As this chapter demonstrates, particular features of the Argentinian business environment has a deep impact on the character and transformation of indigenous firms over time.

Argentina, the country on which this analysis focuses, has been considered a newly industrialized country (Helleiner, 1990), a developing country (Lal, 1975), an emergent country (Contractor, 1998) or a less developed country (Kirkpatrick, 1987; Buckley and Casson, 1985). We consider Argentina to be an emergent country.

Hoskisson *et al.* (2000) indicate that an emerging market economy can be defined as one that satisfies two main criteria: a rapid pace of economic development and government policies favouring economic liberalisation. The term 'emerging country', for Zahra *et al.* (2000) and Ramamurti (2000), also presupposes economic, social, institutional and political instability compared to economically developed countries.

But what are the particular national features that distinguish the Argentinian national context from others? To what extent have the unique characteristics of the national context shaped indigenous businesses? And how have the national business characteristics impacted on the way indigenous businesses organize themselves, transform and respond under competitive pressures? Aiming to understand these questions, this chapter is set up as follows: after this brief introduction, the second section introduces the framework we use to understand the National Business Environment (NBE). The third section develops the analysis of the

31

Argentinian business environment. The fourth section presents some concluding remarks and the fifth section analyses the particular features that make Argentina a hypercompetitive environment during the period analysed in this book and the impact on indigenous businesses.

NATIONAL BUSINESS ENVIRONMENT (NBE)

Our intention now is to develop a framework called the 'national business environment' to provide an understanding of the extent to which the national business features of Argentina have influenced both the development and structure of indigenous businesses in the country.

Our framework of analysis needs to shed light on the process of industrialization in the country so as to spell out the competitive pressures indigenous businesses faced over time and the radical changes Argentina underwent in the 1990s when its business organizations were transformed. It is by understanding the process of industrialization of a country that one becomes aware of the evolution of indigenous businesses (Kosacoff, 2000). Sylla and Toniolo (1991) emphasize that it is important to take into consideration the role of the state and the financial institutions. We will also consider the national culture as it can complement and enhance our analysis of the evolution and organization of indigenous firms. It is not possible to understand organizational and managerial arrangements in isolation from the culture that influences them (Hofstede, 1991).

Figure 3.1 displays the framework used in this research to understand the Argentinian business environment. Then, the elements of the framework are explored for the particular case of Argentina.

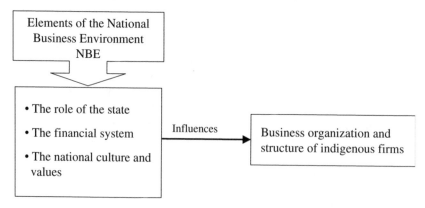

Figure 3.1   NBE and the structure and development of indigenous firms

THE ARGENTINIAN BUSINESS ENVIRONMENT

The Role of the State

There are different theories about the stages of development of Argentinian industry (Kosacoff, 2000; Gerchunoff and Llach, 1998; Llach, 1997; Di Tella and Zimelmann, 1977; Ferrer, 1971). In broad terms, however, three major periods can be identified in Argentina's industrialization process. In each period, the role of the state was a key factor in boosting that process.

The first period was from around 1880 till the crisis of 1930 when the country became integrated with the rest of the world as an agro-export economy. The second period extended from 1930 to 1989, the chief feature of which was the application of so-called import substituting industrialization (henceforth ISI) within a semi-closed economic framework. Finally, a new era for the industrialization process of the country started in 1989 with a stabilisation plan and the structural reforms of the Convertibility Plan.[1]

First Period: the Agro-export Model (1880–1930)

Once its institutional structure was settled, Argentina won a place in the international economy as a dynamic exporter of primary goods and importer of capital and manufactured goods. From 1880 to 1914, the economy was open to foreign investments. The economy was based on the agricultural production of the Pampas. A few major products were developed for export (meat, leather, seeds and wool). There was national and foreign investment in railways, roads, harbours and everything related to the infrastructure. Kosacoff (2000) indicates that during this period, economic fluctuations were linked with both the weather conditions (since the main exports were agricultural products) and the British business cycle (since Britain was the main international trading partner).

During this period the growth of the economy was based on the production of raw materials and the sale of these products to the external market. Exports and imports represented 50 per cent of the GDP (50 years later this figure had fallen to 20 per cent) (Fodor and O'Connell, 1972; Gerchunoff and Llach, 1998). In 1913 Argentina ranked 11th in the world in terms of GDP per capita (Llach, 1997).

The First World War forced the country to develop some industries in an attempt to replace the imports that were no longer arriving from Europe. Textile, shoe and furniture industries appeared at that time. The peak of industrial activity was reached between 1914 and 1929, during which period industrial production grew 127 per cent. Between 1926 and 1929 steel production rose by 48 per cent. Nevertheless industrial growth was in traditional agro-industries and light industries following the pre-war trend. Productivity gains in agriculture played a major role in inducing industrial growth as well as in increasing per capita incomes (Gerchunoff and Llach, 1998).

The state intervened little in the economy and preferred to follow a liberal policy, leaving economic decisions to market forces. However, successive governments during this first stage tried to encourage the export of agricultural products and the special trade relationship with Britain (Floria and García Belsunce, 1992).

The end of the expansion of the agricultural frontier, together with the 1930 international crisis, caused the demise of the agro-export model.

Second Period: Import Substituting Industrialization (ISI) and a Semi-closed Economy (1930–1989)

After the crisis of 1929, the government imposed an exchange control in 1931 and import permits in 1933. As a consequence import tariffs rose. These measures are illustrative of the new way in which the economy operated. The process of substitution of imports was helped by the incipient industrialization already achieved during the first phase. Furthermore, the Second World War made it more difficult for imports to reach the country. This was another incentive for the governments of the 1940s to encourage industrialization in the country.

Industrialization proceeded rapidly under the auspices of the Peronist regime (1946–1955). Perón saw in industry the potential for high employment and consumption. Three mechanisms were used by the government: restriction of imports; a credit policy for new industries through the Banco de Crédito Industrial; and the promotion of specific industrial sectors through the IAPI (Argentine Institute for Industrial Promotion). Nationalization of private companies such as the British railways, telecommunications and electricity, among others, marked this stage.

One problem associated with this attempt at industrialization, which had long-term consequences for Argentinian industry as a whole, was the lack of focus and diversification of industries that developed. The government did not seek advantages in the different sectors. A lot of the industries that developed were not large enough to benefit from economies of scale. The result was a manufacturing industry with high costs, high salaries and few possibilities of exporting (García Vazquez, 1995).

In 1958, the last ISI sub-period began. The most prominent of all the plans during this sub-period was the one launched by President Frondizi

(1958–1961). Heavy industry – such as petrol, gas, paper, chemicals, plastics, metals, machines and cars – was stimulated. Restrictions on imports were very severe. Subsidiaries of multinational companies (MNCs) started to participate extensively to fill the gap left by national industries. All this process took place within the framework of a highly protected economy and was a response to the explicit policy goal of raising the level of national economic self-sufficiency (Gerchunoff and Llach, 1998).

The 1980s would be critical for Argentinian industry. The ISI stage ended in the late 1970s. From 1976 onwards industry passed through a phase of sharp decline. From 1976 to 1982 employment in industry dropped by 37 per cent.

The economic crisis peaked in 1982 but the Military Junta found a way of diverting attention away from the internal problems: it launched the invasion of the Falkland Islands (taken over by Britain in 1833).[2] After a short conflict, the British ousted Argentinian forces. Public outrage alerted the military to the fact that its rule was coming to an end, and signalled the start of a new democratic era in the country.

After the re-establishment of democratic government in 1983, led by President Alfonsín (the Military Juntas were in power from 1976 to 1983), the economy began to suffer severe problems. The interest on foreign debt represented 9.4 per cent of GDP (compared with only 2.2 per cent in 1980) which, combined with increasing inflation, fiscal problems and the stagnation of the economy, meant that the new and inexperienced democratic government got off to a difficult start. Although the government implemented some measures (the so-called 'Plan Austral'), inflation rose dramatically in 1989. In that year, Argentina experienced a record level of 5000 per cent hyperinflation. In the period 1980–1989, the country suffered an economic contraction close to 14.3 per cent (Gerchunoff and Llach, 1998).

Third Period: Economic Openness, Structural Reforms and the Role of Foreign Direct Investments (FDI)

In 1989, the new government led by President Menem embarked on a process of far-reaching changes in the economy. In the course of five years (1989–1994), the country went from being a tightly regulated and protected economy to an open one, where free competition was allowed. The economic plan, which affected virtually every aspect of the economy, was based on three pillars of reform: monetary, fiscal and trade and regulatory reforms.

Monetary reform – from which the convertibility of the currency was developed[3]– and fiscal reforms were necessary to tackle an old Argentinian problem: inflation. Inflation was slashed from its peak of 5000 per cent in 1989 to 0.7 per cent in 1997. Privatizing the state-owned companies and bringing down subsidies helped to reduce government expenditure (Guillén and Toulán, 1997; INDEC, 1998).

While the monetary and fiscal reforms were important for the stability of the country, it was regulatory reform and the opening up of the economy to foreign trade and investment that impacted on the level of competitiveness of the indigenous companies. In one year (1990–1991), the import tariff was reduced from 18.4 per cent to 11.6 per cent. Additionally, deregulation in different sectors of the economy caused the price of services to plummet (Llach, 1997).

As a result of the privatization process and the opening up of the economy, the participation of the state diminished throughout the whole economy. Until 1989 the state was the sole supplier of the basic services: gas, oil, telecommunications and electricity were state-owned enterprises. In 1988, the state controlled seven of the first 15 enterprises (ranked according to turnover). By 1997, the presence of the state in that ranking was reduced to 13th position (The National Lottery). In 1992, the state accounted for 17 per cent of companies among the top 100 companies (ranked according to turnover). In 1996 this figure was further reduced to 2 per cent (Revista Mercado, 1992, 1997) (see Figure 3.2).

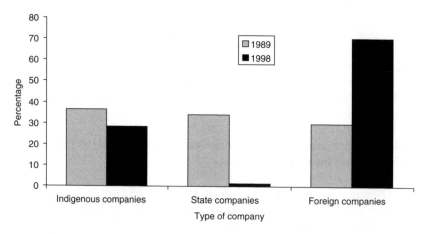

Source: Revista Mercado. This ranking takes into account the first hundred companies in the country in terms of turnover. The ranking shows the variations among these companies in terms of ownership structure.

Figure 3.2   Indigenous, State and Foreign Companies 1989–1998 among the top 100 firms

The Role of the State in the Structure and Development of Argentinian Firms

The participation of the state in the industrialization process of Argentina had a great impact on the genesis of indigenous firms, their growth and decline in the national market. Table 3.1 shows the links between the role of the state in the economy and the type of organizations that were emerging at the different stages of the industrialization process.

At the start of the industrial process, when the state supported the agro-export model, indigenous family firms emerged as the most important presence in the economy. The export of agriculture and meat products was managed by family run farms (*estancias*) (Kosacoff, 2000). After the 1930s, state intervention in the economy in the form of the nationalization of private companies caused a new type of organization to emerge: the state-owned company. The protectionism that prevailed at that moment caused small and medium size companies (hereafter, SMEs for small- and medium-size enterprises) to consolidate. In fact, SMEs acquired their main operating features during the period of ISI (Yoguel, 2000). In the 1980s, indigenous holding companies emerged to fill gaps in activities in which the state did not participate (such as the food sector, among others (Bisang, 2000)).

The deep structural changes that took place during the 1990s, however, merit a longer explanation to account for the decline of indigenous family-owned businesses in the country and the role of the state in that process. Three main processes over the decade analysed shed light on the influence state decisions had on the fate of indigenous businesses: first, it is important to mention the impact of structural reforms on strategic thinking and planning; second, the sudden withdrawal of the state as one of the most important agents in the economy; and finally, the importance MNCs acquired over time through the process of privatization and the merger and acquisition (henceforth, M&A) of indigenous firms.

The structural reforms in Argentina during the 1990s brought economic stability but at the same time competitive pressures and uncertainty for indigenous businesses. The days when nominal macroeconomic indicators were volatile were over. Indigenous businesses were now able to operate in a more stable macroeconomic environment. However, indigenous firms had to confront high levels of uncertainty because of the competitive pressures introduced by foreign firms following the opening up of the economy. As a result of this, indigenous firms had to take strategic decisions of a different nature than they had hitherto been used to. These decisions were based on longer planning horizons – a new concept for indigenous companies used to a small and protected market with low levels of competition (Dal Bo and Kosafoff, 2000; Toulán and Guillén, 1997).

Table 3.1 Stages of Argentinian industrial development and the evolution of business organisations

Type of context and firm	Agro-export model 1880–1930	ISI and closed economy model 1930–1989		Economic openness 1989 onwards
		1930–1976	1976–1989[a]	
General framework	Industrial consolidation. British hegemony	Protected market. Industrial self-sufficiency	Protected market	Stabilization-privatization-openness and deregulation. Higher competitive pressures
FDI	Mainly directed to infrastructure	Directed to production for the protected market		Directed to privatizations, merger and acquisition of indigenous businesses
Role of the state	Supporting the agro-export model	'Development and plan rational' (Whitley, 1991). Protection, promotion and subsidies		Diminished. Focus on deepening structural reforms
Leading companies	Export-oriented local business groups. Semi-artisanal small and medium size companies (SMEs)	State-owned enterprises Subsidiaries of MNCs and SMEs	National holding companies Some SMEs	Subsidiaries of MNCs
Type of organization	Family businesses	State-owned enterprises Family businesses Subsidiaries of MNCs	Holding companies Family businesses	Incipient development of partnerships and collaboration between indigenous groups and MNCs

Note: [a] Except by the period 1979–1981 in which external openness was attempted (Llach, 1997).

Sources: Llach, 1997; Fracchia and Spinetto, 1998; Gerchunoff and Llach, 1998.

The withdrawal of the state from the economy also had a great impact on indigenous firms. However, the strengthening of indigenous businesses did not naturally follow the withdrawal of the state after the process of privatization (1991–1994). The state did not favour indigenous businesses in the privatization process. Foreign firms with the managerial capacity to run the critical state-owned companies were given preference in that process. The state was therefore replaced by foreign firms instead of indigenous firms.

After the withdrawal of the state from the economy, once the privatization process ended, a process of M&As began in which foreign companies acquired a large number of family businesses. This process changed the map of local competition. The arrival of new participants brought pressure to bear on local firms ruled by a less efficient dynamic. The implementation of new business strategies and productive techniques by MNCs implied a breakthrough for the local firms which were by no means as efficient as their foreign counterparts (CEP, 1998).

Foreign companies were responsible for initiating 66 per cent of the M&As over the period 1990–1998. With the privatization process, MNCs occupied the role of the state, and by buying indigenous businesses they consolidated their influence in the national economy. Many traditional family businesses decided to sell their companies to an MNC, while others started to play on a different ground. The survivors were companies that could adapt their firm to the new market requirements. This process of selling off national companies (see Figure 3.3) influenced the market structure, changing the balance between national and foreign companies within the different sectors.

The financial system

According to Zysman's (1983) classification, the Argentinian financial system is closer to the credit-based model (that encourages state intervention) rather than the market-based type (where resources are allocated in competitive markets based on prices). Underdevelopment of capital markets and a limited number of financial institutions traditionally dominated the system. The dominant institutions in Argentina were banks of different sorts (mainly commercial and state-owned banks). This was complemented by strong state intervention that generated a closed financial system for many decades and only began to change after 1990. Throughout the second period of industrialization (1930–1989), the financial system was used by the state as an instrument of development. During that period, the Central Bank was a regulator of the government's industrial policy (CEP, 1998).

In periods of inflation or hyperinflation, commercial credit was not affordable. The lack of loans during inflationary phases necessitated a different business logic. In periods of hyperinflation little working capital

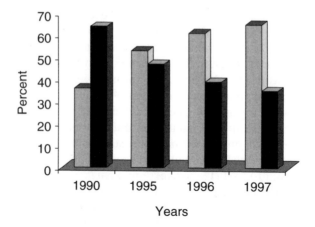

☐ Turnover of foreign firms (as % of total)
■ Turnover of national firms (as % total)

Source: CEP (1998) and Revista Mercado (1990), over a sample of the first 160 companies in terms of turnover

Figure 3.3 The selling off of indigenous businesses in Argentina

was needed (or affordable): buyers had to pay in advance, production was carried out with this money, and the difference due to indexation was collected once the merchandise was delivered (CEP, 1998).

The advent of stability has put a totally different financial system in place. Monetary reform was the most important aspect of transformation of the Argentinian financial systems. The convertibility plan required the Central Bank to fully back the monetary base in the form of foreign assets. The Central Bank was independent of the executive branch, making it accountable only to Congress. This fact reduced the government's ability to use the Central Bank as a last-resort lender. The changes in the monetary system increased the amount of money in the financial system, so commercial credit became available again (Kosacoff, 2000).

The opening up of the capital markets was accompanied by a shift in their composition. Government banks began to play a smaller role, having been replaced by private lenders, both domestic and foreigner.

The Role of the Financial System in the Development and Structure of Indigenous Firms

The credit policy of the state (through its various mechanisms such as the creation of the Banco de Crédito Industrial in the 1950s, IAPI, and the

Development Bank, among others) plus the underdevelopment of the capital markets have strongly influenced the type of ownership of firms in Argentina over time. It is no coincidence that the family structure of the firms in the country lasted so long. Given that it was impossible to rely on commercial credit from the local banks (due to high interest rates or the lack of policy to support certain activities) Argentinian entrepreneurs preferred to draw on family savings to fund their enterprises (CEP, 1998).

Over time, Argentinian companies suffered from capital shortages during periods of high growth and/or the state control of interest rates to support economic development. As a result, banks (private or state funded) allocated money to particular sectors and activities such as export industries (during the Perón presidency) or the heavy manufacturing sector (throughout the 1960s and 1970s). Consequently, indigenous firms found it was more reliable to depend on family funding than to trust in the financial system. Whitley (2000) indicates that direct ownership – as was the case in Argentina – is a direct consequence of low levels of trust in the formal institutions.

The deregulation and liberalization that has occurred since 1990 has produced a radical transformation and modernization of the Argentinian banking system. However, as the CEP (1998) reports, access to commercial credit has varied according to the financial capacity of the firms. While SMEs tend to depend to a large extent on national banks, large indigenous businesses tend to be customers of private and international banks. However, the main source of funding for investments is still family savings and net worth (CEP, 1998).

The national culture and values
To undertake the analysis of national culture and values in Argentina, we used Hofstede's (1980, 1985, 1991) analysis, which proposed four national culture dimensions: power distance; uncertainty avoidance; individualism and collectivism; and masculinity–femininity. This is the only study in which Argentinian culture, among others, is analysed on a quantitative basis. Moreover, the study provides a framework for understanding how Argentinian culture has changed over time.

Power distance is the extent to which people believe that power and status are distributed unequally and indicates their readiness to accept an unequal distribution of power as the proper way for social systems to be organized (Hofstede, 1991). Power distance in Argentina is increasing over time. A recent study (Friedrich *et al.*, 2006) states that Argentina scores significantly higher than other countries in Latin America regarding the role of authority in organizations. For Argentinians, it is important who has the authority to lead a group from the start. Hierarchy and authority is all important to them.

Table 3.2   The Argentinian national culture compared with Latin American countries and the United States[a]

Country	Power distance[b]	Uncertainty avoidance	Individualism[b]	Masculinity
Mexico	81/70	82	30/33	69
Venezuela	81/66	76	12/28	73
Brazil	69/72	76	38/37	49
Colombia	67/75	80	13/18	64
Peru	64/69	87	16/22	42
Chile	63/56	86	23/38	28
United States	40	46	91	62
Argentina	49/56	86	46/47	56

Notes:
[a]   The scores presented in this table corresponds to the findings of Hofstede's work (1980, 1991).
Power distance score: the higher the score the higher the power distance. Scores above 44 are considered to be an indication of a high level of power distance.
Uncertainty avoidance: the higher the score the higher the uncertainty avoidance. Scores above 56 are an indication of a high level of uncertainty avoidance.
Individualism: the higher the score, the higher the individualism. Scores above 50 are considered an indication of a high level of individualism.
Masculinity: the higher the score, the higher the masculinity. Scores above 50 are considered to be an indication of a high level of masculinity.
[b]   The second value in the table corresponds to predictions of the evolution of the value over time (Hofstede, 1991).

However, Argentinians do not trust all types of authority. Authority deriving from the state is therefore looked upon with suspicion and state actions are seen as corrupt (*Economist*, 30 June 2001).

A study carried out by Gallup (Escribano, 2001) confirms that Argentinians have little faith in their institutions. Only 38 per cent of the people interviewed said they trust institutions in general. The Church and educational institutions were considered the most trustworthy institutions (with 60 per cent and 74 per cent respectively). Political institutions such as Parliament and political parties are not trusted by Argentinians (only 11 per cent and 10 per cent of interviewees respectively considered those institutions to be trustworthy).

Collectivism versus individualism is the extent to which individual identity derives from the collectivity as opposed to the self. Individual cultures are loosely coupled. Individuals are expected to look out for themselves and their immediate families. Status derives from individual accomplishment. Collective cultures rely on membership in groups – social classes, companies, communities, or extended families – for identity and status. People are protected by the group, depend on the group, and are expected to act in the group's best interests (Hofstede, 1980, 1985).

Argentina is more collective than individualistic, owing, in part, to the high number of immigrants of Spanish and Italian extraction. Hofstede (1991), however, indicates that there is a slight tendency towards more individualism among future generations. The collectivist culture prevalent in Argentina is perceived to derive from a sense of duty and obligation to the family. This is understandable in a society that rejects the state as a reliable authority and falls back on the family or other social institutions (such as the Catholic Church) as trustworthy (Escribano, 2001).

Uncertainty avoidance is the extent to which people are threatened by uncertain, unknown, or unstructured situations (Hosftede, 1980). Uncertainty avoidance is high among Argentinians who are tired of economic and political turmoil (Friedrich *et al.*, 2006). Argentinians always search for the right way to make transitions as quickly as possible. The lack of clear-cut answers and the number of years required for complete transitions encouraged people to retreat into old habits such as avoiding initiative and innovation. These attitudes have been clearly reflected throughout Argentinian history when strong opposition from society has flared up after long periods of economic turmoil (Gerchunoff and Llach, 1998).

Finally, Argentinians have a tendency towards masculinity in Hofstede's (1991) masculinity-femininity dimension. Masculine cultures are characterized by doing and acquiring, rather than thinking and observing. They value affiliation and view failure as much less important. Hofstede (1991) illustrates the masculine character of a society in terms of the way countries resolve international conflicts. He states that feminine countries compromise and negotiate. However, masculine countries fight. As an example of this, Hofstede (1991: 100) cites the way the Falkland crisis was handled. The Argentinian military government occupied the islands in April 1982, as a result of which the British sent an expeditionary force to rebuff the occupiers. Argentina and the UK are both masculine countries in Hofstede's dimensions, and fighting and acquiring was the way both countries preferred to handle the conflict.

The Role of National Culture and Values in the Structure and Development of Argentinian Firms

How can the features of Argentinian culture and values affect the business organization? The national culture and values mainly affect the governance structure of the firms, the ways in which people deal with each other and other organizations, and the patterns of work organization and control (Whitley, 2000).

In organizations, power distance, as shown by Argentina, increases the extent of formal hierarchy and the degree of centralization. On the other hand, it decreases the level of participation in decision making (Hofstede, 1980; Trompenaars, 1992). Trust and authority relations are also affected. Argentinian managers' unwillingness to delegate authority and employees' unwillingness to take the initiative are emblematic of a higher power distance. In Argentina, the organization is seen as 'a pyramid of people' (Hofstede, 1991: 141; Friedrich *et al.*, 2006).

Indigenous businesses in societies with high power distance are characterized by a paternalistic culture. However, due to the increasing power distance in Argentinian society, paternalism is remote rather than reciprocal (Whitley, 2000). Remote paternalism implies a high degree of social and moral distance between leaders and led. This paternalistic culture influences the corporate governance structure of indigenous firms. These structures are characterized by a low level of managerial participation and the lack of clear boundaries between the role of ownership and management (Whitley, 2000; Carney and Gedajlovic, 2002).

Argentinian employees' reluctance to take individual responsibility is partly a reflection of their collectivism. The clarity of rules, procedures, job security and systems organizations that companies try to build up, on the other hand, is a clear sign of uncertainty avoidance. Reliance on clear procedures, well understood rules, and detailed job descriptions helps employees reduce uncertainty and cope with their discomfort with unknown situations. Finally, the masculinity and collectivity of Argentinian society will attach importance to group rewards and group empowerment rather than individual performance rewards (Hofstede, 1991) (see Table 3.3 for more details).

Hofstede's categories of analysis are taken up by Hamed and Miconnet (1999) in their study of the diffusion of process management practices in the Swedish company Ericsson in three different countries: Sweden, New Zealand and Argentina. Regarding the case of Argentina and its uncertainty avoidance, Hamed and Miconnet (1999) provide evidence of how employees in Ericsson Argentina are more likely to accept clearly defined reporting systems and responsibilities than their counterparts in New Zealand and Sweden. In addition, reward systems associated with the idea of taking risk, for instance performance-related pay systems, are rejected by Argentinian employees who are sensitive to uncertainty. They also suggest that Argentinian employees are less individualistic than their counterparts in New Zealand and Sweden, making it easier to foster teamwork, as the research fieldwork in Ericsson Argentina showed.

Table 3.3 Implications of national culture for Argentinian businesses

National culture factors affecting firms (Whitley, 2000)	High Power Distance	High Uncertainty Avoidance	Collectivism	Masculinity
Governance	• Top-down leadership • Paternalist-remote governance	• Important to know who has the authority over whom, and whom to obey	• Tendency towards multiple reporting	
Relations (within the organizations)	• Hierarchy is important • Distant relation between top management and employees • Favours upward delegation • Employees with low level of participation of decision making.	• Well defined hierarchy • Consensus important • Avoid conflict • Rules and procedures needed to be clear	• Hierarchy reflects personal status rather than achievement • Emphasis on relationships rather than tasks • Appeal to collective identity	• Group empowerment
Work organization and control	• High levels of centralization of decision making • People do not feel responsible for results • Risk-taking at the top • Change is a top-down process • High resistance to change	• Formalization of decision making • Tight control, based on well-established rules and standards • Emphasis on precision and routines • Innovation avoidance • Change perceived as a threat. High resistance	• Requires more control and dedication to norms of behaviour • Responsibility tends to become diluted within the group • Change is seen as a challenge to the group • Change is slow and shared	• Rewards for status difference not for performance difference

Sources: Hofstede (1980, 1985, 1991); Laurent (1986); Trompenaars (1992); Granell *et al.*, 1997.

CONCLUSIONS

The structure and development of indigenous firms are to a large extent the reflection of the institutions, values and assumptions of different societies. The analysis of the Argentinian business environment in terms of the role of the state and financial institutions in the industrialization process and national culture and values reinforces the fact that specific national factors play an important role in explaining differences in business organizations.

The Argentinian case is a good example of a country and a business system that, despite undergoing a radical transformation and modernization in a very short period, is significantly imprinted by its past institutional legacy. Indigenous firms were also shaped by the changes in the national business environment. Their rise, growth and decline can be explained as a product of the business environment in which they are embedded.

The previous analysis also reflects how certain nationally dominant socio-economic configurations persist over long periods and influence firms' behaviour. Moreover, national peculiarities are a critical element shaping the competitive advantage of both companies and industries. Indeed, the origin of any successful industry is specific to national attributes and not firm factors (Porter, 1990).

IS HYPERCOMPETITION A FEATURE OF THE ARGENTINIAN BUSINESS ENVIRONMENT?

Pettigrew and Whipp (1991) point out that the characteristics of a particular environment influence the adaptive responses of the firms. Firms respond differently depending on whether they are in stable or turbulent contexts (Volberda, 1999). But what attributes of an environment are likely to make it more turbulent than most other environments?

Several researchers have stated the differences between stable and turbulent environments. Emery and Trist (1965) highlight these differences by saying that, compared with stable environments, turbulent ones have an increasing rate of change, complexity is higher, as is the level of connectedness between the firm and the environment.

Khandwalla (1977) states that a turbulent environment is dynamic, unpredictable, expanding and fluctuating. It is an environment marked by changes, compared with stable environments in which little change occurs. Miles *et al.* (2000) suggest that unpredictability and dynamism characterize a turbulent environment. Unpredictability is understood as changeability and instability, while dynamism is defined by the rapidity of change.

D'Aveni (1994) has coined the word 'hypercompetition' to refer to highly turbulent environments. Hypercompetitive environments are different from stable ones for D'Aveni in that the former escalate towards higher levels of uncertainty, dynamism, heterogeneity of the players and hostility.

Endorsing the different ideas explained above, Volberda (1996, 1999) proposed three dimensions for analysing environmental turbulence: dynamism, complexity and unpredictability. Dynamism is defined in terms of frequency and intensity of change. Complexity is defined as the number of factors considered to be drivers of change and their interconnectedness. Finally, unpredictability will depend on the information available to enable managers to predict future developments. The application of Volberda's (1999) approach to analysing the environment faced by indigenous firms in the 1990s produces interesting results.

In terms of dynamism, indigenous firms went through a relatively stable period of three decades (from the 1960s to the 1980s). Firms were used to long product life, similar competitors and well-established regulation. In the 1990s, the pace of change increased. It saw the opening up of the economy and the lifting of regulations that affected the pharmaceutical industry directly (that is, through deregulation measures and a new legal framework) and the edible oil industry indirectly (that is, through deregulation in transport). Regulations that had previously fended off competition were lifted, making way for new competitors and new products to enter the market, and consequently increasing the level of complexity of the industry.

Unpredictability is the outcome of a far-reaching process of transformation both at the national and industry level. Before the 1990s it was easier for the different companies to predict each other's movements. Changes in the economy and the entrance of new players with different technology and business strategies, however, brought unpredictability into the industries during the 1990s.

The competitive environment for both edible oil and pharmaceutical industries changed from a stable context over 30 years (1960s to 1980s) to a turbulent environment in the 1990s, with each of the factors mentioned by Volberda reaching particulary high levels. In such a situation, Volberda (1999) suggests that we are in presence of a hypercompetitive environment.

Summary

In a hypercompetitive context, questions arise regarding the adaptive responses of indigenous firms in such an environment. How did the firms in our case studies react in a highly changeable environment? Were the firms able to adapt and change quickly or were they laggards within their industries? If so, why? What strategies did the firms implement to enable them to face the environmental changes? And what organizational and managerial changes did they try? And finally, what made the companies under study decide in favour of either strategy and organizational change? The following chapters aim to understand those adaptive responses by highlighting the differences in the way flexible and less flexible firms confronted the high levels of competition present in their industries.

NOTES

1. The economic crisis in Argentina that began towards the end of 2001 may imply the beginning of a new economic era in the country. These are, however, early days to make predictions about the economic future of the country. Economic and social stability is needed to understand the far-reaching consequences of the recent crisis.
2. The Falkland Islands are called Islas Malvinas by Spanish speakers.
3. The convertibility plan created a currency board that pegged the Argentinian peso with the US dollar in a one to one parity.

4.   Adaptive responses under competitive pressures

Chapter 3 underlined the competitive pressures firms underwent during the 1990s. We described these firms as being in a hypercompetitive or highly turbulent environment. Craig (1996) and Volberda (1999) point out that hypercompetitive environments have precipitated far-reaching changes in firms' competitive position and have forced them to transform in order to compete effectively. The adaptive responses of firms under hypercompetition would therefore vary according to the extent to which the transformation process was undertaken (Volberda, 1997). The adaptive responses of the companies under analysis are, therefore, the main concern of chapters 5–8.

In his seminal work, D'Aveni (1994) points out that in hypercompetitive environments, competitive advantages are quickly eroded. Companies therefore have to be more concerned about creating new competitive advantages than sustaining old ones. D'Aveni (1994) suggests that companies have to disrupt their own advantages and the advantages of competitors. These strategies need speed and surprise to enable companies to seize opportunities first. Questions arise as to what strategies are needed in such highly competitive environments? And what organizational and managerial challenges are required to allow a company to face hypercompetitive environments?

At the strategic level, the literature has emphasized the importance of product innovation, process and knowledge as competitive and disruptive advantages. In presenting a model for understanding firms' competitive advantages, Nault and Vandenbosch (1996: 342) assert that in hypercompetitive markets companies should cannibalize their own advantages. For them it is better to 'eat your own lunch before someone else does'. Such a strategy requires companies to invest and launch the next generation of advantages (that is, product, process or knowledge) while current advantages are still profitable. This pre-emptive strategy implicitly considers the importance of first mover or early adopter strategies.

Being a first mover is widely accepted in the literature on hypercompetition as a protective and anticipatory strategy. Craig (1996) shows the importance of the first mover advantage in the Japanese beer industry and how competitors in that industry were surprised by a competitor's introduction of a new product. As Craig (1996) indicates, the first mover advantage can change the rules of competition in an industry. Eisenhardt and Tabrizi (1995) and Brown and Eisenhardt (1997) also point out the importance of the first mover advantage in product innovation in a high velocity environment.

The need for competitive rather than sustainable advantages means organizations have to engage more in the exploration of new strategies rather than incremental exploitation of existing ones (Ilinitch *et al.*, 1996). March (1995) indicates that environmental volatility and uncertainty requires change and flexibility if a company wants to explore new horizons. If the environmental context changes rapidly and organizations do not maintain a steady stream of exploration efforts, they may fail to adapt.

Pettigrew and Fenton's (2000) comprehensive study of new forms of organizing in Europe sheds light on both strategic and organizational decisions faced by firms in rapidly changing organizational contexts. The analysis includes economies of scale, concentration on core activities rather than diversification, focus on competencies, and outsourcing and downsizing rather than vertical integration.

In the course of this analysis, Pettigrew and Fenton (2000: 39) found that outsourcing and alliance activities increased by 65 per cent over the period 1992–1996. However, only 11 per cent reduced diversification. The de-diversification process was small and diversification among related business high.

Pettigrew and Fenton (2000) also underline the importance of new managerial processes in allowing companies to cope better with the complexities of a rapidly changing environment. These processes include, among others: diversity among the top team; empowerment; employee participation in decision making; knowledge creation and knowledge transfer; collaboration and communication.

It is important to highlight that the conclusions of Pettigrew and Fenton's research refer to studies carried out in companies in developed countries. Khanna and Palepu (1997) suggest that while Western economies stress the importance of core competencies and focus, emerging markets emphasise the critical role of diversification. Khanna and Palepu (1997, 2000) indicate that these differences in organizing between more advanced Western economies and emerging economies stem from their different institutional settings. The unpredictability of government actions and the lack of access to the advanced technology, capital markets, cheap financing and technical knowledge available in Western economies forces companies in emerging markets to rely on diversification as an organizational form to fill the institutional voids existing in their countries (see also Ghemawat and Khanna, 1998).

Broadening the scale and scope of the business was also considered important by those who carried out empirical research in Argentina.

Carrera *et al.* (2000), in a study of the strategic responses of Argentinian companies throughout the 1990s, show that indigenous businesses strengthened both diversification of related activities and vertical integration. Thus, widening the scope of the business rather than concentration on core competencies was the strategy followed by indigenous businesses. Carrera *et al.* (2000) explain that the institutional context in Argentina features a lack of highly developed intermediaries in the market, so the increase in scope was necessary to overcome that shortage (for example the impossibility of outsourcing some activities due to the lack of a reliable supplier).

While Pettigrew and Fenton (2000) emphasized the importance of alliancing, Yoguel and Milesi (2001) – in a survey carried out in Argentinian firms – found that only 25 per cent of the companies signed cooperation agreements during the 1990s. The vast majority relied on informal connections rather than formal còoperation.

Internationalization of indigenous firms' activities was also considered important in companies facing severe competition in the internal market in the 1990s. Guillén and Toulán (1997) show how the intense pressures brought into the Argentinian market by foreign investment made indigenous firms start to internationalize their activities as a way of balancing out the loss in the internal market.

Changes at the organizational and managerial level were also indicated by Guillén and Toulán (1997) and Yoguel and Milesi (2001). These writers depict the challenges faced by companies in different sectors in Argentina during the 1990s and how most adaptable firms changed their organizational design from a functional hierarchical structure to one based on business units.

New managerial capabilities also needed to be developed. Batley (2000) analysed the water industry in Argentina and highlighted the importance of operational autonomy as a way of confronting the speed of environmental changes. In practice, this operational decentralization meant improving efficiency and effectiveness mainly by freeing managers from bureaucratic rules and controls. Yoguel and Milesi (2001) and Guillén and Toulán (1997), on the other hand, stress the importance of having managers with broad state-of-the-art techniques and skills. This was a crucial factor for firms that attempted to transform and adapt their businesses during the period of structural adjustment in Argentina in the 1990s.

In the light of the foregoing analysis, questions arise regarding the adaptation responses of the flexible and less flexible companies in this study. We have already shown the differences and similarities in studies that consider the adaptation process of firms operating under high levels of competition in developed countries and in Argentina. So, did the companies in this study focus on core competences or diversify their activities? Did the firms dismantle the value chain or strengthen it? What were the most important strategies followed by the companies? What organizational and managerial aspects were the focus of their transformation process? And, finally, what were the differences between the adaptation behaviour of flexible and less flexible firms?

Chapters 5–8 are transformational accounts that shed light on the adaptive responses of the flexible and less flexible firms selected for the analysis. In Chapters 5 and 6 the transformation of Sidus and DERSA in the pharmaceutical industry is explained, while in Chapters 7 and 8 the transformation of AGD and St Martin in the edible oil industry is examined.

To facilitate comparison between the companies analysed in this book, the structures of the chapters are similar. In each, we briefly analyse the history of the firm from its foundation to 1999. However, the cases center on tracing key issues chronologically over the period 1989–1999, namely: strategic initiatives (in the case of flexible firms) or market and products (in the case of less flexible firms); changes in the structure of the company; changes in the management; changes in the governance; and finally, unresolved issues and challenges for the future.

5. Case Study: Sidus Group

OVERVIEW OF THE HISTORY OF SIDUS 1938–1999

Founded in 1938 by Miguel and Antonio Argüelles, today Sidus[1] is a diversified group that participates in the pharmaceutical industry at various points in the chain of value. By 1999 Instituto Sidus, the mother company, was the fourth largest laboratory in the ranking of pharmaceutical companies in Argentina (IMS, 1999). Another company in the Group, BioSidus, was considered the most important biotechnological company in Latin America (González García *et al.*, 1999). BioSidus was also considered one of the few companies that successfully weathered the economic recession that affected the country over the period 1998–2001 (Ramos, 2001).

Both Miguel and Antonio married and had children. Miguel had three children: Estela, Irma and Fernando. Sadly, Fernando died at the age of 18. Antonio had two children, Marcelo and Silvia. None of the female children entered the business and the only male heir was Marcelo, who started to work in Sidus in 1963. By 1984 the company was in effect run by Marcelo Argüelles, although the founders were still alive. Antonio died in 1985 and Miguel in 1987.

From the very beginning, the founders emphasized the importance of product innovation as a key factor for success. Product innovation promoted the growth of the company throughout the 1960s and 1980s.

The 1980s saw significant changes in the company. In 1980, Instituto Sidus set up a small biotechnological department. This investment would become the star project of the company a decade later: BioSidus.

> In those days we could see that there were two clear alternatives: one was the pharmo-chemical projects that were popular at the time in Italy and Europe, on the basis that Italy was the supplier [of raw material] for the countries without patents; and the other was integration from the biological point of view. We took the risk of heading towards biological integration.[2]

It was during the tenure of Marcelo Argüelles that the company took off rapidly. In 1988 the opportunity arose with the first and only strategic alliance in the industry at that time.[3] A deal with Merck, the world's largest medicinal laboratory in 1988, made it possible for Instituto Sidus to jump from 22nd position in the ranking of pharmaceutical companies to third

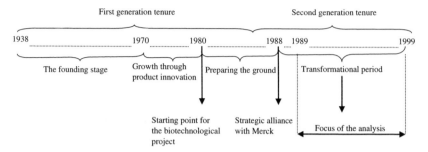

Figure 5.1   Stages in Sidus' history

position in Argentina. The 12-year agreement (until the year 2000) with Merck can be considered the most important milestone in the growth of the company during the 1980s (see stages of the firm in Figure 5.1).

After the Merck deal, however, the differences between Sidus and the rest of the companies in the industry widened. In 1989 Sidus pulled out of CILFA, the professional association that Sidus' founders had helped to set up.

Although the agreement had boosted Instituto Sidus' position in the pharmaceutical industry, it was clear that once the deal was over, Instituto Sidus was in a potentially very fragile position. A strategy of diversification and spreading the activities of the company throughout the value chain had begun immediately after the deal with Merck. Figure 5.2 shows both the evolution of the Group after the deal with Merck and the main macro-environmental changes affecting the industry.

Sidus embarked on various projects over the period 1989–1999. In 1989 the company set up what would become the first biotechnological company in Argentina and Latin America (Katz, 1992). The former biological department at Instituto Sidus emerged as the driving force of the group some years later.

In 1990 Sidus also set up a distribution company. This step was necessary to enable Sidus to commercialize all its own products and the products that Merck was pouring into the company. In 1992, Tecnoplant, a division of BioSidus, was established. It was a step towards developing markets for new bio-products of plant origin, as well as the production and multiplication of transgenic plants, among others.

The year 1995 saw the company moving forward in the chain of value with its attempt to set up a company called Lasifarma, established to commercialize OTC (over-the-counter) products. However, the project failed and by 1999 Lasifarma was a small and shrinking company.

The end of the decade would show Sidus returning to the mass consumption market but in a different way: investing in retail through buying

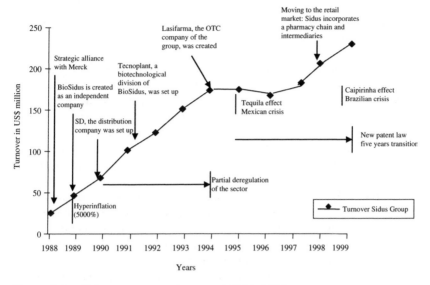

Figure 5.2   Sidus group over the period 1988–1999

a chain of pharmacies and intermediary companies. In 1998 Sidus, in a move unlike other companies in the industry, bought a franchise of Vantage pharmacies, set up its own outlets and also bought stakes in another chain. The move prompted Sidus to participate in intermediary companies that operated between the pharmacies and the unions and the social security system. This strategic move positioned the Group all along the value chain, from production, research and development to commercialization, distribution and retailing.

CHRONOLOGICAL AND ANALYTICAL TRACING OF KEY ISSUES

The Strategic Initiatives: Biotechnology

In 1980, Marcelo Argüelles, the son of the then CEO of Instituto Sidus, decided to embark on a risky but, as it proved, successful project: the setting up of a biotechnological department within Instituto Sidus. Both founders, Antonio and Miguel, backed Marcelo in this venture:

> When you spin things out, you realize that there was something at the back of Marcelo's mind: biotechnology is the development of products under their own brand names. Having a licence means that you have a certain length of time to

commercialize your products. When the time is up, they go, you have lost them. Today, we are using biotechnology to replace what we are going to lose once the Merck contract is over.[4]

Marcelo Argüelles' vision is also related to the situation of both the pharmaceutical and biotechnology industries in Argentina in the 1980s: while Argentina was 30 years behind countries such as the UK or the USA in terms of pharmaceutical research and development, the biological area was still an unexplored field worldwide. Furthermore, Argentina had produced three Nobel prizes in the field of biology: Hussay, Leloir and Milstein.[5] The country had the human resources necessary to undertake such a project (Bercovich and Katz, 1990; Diaz, 1993).

Thus, in 1980, Instituto Sidus hired three biochemists to set up its new biological department. The basic plan was that, by means of scientific investigation, Instituto Sidus would work with Interferon to combat viral infections. In 1982, the number of scientists rose to 20. Between the years 1982 and 1984, Instituto Sidus financed periods of study leave for its group of scientists and researchers. The team was trained in three disciplines: genetic engineering, cell cultivation and protein purification. In 1986, Instituto Sidus bought laboratory facilities in the city of Buenos Aires. Cultural differences between the scientists and Instituto Sidus personnel speeded up the decision to move to a different location.

1989–1999: the investment bears fruit

It was not until 1989, however, that BioSidus was established as an independent company and part of the Sidus Group:

> Imagine that year, 1989, everybody in the industry thought we were mad. That year inflation rose steeply and we had a company that still did not have a product. We were in the last stages of our clinical trials. The situation in which the country was submerged made us fear for the project's survival.[6]

In 1990, BioSidus was in the final stages of releasing its first product, the recombinant human erythropoietin, which is used to combat anaemia. Although the plan had been to release Interferon first, the company shifted strategy due to changes in the market. There were two main considerations that caused them to change strategy: first, erythropoietin was much more profitable than Interferon; second, and as an additional advantage to producing erythropoietin, Interferon already existed in the country but not erythropoietin. Hence, in 1987, the company halted the Interferon project and brought out erythropoietin.

The product was launched in the United States in 1989, and in Argentina in August 1990. The strategic move to release erythropoietin was rewarded by

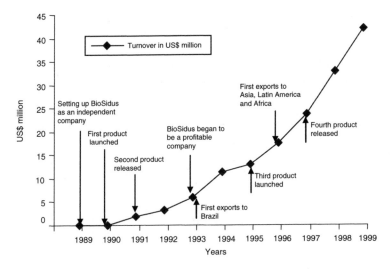

Figure 5.3   Evolution of BioSidus over the period 1989–1999

the market. The product has held 70 per cent of the market share in Argentina while four products are competing for the market. Moreover, BioSidus is considered one of the three largest producers of erythropoietin worldwide along with Amgen and Genetech of the United States (Diaz, 1993).

BioSidus released two more products. In 1991, the Interferon was launched and, in 1995, it launched the G-CSF, a product for patients who have undergone bone marrow transplants and for those undergoing chemotherapy. In 1997, the last product was launched, which was the hormone to treat growth problems in children (Figure 5.3 shows the evolution of products released and turnover obtained in the period 1989–1999).

Internationalizing the group through BioSidus

The investments the Group made in the first two products meant that the company could not afford to write off the debts incurred by the investments without looking beyond the Argentinian market. Thus, BioSidus created a foreign sales department. The first target market was Brazil. In 1993 BioSidus was in a position to register its products in the biggest market in the region. The company sold both products in Brazil (erythropoietin and Interferon), attaining 70 per cent of the Brazilian market. This was when BioSidus leapt ahead. In 1993 the company had achieved economic independence from Sidus.

While the company entered the Brazilian market with a partner, Biosintética, it granted licences to MNC pharmaceutical companies to commercialize its products in the next stages of the internationalization process in Asia, Africa, Latin America and the Caribbean. This new stage of internationalization began in 1995. While Biosidus had an important worldwide presence, there were certain markets – for example, the European, American and Japanese markets – which, due to tight regulatory policies, were difficult to access.

BioSidus had created the 'tit for tat' phenomenon. For example, Schwartz, a German company, had granted Instituto Sidus the licence to produce a series of products and BioSidus had granted them some other licences. This would allow BioSidus to enter the Chinese market within a few years by forming an alliance with Schwartz which already had a company in China.

The investment in biotechnology was also helping the Group to keep the average price of its products above the average price of the industry as a whole, as Figure 5.4 illustrates.

Challenges for the future

BioSidus faces three main challenges in the future. The first one is to release a broader range of products. The second and third challenges are related to building plants in Brazil and Canada.

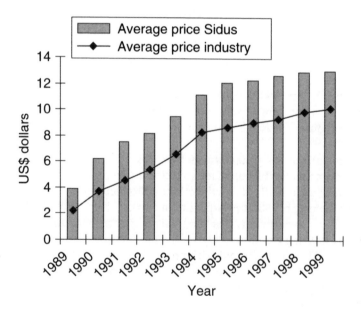

Figure 5.4   Average price of Sidus' products and prices in the industry over the period 1989–1999

There are some lines of products the company wants to bring out in the next few years. The new products, however, are for niche markets such as those related to Alzheimer's disease, bone marrow transplant, thrombosis, osteoporosis and a regulator of intestinal flora, as well as products considered appropriate for illnesses more prevalent in developing countries such as chagas and cholera.

A second challenge would be to build a plant in Brazil. The Group signed a joint venture with a Brazilian partner and founded a company called Biolatina: 'At the moment this project is well under way, but it is hard to set up a bi-national company with Brazil, it is difficult to get finance which fits the economic climate of both countries.'[7]

The final challenge for BioSidus would be to install a plant in Canada. The Canadian context supported this idea. Canada had its first patent law in 1989. It was a very moderate one which was modified in 1992:

> The fact that some products are non-patentable in Canada gives us a great historical opportunity. The most interesting thing is that we can develop technology here, manufacture in Canada and obtain a certificate which says made in Canada, which is an easy way of getting into the States and Europe.[8]

The Strategic Initiatives: Retail Market

From the laboratory to the pharmacy
A recent move Sidus made in the market was in 1998, when it decided to jump from one point in the chain to another, from production and research and development straight to the retail market, by setting up a chain of pharmacies. The original project was to invest US$15 million and establish 50 outlets. However, the plan was modified when Sidus realized that two foreign companies wanted to set up a franchise of pharmacies in the country. The Group thereafter bought only seven pharmacies and a franchise – Vantage – the first and only franchise in Argentina up to 1999.

Having a franchise allowed the Group swiftly to increase its level of participation in the retail market. With the franchises (200 pharmacies) and its own pharmacies, the Group sought to find mutually beneficial arrangements. In 1998, Sidus bought 30 per cent of the shares of a very important chain of pharmacies. The last acquisition was explained as an attempt 'to learn the business from the most important company in the sector and to achieve synergies with our own pharmacies. Thirty per cent of the shares was enough to accomplish this.'[9]

In one year then, Sidus shocked the pharmaceutical industry by entering a field that had not been explored by other pharmaceutical companies, buying the first and only franchise in the country, acquiring seven pharmacies and buying a share in another chain (Manzone, 2000). 'Our entrance into the market was a shock for the rest of the industry. They did not expect us to make this move. Again we were in the forefront, the first to move ahead, and setting ourselves apart from our competitors.'[10]

In 1999, Sidus also decided to get involved in another activity which complemented its investments in the retail market. That year, it bought 60 per cent of two intermediary companies. They traded between the pharmacy and the social security system, agreeing contracts and discounts. In 1999, Sidus also bought 30 per cent of a technology company that provided services to the pharmacies. The purchased firm had no competition because it was the only company providing this type of service: 'By buying these companies what Sidus did was it distanced the company from the rest of the industry.'[11]

The incomplete tasks

From the moment the pharmacies were opened, the volume of products sold by Sidus increased. The new businesses, however, were still far from being profitable. Sidus' own companies did not reach the break-even point. Furthermore, the Vantage franchise was also seeing losses.

> Our main aim in 2000 and 2001 is to break even in the three projects. All three of them are strategically important but we are not earning money with them; on the contrary, we are losing money. We need to own at least 20 pharmacies to gain scale. This, with a good management of the outlets, will give us profits. We need to have a level of turnover of 6 million a month to be able to absorb the costs of such a structure.[12]

On the other hand, companies such as the intermediary or the technology firms are also running at a loss:

> The whole idea is great. It is an important step forward to be the first to get a grip on this part of the industry. The companies, nevertheless, are operating below the breakeven point. When we bought them they were losing money. As you can see, money was not the main reason for buying them. But now, we have to sort things out and start to make profits.[13]

Changes in the Structure

The effects of Sidus' decision to diversify are clearly reflected in the structure of the company. While in 1989 the structure of the company was a functional one, in 1999 the group split up into five companies that are divisions of Sidus Group (that is, BioSidus, Sidus, SD, Lasifarma and Retail Businesses).

The changes in the structure were decided in 1989 once BioSidus was established as a separate company. The Board believed that BioSidus had a different nature and this was demonstrated by the cultural clashes the group of scientists experienced while sharing the same space with Instituto Sidus' personnel. The Board therefore decided that BioSidus should have its own space 'to express and develop itself'.[14]

With the other emerging areas such as the distribution company (SD), the OTC company (Lasifarma) and the retail businesses, the company used a similar strategy. The aim, as the CEO stated, was 'To avoid bureaucracy in decision-making. Having different companies with the freedom to make decisions and a structure focused on their particular businesses helped us to be fast and first.'[15]

After the creation of the second company – SD – in 1990, the Group started to reorganize the areas within Instituto Sidus (the mother company) to gain, as some managers stated, 'economies of scale' and 'efficiency'. The different support areas that previously gave their services to the main company were transformed into support areas for the whole Group. In so doing, the company avoided overlapping functions and activities.

New support units emerged in this process, such as the Human Resource department in 1994, which replaced the old Personnel Department, and the area of Communication and Image to unify the corporate message of the whole group. Finally, the Logistics Department was set up to achieve economies of scale throughout the companies of the Group.

Not only were new areas created but a new concept also emerged as central to running the businesses at Instituto Sidus: the business units. The reorganization sought to give more power to the people in charge of the business units: 'By doing this we wanted to infuse the areas with more dynamism, and we thought that the form of business units suited our objectives.'[16]

While the different companies of the Group benefited from the support of some units at the headquarters, the Board also decided they needed to update the units that depended directly on the Board. This is how three new areas emerged: Regulation and Legal Analysis in 1990; Sectoral Analysis in 1990; and finally, Macroeconomic Analysis in 1997. In all three cases, these were areas that aimed to look into different aspects of the context surrounding and affecting the company.

Changes to the structure were effected smoothly and without resistance. The fact that the company was expanding did not alter its normal development. As some managers stated:

> The changes in the structure passed without notice. The company was expanding its activities, and the fact that it was decided that each new venture would become a new company meant that we did not notice the impact of the change. This was probably the success of the structural change.[17]

> If you compared the structure now and ten years ago, there have been huge changes. I think this is something the Board was working on hard to try to avoid the normal problems these changes usually bring about.[18]

Changes in the Management of the Company

A wave of new professionals

From 1980 when the company first started to diversify its activities, its management began to shift and become more professionalized. It was BioSidus that marked the difference between the old-style management and the new. Furthermore, BioSidus brought young professionals with a different profile into the organization:

> BioSidus was a rare experience for us. The new professionals, scientists and technicians differed greatly from the rest of the employees in the company. They were better prepared and could take decisions on their own. They were very efficient and had tools that we did not have.[19]

The rest of the company's ventures began to add more variety to the already established management in the company. Splitting the Group into a series of companies helped Sidus to start to professionalize the different businesses from scratch:

> One of the advantages that we found in exchanging the functional structure for a structure dominated by the different businesses is that professionalizing was not painful at all. I would not have liked to imagine the situation if all these new ventures had not been independent companies. We would never have achieved the efficiency and level of professionalization these companies have today.[20]

While the new companies benefited from professionalization from the moment they were set up, Instituto Sidus went through a different process:

> Changes at the managerial level were needed at Sidus. We were laggards within the Group and the rest of the companies in the Group saw us as the steam train. Changes here had a different pace. There were areas that were keener on professionalizing and other areas that still needed more work.[21]

The new and more sophisticated product lines Instituto Sidus incorporated over the 1990s (that is, odontology, biotechnology and ophthalmology among others) helped the firm to renew the largest section of its work force: the sales team. As Table 5.1 shows, entry requirements for those seeking employment with Sidus were tougher, thus boosting the level of professionals incorporated in the firm over the 1990s. By 1999 the sales force of Sidus had increased in number from 20 in 1989 to 200 in 1999, reducing the average age from 49 to 39 years. Similarly, the average amount of working experience was reduced from 15 years to 5 years. Table 5.2 illustrates the changes in average age in different areas of the company.

Although Sidus considered it advantageous to shift towards a more professionalized company, it was also aware of the disadvantages of this move:

Table 5.1   *Degrees and requirements for entering Sidus over the period 1989–1999 (selected areas)*

Areas	1989	1999
Marketing	• Experienced medical visitor • At least 10 years' work experience in the industry	• University degree • Age between 25 and 30 • 3 years' average experience (not exclusively in pharmaceuticals)
Finance	• University degree in accounting or economics • Several years of experience in banking or pharmaceutical industry	• University degree, preferably accounting, economics and business administration • Experience in different industries is welcomed
Human Resources (Personnel in 1989)	• Not specified. The personnel area focused on administrative matters therefore, no specific requirements for entering the area	• University degree • Having done training or internship in a company before • Experience outside the sector welcomed

Table 5.2   *Average age of personnel in selected areas of Sidus Group*

Area/Company	1989-Average age	1999-Average age
Marketing	49	39
Production	54	42
Administration	48	37
BioSidus	33	32
Vantage Pharmacies	Did not exist	30

Previously, executives were very intuitive, they based their relationship with the company exclusively on trust, within surroundings which needed very little control. They had a nose for the market, very few managerial skills, but put in lots of effort. The new professional is someone with many skills, who is well trained, and who has less intuition but more intention.[22]

At Sidus they asserted the importance of old and new managers as having a complementary role in the running of the company:

The Board is convinced that old managers can help to preserve old values that are our foundation, and new managers would bring those values and tools that the company needs. I would not say that the coexistence is easy, but it works and we learn from each other.[23]

Control and planning process

In 1988 Instituto Sidus hired a consultant from Arthur Andersen to become its Administration Manager. He was given an important task by the Board: to set up the control systems of which the company had very few.

The administration manager spent his tenure setting up the whole area of administration, including the clarification of costs, preparation of budgets and the area of taxation. The emphasis of his work was on information systems and control processes:

> The philosophy I encouraged, in agreement with the General Director, was to prioritize the sharing of information, the sharing of transactions, for which we installed a single database for the whole of the company. We created the control boards that allowed managers from different levels and the Directors to have access to different indicators of the company and its performance. Besides that we improved horizontal communication[24] (see Table 5.3).

It was not an easy task to convince the Board of the benefits of having more control: 'We were afraid of control mechanisms. I was against them. We did not want to lose one of our virtues which was being able to make

Table 5.3   *Indicators used by selected areas over the period 1989–1999*

Area	Indicators in 1989	Indicators in 1999
Marketing[a]	• Sales budget	• Sales budget • Spending budget • Investment budget
Production[b]	• Estimates of cost per unit released	• Per cent productivity • Quality of products released • Cost efficiency (cost over total units)
Human Resources[c]	• Per cent absenteeism	• Per cent absenteeism • Specific indicators for training, welfare policies and working conditions • Selection and performance

Notes:
[a] In 1999 the indicators correspond to the different business units of product lines.
[b] Corresponds to the Manufacture areas in 1989 and the Technical Operation in 1999.
[c] Personnel department in 1989.

decisions quickly. In other words, we wanted to avoid becoming a bureaucratic company.'[25] The administrator manager pointed out the difficulty of formalization in a company that was not used to controls and processes:

> It took me years to convince them to introduce technology, to introduce a budget. It seems incredible to me, today, to hear the CEO asking the managers to justify how they have spent their budgets, when a few years ago he would say to me that if we set budgets the company would turn into a public and bureaucratic company.[26]

Board of Directors: Governance, Strategy and Family

Governance and family alignment

When the founders were still alive, Antonio was the President of the company and Miguel its Vice-President. In 1985 Antonio died and Miguel took over the post of President, though only for a short period of time before his death in 1987. As mentioned before, Marcelo Argüelles, Antonio's son, was in effect running the company from 1984. Marcelo was the natural candidate when Miguel Argüelles died.

The Board that was created after the founders' death to represent the whole family, however, changed over time. By 1999, the board was composed of three directors representing the stakes of the whole family.

Over the years the Board settled down and the Directors started to work together:

> We can say that it was not a promising start for this Board. We did not get on very well. But you know, this is a family company, and we retain many family values in terms of the way that none of the things we have lived through has weakened our relationship and for us this is incalculably important. I have to say that I never found any obstacles to anything; I always found collaboration, willingness, help and support both for the things which turned out well and those which turned out badly.[27]

While one of the directors was responsible for finance and SD, the other was responsible for production and Lasifarma:

> He [Marcelo Argüelles] is great at strategizing. So we let him go ahead. We are more the administrative type. We put order in Marcelo's turmoil. This is the best, and only way we found of working together, complementing each other.[28]

In 1990, the Directors agreed to sign a family protocol, thus avoiding any rows between the third generation of family members. Some of them were already working in the company in 1990. The protocol made the entry conditions for family members tougher.

Strategy, delegation and control

It was the Board's idea to reorganize the company in the early 1990s and create a group of companies. This decision had a specific aim concerning the strategic decision making of the company:

> I am overwhelmed by the bureaucracy a large organization generates. In this aspect, our relationship with Merck had too much of an effect on our structure. I did not want this company to become a leviathan. I wanted to keep the speed in our decision-making process. I think that this was our principal advantage.[29]

The reorganization of the company in the early 1990s was helpful in tackling the task of avoiding bureaucracy in decision making and allowing the Board – and its President – to focus on strategy.

> In this business, as in others I imagine, you have to have time for thinking about strategy, to have a vision. The main difference between the 1980s and the 1990s is the time you spent grounding and developing the strategy. What we [the Board] wanted to achieve with the changes in the company, was to have more time for thinking strategically and being open to changes in the context.[30]

A process of delegation started once the second company of the group was created (that is, BioSidus). It was a necessary and natural process that otherwise 'would have trapped us in a terrible deadlock.'[31]

Strategic decision making, however, was centralized in the Board. Mr Argüelles made it clear that there are some decisions that are not being delegated because 'they represent critical aspects of the company's life and future.'[32] Table 5.4 shows those decisions considered to be strategic and that only the CEO and Board would take.

The most important way the Board of Directors exercises control is through these strategic decisions:

Table 5.4   Strategic decisions needing the CEO's intervention

Areas/Companies	Strategic decisions
In all the companies	• Strategic alliances • Associations or joint ventures • Investments • Launching a bid to buy a company
BioSidus	• Development of new products • Licences to be given
Marketing business units	• Licences to be taken

This is how the Board has a grip on the different businesses. There are meetings in which the different critical areas analyse the different businesses. The Board is more interested in the strategic part of the presentation. They assume that you should be responsible for the operation. Another outcome of the Board's change of attitude toward the businesses is that it has forced managers to provide the Board with more accurate indicators and information, something that was impossible a decade ago.[33]

The incomplete tasks

Many tasks have yet to be fully accomplished. However, two issues have preoccupied, and sometimes vexed, the managers.

The first issue relates to the communication of strategy. For some managers, there is a lack of communication of strategic issues that sometimes undermines the feeling of belonging to the company and distorts the alignment of operational issues to strategic issues. As the HR Manager stated:

> I think that Marcelo [Argüelles] should try to explain better, to the managers, the whys and wherefores of the strategy he is working on. . . . Sometimes this lack of communication causes misunderstandings, lack of motivation and duplication. Improving strategic communication is a challenge for the Board and its President.[34]

Another issue that has worried some managers is the delegation of some aspects of decision making. While the delegation process worked in the different companies that are part of the Group, the situation at Instituto Sidus is different:

> In the different companies of the group the wheels of the delegation process were well oiled. With Instituto Sidus it is different: the President is sometimes caught up in the day-to-day running of the company. He loves marketing and so he is always involved with that.[35]

The Unresolved Issues

Two issues regarding the future of the company concern the Board and managers. The first issue is related to the participation of the third generation of family members in the Board and the second is related to the opening up of the company to the public.

The problem of succession and family participation in the Board is one issue that could potentially harm the governance of the firm. Marcelo Argüelles's children are very young compared with the others in the third generation, thus making it difficult to decide who will be Argüelles's successor.

An idea shared by the human resource manager (hereafter, HR manager), a family member, was the creation of an executive committee between the Board and the managers:

This would be a way of starting to participate in the decisions, a committee in which top managers from the different companies of the Group – both family and non-family members – participated.[36]

I am trying to sell this idea to the Board. It is the best way of avoiding tension between generations of family members and a way of having a participative organisation.[37]

A second issue, which is equally important but not so pressing, was the possibility of floating BioSidus on the stock market. The company had a concrete plan which was to open BioSidus up to the public. The idea was to sell between 15 and 20 per cent of the shares. This was planned for the year 2001: 'It will change a lot of things for us. The plan is to consolidate the company first and this undoubtedly will take us a couple of years.'[38]

NOTES

1.   In 1989 Instituto Sidus became a Group of companies, so, we will use the words Sidus, the Group or Sidus Group to differentiate them from Instituto Sidus the mother company.
2.   Interview with CEO.
3.   To date there has not been another strategic alliance in the pharmaceutical industry in Argentina.
4.   Interview with family member and Executive Director of Retail Businesses.
5.   Milstein studied in Argentina but won the Nobel Prize at Cambridge University.
6.   Interview with Business Development Manager of BioSidus.
7.   Interview with Executive Director of BioSidus.
8.   Interview with CEO.
9.   Interview with family member and Executive Director of Retail Businesses.
10. Interview with family member and Executive Director of Retail Businesses.
11. Interview with family member and Executive Director of Retail Businesses.
12. Interview with Manager, Vantage franchise and own pharmacies.
13. Interview with family member and Executive Director of Retail Businesses.
14. Interview with CEO.
15. Interview with CEO.
16. Interview with CEO.
17. Interview with Controller.
18. Interview with ex Marketing Manager, current head of New Businesses Unit.
19. Interview with CEO.
20. Interview with CEO.
21. Interview with HR Manager.
22. Interview with HR Manager.
23. Interview with HR Manager.
24. Interview with HR Manager.
25. Interview with CEO.
26. Interview with HR Manager.
27. Interview with CEO.
28. Informal talk with one of the Directors.
29. Interview with CEO.
30. Interview with CEO.
31. Interview with CEO.

32.   Interview with CEO.
33.   Interview with family member and Executive Director of Retail Businesses.
34.   Interview with HR Manager.
35.   Interview with HR Manager.
36.   Interview with family member and Executive Director of Retail Businesses.
37.   Interview with HR Manager.
38.   Interview with CEO.

6.   Case Study: Laboratorio DERSA

OVERVIEW OF THE HISTORY OF DERSA 1930–1999

Founded in 1930 by two Frenchmen Jean Dufour and Patrice Patou, DERSA[1] was in 1999 a leading company in the dermatological sub-market of the industry (IMS, 1999). DERSA was among the leading 20 companies in Argentina (IMS, 1999).

Until the definitive split between the partners, that occurred in 1950, the company had commercial or industrial outlets in 19 countries.[2] When the partners split, they shared the brands and branches between them. They also granted each other the right to found businesses in countries where DERSA had not already established itself.

Jean Dufour carried on with the internationalization process in different countries such as Chile, Brazil, Argentina, Paraguay, Uruguay, Colombia and Mexico. The headquarters of the new DERSA was in Argentina.

In 1979, Jean Dufour died, leaving eight children. That year, the family situation took its toll on the organization because the shares were held by so many private individuals that there was no impetus to continue as a group.

A gradual exit from the world of business, the loss of group identity and family continuity in the Southern Cone area were the three phenomena which marked 1979. The only part of the family to persevere with the business was the family that remained in Argentina and which took over operations in Uruguay and Paraguay under the son of Jean Dufour, Émile. The remaining companies of the group were sold off. The Argentinian market is the most important for DERSA both in terms of volume and value of products sold in US dollars (75 per cent and 88 per cent respectively).

While Jean Dufour was still alive and running the Group, Émile Dufour was not involved in the business because his father did not want his children to get caught up in the company. Thus, when Jean Dufour passed away and Émile inherited the Argentinian branch (Paraguay and Uruguay were included here), he decided to retain Daniel Alcorta as CEO – formerly the CEO of the DERSA Group.

In 1983 the CEO died and Andrés Gali took his place. Émile Dufour stayed on the sidelines. Over 50 years old and with little experience as an executive, he preferred to employ an experienced manager to run the company. Andrés Gali ran the company until 1997.

My father had no alternative. Gali's period represented a solution for my father. He could not manage the company so he had to rely on somebody else. Gali seemed to be the right person at the time. The problem is that he [Gali] lasted for a long time and the market changed a lot but the company did not.[3]

In 1988, Michael Dufour (the son of Émile) entered the company when he was co-opted to the Board. However, it was not until 1993 that he started to have an important role in the company. That year, he set up the OTC (over-the-counter) department, and in 1996 he became the Commercial Manager, a role which involved the management of 'ethical' products, promotion and sales and marketing of OTC products. In 1997 he became the CEO of the company, replacing Gali.

On the day Michael Dufour took over responsibility for the company, 22 managers were dismissed, the first step in a 'shock strategy', as the company likes to define it.

The new CEO undertook several changes to bring the company out of the stagnation of the previous two decades. Strategic focus on dermatology products, financial order and organizational restructuring were critical issues for the new management (see Figure 6.1 and Figure 6.2). However, by 1999 many difficulties were still jeopardizing the company's growth. The changes in strategies, although clarifying the long-term objectives of the company, put the firm in a niche of the market that limited its possibilities for growth.

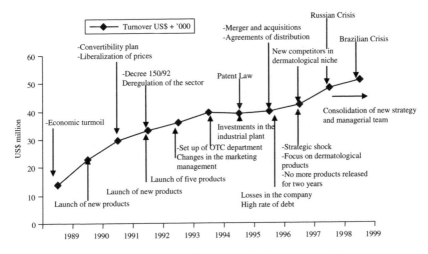

Figure 6.1   DERSA's evolution 1989–1999

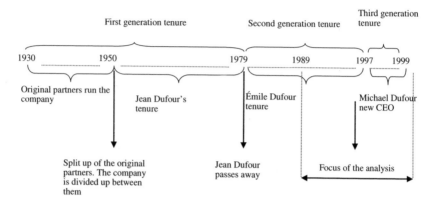

Figure 6.2   Stages of analysis in DERSA's history

CHRONOLOGICAL AND ANALYTICAL TRACING OF KEY ELEMENTS OVER THE PERIOD 1989–1999

Market and Products: Finding out the Strategic Focus of the Company

From 1978 to 1997, the company followed a simple strategy: investing in those niches that were fast-growing and which could offer opportunities, no matter what the niche was.

DERSA participated in all the therapeutic niches in the pharmaceutical market. The fact that it had been an international company made the board believe that they could profit from the different products they already had, and add new products to the already existing ones: 'Many products were launched in the different therapeutic niches in the conviction that anything would add value and everything would have the potential for commercialization. After a while these products were withdrawn because the return on the investment was negative'.[4]

However, the regulation of the market and the tight price control in the 1980s allowed the company to keep this policy of trying a new product in the market without taking heed of the long-term consequences.

This strategy, which many managers in the company called 'diffused', or 'blurred', or characterized as having a 'lack of vision', 'no vision' or 'lack of strategic orientation', was supported by a system of promoting the products to the distribution chain instead of via the normal channel of promotion (that is, the doctors). The APMs (promotional and sales team) offered huge discounts to the wholesaler so they could reach the estimated sales levels: 'Almost a whole month's worth of sales laid dormant in the wholesaler

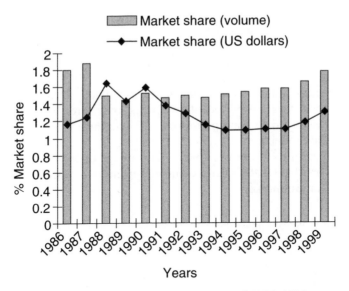

Figure 6.3   DERSA's market share over the period 1986–1999

warehouses because of this policy, which is obvious because when the wholesaler gets a discount he buys more.'[5]

The 1990s, however, proved the inconsistencies of this strategy: 'In 1990 we faced the impossibility of launching new products. We were losing market share. We thought about selling abroad, but the export strategy also failed.'[6] Figure 6.3 demonstrates that the firm's strategy was not rewarded by an increase in market share. On the contrary, DERSA was losing ground in the pharmaceutical market for most of the decade.

While the market conditions allowed the company to increase its turnover until 1994, after this date sales stagnated and started to decrease, and financial indicators began to give the owners cause for concern. In 1995, Michael Dufour and a group of managers studied the performance of all the products released by the competitors and DERSA over the period January 1990 to December 1995. A successful performance was defined as a product with a turnover of one million US dollars per year two years after being launched, or a product that could have cornered 10 per cent of the market share in its niche with a turnover of at least US$ 250 000 also two years after the launch of the product. The results were disappointing for the company.

The proportion of successful launches in the industry was around about 30 per cent. DERSA had a proportion of 22 per cent. We were more effective in the dermatology product market where the proportion was 60 per cent. But we kept on trying new niches in which we were not effective. In fact, the money fed into the other niches came from our cash-cow products, the dermatological ones.[7]

The analysis carried out by the company in 1995 underlined the ineffectiveness of the product launches in the different niches. Of 14 products launched over a period of five years, only three were considered effective releases with good performance. These three products were dermatological products.

The study in itself did not change the strategy of the company, but it made it clear that DERSA had a definite propensity for working in the dermatological sub-market:

> The most important outcome of this study was to make my father realize that we were on the wrong track. However, Gali was against this idea of focus and nothing happened. Never mind, I said to myself, this is the first step towards a big change in the company. This change took two long and painful years to happen.[8]

The critical years: 1995–1997

The Mexican crisis in 1995 hit the whole industry hard. Until 1994 deregulation benefited all the companies in the industry. Turnover increased due to an increase in prices rather than units sold.

However, after 1995, sales stagnated and DERSA's debt grew. The company found it difficult to recover from that situation:

> The company was in a critical situation. In spite of important decisions taken as part of our business plan, like the increase in the price of our most important brands, the financial problem could not be solved.[9]

> The company was rather slow to react to the threats it faced. It did not update its products nor did it launch any successful products – the worst possible situation for the company.[10]

A general audit of the company was carried out, showing a certain number of aspects that were out of date, a lack of order and – most strikingly – rampant corruption.

By the end of the year, Gali's power was in tatters and the Board of Directors had been restructured. Michael Dufour and Émile Dufour Jr were now Directors. The Board asked Michael to prepare a plan to get the company out of the crisis. Along with Fernando García, who joined the company in 1997, he prepared a new strategic plan for the company. That plan was finally approved.

The Shock Strategy: 1997

I presented the plan to my father in 1997 and he backed it. It was decided that Andrés Gali would step down and I would take over his job.[11]

On that day, the new CEO took over his post, he dismissed 22 managers. The new strategic plan was communicated and the main aspects of the strategy were highlighted:

- The company would focus on dermatological products. A strategy of niche products replaced the more generalist view of the former administration.
- Reduction of the company's debt (that is, US$ 5.3 million, which represented one and a half month's sales).
- Investments in infrastructure to update the old facilities.
- Decision to suspend the launch of any new product for two years.
- To achieve 25 per cent of market share of the dermatological niche by 2003.

We worked hard on the idea of differentiation. We asked ourselves what made us stand out from our competitors – did we do anything better than them? Should we highlight that aspect? DERSA runs 1.1 per cent of the total market. But in the dermatology sector it has 17 per cent, followed by another company with 5.8 per cent. At DERSA this unusual asymmetry made us think.[12]

Having strategic focus has huge advantages which consist of ensuring the organization has a meaning, direction and a logical *raison d'être* when it comes to running things. It makes decision-making easier.[13]

Once the strategic focus was defined, once it was decided that the company was going to commercialize dermatological products, the remainder of the company's products were considered 'peripheral'.[14] Thus, some peripheral products were used to acquire new brands in dermatology.

Supporting the strategy

In 1998, Michael Dufour started to implement changes in the area of Promotion and Sales. It was necessary to build up a support system to boost the strategy Michael Dufour wanted to achieve. A new head of the department was appointed. The old policy of focusing on the wholesaler was changed by stressing the importance of the demand (the doctor).

We changed the paradigm for the way we commercialized products in the firm. We did not expect the wholesaler to sell one unit more of my product, because it is not up to them to generate the perception of a brand. We needed to generate this perception in the person who makes the purchasing decision, which is the doctor.[15]

By mid-1998, the company ran for almost 45 working days with short-term liabilities and no way of paying wages. The situation worsened because the dismissal of 22 managers meant that a great deal of money was paid out in redundancy payments throughout 1997. By the end of 1998 the crisis was much more pronounced because of the lack of raw materials needed for use on the production line for the suntan lotion campaign. These crises made the company consider even more far-reaching changes in the logistics department. By 1999, none of the suppliers that used to provide raw material to the company were still working with DERSA.[16]

> I took over the company when it was nearly collapsing. These crises were inevitable. What happened with these crises throughout 1998 was that we reached rock bottom. However, we did not change our path, we stuck firmly to our vision. Those crises, however painful, were helpful because they introduced more changes that would otherwise have been difficult.[17]

In 1999, the company had paid off its debt and started to generate its own resources. In that year, the company launched one product (after two years without releases) and bought up four new brands.

Changes in the Structure of the Company

From 1989 to 1996, the structure remained largely unchanged. The main change was in 1993 when Michael Dufour created the OTC department and later in 1996 when he became the new Commercial Director of the company. Creating the OTC department in 1993 allowed the company to be more dynamic in the commercialization of the OTC products that were one of its strengths.

The main changes DERSA experienced related mainly to the merging of areas to create a structure more suitable for the new competitive arena. However, DERSA was still structured in a functional way in 1999.

As one manager explained:

> I remember that the structure of the company was like an octopus. The CEO made all the decisions and the head of each department was taking all of the decisions related to his section. Today, although there is a lot of work to be done, the company has decompressed the situation a lot by creating different areas within the different departments.[18]

> I do not think you will have many problems analysing the structure in 1989. It was a very easy structure: everything was centralized in the General Manager Gali.[19]

The old structure had two main problems. Firstly, hierarchy was more important than anything else, so decisions were delayed for ages. But secondly and probably most importantly, the old structure lasted a long time, until I took over the post of CEO.[20]

Since 1999 DERSA has had a structure in which positions have been consolidated and the structure itself evened out. But there are still some unresolved issues to be considered: first, there are still many layers in the different structures of the departments. This fact made decision making more difficult and bureaucratic processes became very complicated:

> We still have on average six layers. That is a lot. There is not a great difference in the number of layers now and in 1989. This is one of the most important aspects we have to tackle. We have started to work on that issue though but it is not easy.[21]

Changes in the Management of the Company

Between 1989 and 1996, the managerial structure of the company remained largely unchanged. The style of the CEO marked the period: 'Gali was rather authoritarian. This did not allow him to surround himself with the right people to make the changes the company needed.'[22]

The main criteria for hiring managers were, as some managers stated, age and experience in the industry: 'Age was very important. Previously [in the 1980s] there were a lot of old people in the company who relied on their years of experience in the industry'[23] (see also Table 6.1).

The relationship between the managerial team and the CEO was not always amicable: 'Gali's management was characterized by a lack of any kind of communication between the different levels of the company, accompanied by the strict control of operations. Decisions were never discussed.'[24]

In 1993, when Michael Dufour set up the OTC department, changes in the managerial team started to take shape:

> Setting up the OTC area was a big challenge for the company, not only because of the commercial implications but in terms of the managerial team. I hired new people, professionals, different from the old professionals that were in DERSA at that time. The differences between the people working in OTC and the rest of the company were so huge that there was a lot of tension in the organisation.[25]

After the crisis the company went through during the period 1995–1997, Michael Dufour took over as the new CEO of the company and started to change things. Dufour's first decision was to reshuffle the management team by dismissing 22 managers:

> In 1996 we were working on the new strategic plan and, while doing so, I was assessing the different managers of the company. I started to see behaviour that

Table 6.1   Entry requirements for the different areas in DERSA. Selected areas

Areas	1989	1996	1999
Logistics (we take the case of Production and Technical Department in 1989).	• Age (*'the older the better'*). • Experience in logistics in other pharmaceutical company.	• Idem 1989.	• Young professionals (engineers). • Experience in other industries.
Administration and Finance (we take the case of Accounting and also Finance in 1989).	• Accountant and tax specialist.	• Accountancy • Business Administration	• Accountancy • Business Administration
Marketing OTC and Marketing Ethical Products (Commercialization in 1989).	• Promotional and sales team (APM): very experienced in the industry. • Mktg: Experience in the industry.	• APM: Idem 1989 Mktg: New OTC area introduced new and younger professionals with experience different from the pharmaceutical industry. The rest of the commercial area had similar features to those in 1989.	• Big changes in these areas. Reshuffle of APMs: younger, with university degree or technical degree. Experience in the industry was not a requirement. • Other professionals: younger with university degrees were welcomed. • Experience in the industry was preferable.

was less than loyal to the company – people with very difficult personalities. To avoid any type of resistance I got rid of those who I saw as an obstacle to change.[26]

However, the managerial team was not ready in 1999:

I think by the end of the year 2000 we are going to have our structure settled with all the boxes of the structure filled. I take special care when selecting those who are going to be part of the managerial team.[27]

With the new managerial team, vertical and horizontal communication has improved:

Communication is clear now, in contrast to the closed system operated by the previous CEO. Before 1997 there was no communication between managers and employees. The worker found his way by drawing his own conclusions.[28]

Supporting the managerial change process: the HR area

Until 1997 there was no HR Department in DERSA but a Personnel Department dealing with administrative matters. In July 1999 the first HR manager started work in the company. 'When I started work, there was no HR policy within the company. There was a lack of HR policy, widespread demotivation and a lack of integration in the organization. Furthermore they did not consider HR to be a strategic resource for the company.'[29] However, the new CEO wanted a change: he wanted DERSA to become a company that focused on people rather than on the hierarchy.

The HR area was set up to support the new changes in the company. Michael Dufour and the new HR manager established the objectives of the area in the medium term: first, to avoid the bureaucracy that had been a problem in the company; second, to bring people closer to the Board; and, finally, to improve the selection process and create a training programme for young professionals (Table 6.1 shows the evolution of the entry requirements for selected areas in DERSA).

One of the problems I encountered was a terrible bureaucratization in the company. The information it produced was not trustworthy, it was erratic and there were no statistics. We are now working with the areas in creating trustworthy indicators.[30]

Another aspect we are working on is encouraging contact between the Board and the different levels of employees. Employees did not know the Board, they did not know what they were like. Using the tactic of holding conversation sessions with 20 people each time, Michael Dufour was able to comment on the company's strategy and let them know what changes the company was going through.[31]

The last aspect human resources was working on in 1999 was the selection process in the company. One of the most ambitious projects in the area today is what they call the 'DERSA seedbed'. The company's aim was that by February 2001 there would be a group of ten trainees who can either replace or join the current managerial team in the medium term.

For the CEO, selection has another important effect:

Selection is very important. Through selection I am trying to get all the heads of departments to share similar values. On the other hand we would like young people without experience to join the company. Why? Because the company would be their school and we will shape them with our mould.[32]

Board of Directors: Governance: Strategy and Family

Corporate governance in DERSA

While the founder Jean Dufour was still alive, the whole group of companies followed the orders of his right hand man, the Argentinian Daniel Alcorta. There was neither a Board of Directors nor a committee that tried to establish general strategies for the group. Both Jean Dufour and Alcorta took decisions.

When Jean Dufour died in 1979, and the group split up into different companies, the responsibility for the Argentinian branch (including Paraguay and Uruguay) fell to Émile Dufour – the son of Jean Dufour. His inexperience in the business and his shy personality made him back out and delegate the management of the company first to Daniel Alcorta and then to Andrés Gali until the third generation took over the administration of the company.

In 1986, when Émile Dufour Jr joined the company they decided to set up a Board of Directors as a way of improving the communication of strategies to the future heirs. The Board was formed by Émile Dufour (father and President), Émile Dufour Jr (eldest son and Vice-President) and Andrés Gali (CEO). In 1988, Michael Dufour was co-opted to the Board.

However, the Board of Directors was not meeting its objectives: 'It did not make any difference when my brother and I joined the Board. We were inexperienced, and my father relied on Gali. So, we went there to listen to what Gali had already decided.'[33]

There was a transitional stage in the Board's life between 1993 and 1996 when the brothers started to have more power. Émile Dufour Jr assumed responsibility for institutional communication and Michael Dufour for the new and profitable OTC area. By 1996, the success of both brothers, but mainly the achievements of Michael Dufour in his new post (Commercial Director), started to pay off and reshaped the role of the Board:

> Our father started to be more open towards what was going on in the company and he started to listen to us. We were working hard and our accomplishments were helping us to be heard.[34]

In 1993, Michael Dufour took over the project of the OTC area in DERSA with great success (in three years he increased the volume of OTC products sold fivefold). By 1996, achievements in the OTC area led Michael Dufour to become Commercial Manager of the company, a critical role in a company that was struggling to survive.

> Michael [Dufour] set about taking on more of the company's problems until he actually replaced Gali. It was a natural process and that gives added value to the

leadership Michael achieved within the company. The whole process was accomplished thanks to Michael's amazing strategic vision.[35]

In 1997, when Michael Dufour took over control of the company, the Board was composed of three members, all of them family members: Émile Dufour, Émile Dufour Jr and Michael Dufour.[36] Émile Dufour was the President of the company, Émile Jr the Vice President. He dealt mainly with Public Relations and issues concerning the industry. Michael Dufour, on the other hand, was both CEO and a Board member.

Émile Dufour has delegated a lot to his son Michael, who has responded by achieving great success. This constituted the mainstay of the restructuring process. Michael is quite an autonomous figure. Émile Jr has a very good relationship with Michael because their different personalities complement each other: Michael is more thoughtful and Émile more intuitive, less respectful of forms, less willing to take risks, with less theoretical base to his actions but a wide knowledge of the day-to-day reality. By contrast, Michael has done more formal training, which helps him to be more sure of his concepts, taking risks in things which make up the business.[37]

Strategy, delegation and control

The old company was very dull and bureaucratic, decisions were far too reliant on the centre of power: Andrés Gali, the Managing Director. This person presided over a golden period in the company's history and another period of bad luck. He nearly compromised its survival.[38]

The Board did not agree with decisions being made at the lower levels, but insisted that everything be studied by them, an attitude which remains today but to a lesser degree now.[39]

Under Gali's administration, decision-making took ages because two or three people in the company decided everything, every single detail.[40]

Centralization of decision making not only seems to have been an old problem but continues to be one: 'I am trying to delegate decisions to the managers, but this will take time. The management team is new and we first need to make them work as a team.'[41]

The Board and the CEO are very much involved in the different operative activities of the company:

We are still very dependent on the owner. Although the company is family-run and the owners are professional in their actions, they continue to make the same kind of gut decisions typical of this sort of company. Decisions are made more according to the owners' whim than by obeying business logic.[42]

Control mechanisms were always stringent in DERSA. However there was a difference in nature.

> Under Gali's management the Board was very keen on obtaining information and controlling. They were always on people's backs . . . This type of control generated harmful behaviour in the managers and workers.[43]

> Today's control is different. I would say that control is tighter now than before but is more consistent.[44]

However, there was a general feeling among managers that the control mechanisms were still excessive:

> The nature of this business, and all businesses, is that decisions and counter-decisions must be taken throughout the progress of the different activities. These decisions have to be made on a daily basis. The problem we have is that the CEO and Board want to participate in each decision.[45]

As many managers recognized, the higher degree of centralization and control impeded the company's ability to respond quickly. However, Michael Dufour stated that:

> The company came from a very low level. We were at rock bottom. So the first commitment I had was to reach a level of performance that allowed us to survive. Tight control of operations has allowed DERSA to perform well over the last two years and is still necessary. As soon as we achieve stability and a continuous and better performance we are going to whip up support for delegation.[46]

The Unresolved Issues

Two issues regarding the future of the company concerned the Board and, in particular, the CEO. These two issues are related to the possibilities of growth in the medium and long term, and the succession process.

There is one big challenge for the company in the medium term. As many managers mentioned, the niche strategy was good for taking DERSA out of the crisis it went through. However, they also saw the strategy as a limitation for growth:

> I agree that concentrating on one area was the best for the company in the mid-1990s. However, now that the strategy is consolidated, DERSA is suffering a growth crisis. DERSA wants to grow in a market that is in decline.[47]

Figure 6.4 shows DERSA's increasing importance in the dermatology sub-market. However, as can be seen in the figure, the importance of the

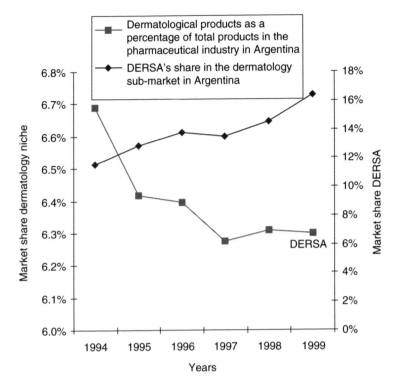

Figure 6.4   DERSA's strategic focus on dermatological niche

dermatological sub-market within the pharmaceutical market in Argentina is shrinking. This reduction of the share of the dermatological sub-market in Argentina is a product of the maturity of such a sub-market and the lack of investments in R&D and innovation in it. These two factors (that is, R&D and innovation) have impacted on the average price of dermatological products which is below the industry average. The heavy dependence of DERSA on such products, as shown in Figure 6.5, has impacted negatively on the average prices of the products sold by the company.

Growth is not going to be feasible for our current dermatology products because they are nearly hitting the roof. To achieve our objectives by 2003, that is to increase the company's share of the market in dermatology products to 25 per cent, there are various alternatives. One is to buy up new brands, but it is difficult to do so because the brands which stay on the market are the biggest and it would mean an extraordinary investment for DERSA, an amount of money that we do not have. The second alternative consists of developing products in those niches where we have not yet participated.[48]

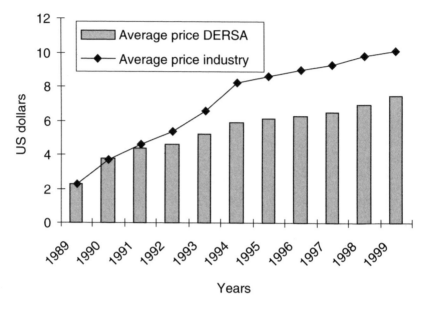

*Figure 6.5   Average price at DERSA and the industry over the period
1989–1999*

The succession process and the entrance of the fourth generation of
family members are the other issues that concern the Board. Measures have
not yet been taken to ensure a planned and smooth succession.

> My father is 73 years old and one of the matters on the agenda is to see how con-
> tinuity will be affected in the future. It is a challenge we will face in the future.[49]

The managers see succession as a problem that might not only damage
family relationships but something that could endanger the future of the
company. There is also a widespread ignorance of family arrangements
among managers in the company.

> I do not know how the shares are spread between the family members, nor
> whether there is any agreement between Émile Dufour's children about what will
> happen when he leaves the Board. The situation is very complicated seeing as in
> this kind of company it is very difficult to distinguish between company and
> family. [. . .] We [the managers] do not know anything about the family.[50]

NOTES

1. Some of the data (dates, names among others) of the firm has been changed to preserve
    its anonymity.

2. Argentina was the first branch set up outside France.
3. Interview with CEO DERSA.
4. Interview with Technical Director DERSA.
5. Interview with Manager of Promotion and Sales.
6. Interview with CEO DERSA.
7. Interview with CEO DERSA.
8. Interview with CEO DERSA.
9. Interview with regional manager DERSA.
10. Interview with Technical Director DERSA.
11. Interview with CEO DERSA.
12. Interview with CEO DERSA.
13. Interview with CEO DERSA.
14. Interview with CEO DERSA.
15. Interview with-Promotion and Sale Manager-DERSA.
16. Interview with Logistic Manager DERSA.
17. Interview with CEO DERSA.
18. Interview with Technical Director in DERSA.
19. Interview with OTC Marketing Manager in DERSA.
20. Interview with CEO DERSA.
21. Interview with HR Manager DERSA.
22. Interview with HR Manager DERSA.
23. Interview with Logistic Manager in DERSA.
24. Interview with regional manager DERSA.
25. Interview with CEO DERSA.
26. Interview with CEO DERSA.
27. Interview with CEO DERSA.
28. Interview with Finance Manager in DERSA.
29. Interview with HR Manager in DERSA.
30. Interview with HR Manager in DERSA.
31. Interview with HR Manager in DERSA.
32. Interview with CEO DERSA.
33. Interview with CEO DERSA.
34. Interview with CEO DERSA.
35. Interview with HR Manager in DERSA.
36. By 1999, Émile Dufour was 73, Émile Dufour Jr was 47 and Michael Dufour 45.
37. Interview with HR Manager in DERSA.
38. Interview with HR Manager in DERSA.
39. Interview with HR Manager in DERSA.
40. Interview with OTC Marketing Manager in DERSA.
41. Interview with CEO DERSA.
42. Interview with OTC Marketing Manager in DERSA.
43. Interview with Promotion and Sales Manager in DERSA.
44. Interview with HR Manager in DERSA.
45. Interview with OTC Marketing Manager in DERSA.
46. Interview with CEO DERSA.
47. Interview with OTC Manager DERSA.
48. Interview with Finance Manager DERSA.
49. Interview with CEO DERSA.
50. Interview with HR Manager in DERSA.

7. Case Study: AGD Aceitera General Deheza

BRIEF OVERVIEW OF THE HISTORY OF AGD 1948–1999

Founded in 1948 by Adrián Urquía, AGD (Aceitera General Deheza) transformed itself from a small oil-processing factory into the biggest indigenous firm in the industry. Nowadays AGD is a leading edible oil export company and also one of the frontrunners on the retail market for bottled oil with several successful brands. It ranked 40th among the 1000 top companies in terms of turnover in Argentina in 1999 (US$841 million), and it is considered the fifth most important exporter in the country (Revista Mercado, 1999).

After the changes the country went through in the 1990s, the company was able to adapt and thrive in an industry in which most indigenous businesses did not manage to survive. Nevertheless, the roots of AGD's success do not date from the 1990s but long before, in its thinking ahead about ways of improving technology, scale and cost-effective measures – a trio of decisions that would prove to be the right combination for survival and success.

The first generation tenure of the firm lasted 37 years: from 1948 to 1985, when the founder bowed out from the executive direction of the company and became its President. This foundational period can be split into three sub-periods: the founding period from 1948 to 1968, the crisis in 1968, and finally, the consolidation of the company between 1968 and 1985 (see stages of the history of the firm in Figure 7.1).

The first generation tenure is shaped by the figure of its founder, Adrián Urquía, who was absolutely determined to set up an oil factory in the countryside in the Province of Córdoba. His enthusiasm and commitment, plus the importance Urquía attributed to technology and process flexibility, were key factors in the success of the firm:

> He [the founder] worked permanently to increase production volume in order to improve economies of scale. Optimizing logistics, achieving efficiency and lowering costs were particular preoccupations of his. Another distinctive attitude was the systematic incorporation of technological developments.[1]

However, there were a number of obstacles in the way. The year 1968 was a milestone for the company. AGD was forced to shut down. An unfortunate combination of events – such as a worldwide increase in oilseed prices and the lack of a commercial strategy – forced the company to rethink its strategy.

From 1968 to 1985 the consolidation process took place until AGD had reached a leading position in the industry. In 1985 the company was 100 per cent export-oriented, selling bulk products made with state-of-the-art technology.

Urquía's children not only inherited the company, but also some of their father's fundamental values that were and still are deeply rooted in AGD's culture – paternalism, and directors who know the operations and who are constantly attentive to what is going on both within the industry and outside it.

In 1985 the founder withdrew from the daily operation. The year 1985 is also an important date because that was when Urquía's youngest child, Adriana, started to work in the company. His sons Roberto and Adrián Jr. had already joined the firm several years earlier.

The period from 1985 to 1999 was characterized both by times of turmoil and spells of stability in Argentina. Changes in macroeconomic policies prompted companies to rethink their businesses and strategies. AGD did just this and ahead of the other companies in its industry, it launched two strategic inititatives: first, it started to manufacture brand products to compete with the retail market; and second, it set about strengthening the logistics chain to achieve cost effectiveness. A second stage began in 1995 when the company took a good look at its internal organization – a process which triggered changes affecting the structure, management and governance of the company.

In November 1996, the founder died. By that time, the firm was a leading indigenous edible oil producer.

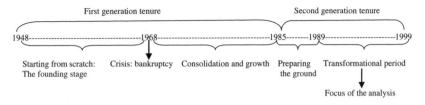

Figure 7.1 Chronology and stages in AGD's history

UNDERSTANDING THE TRANSFORMATION OF AGD: CHRONOLOGICAL AND ANALYTICAL TRACING OF KEY ELEMENTS OVER THE PERIOD 1989–1999

Strategic Initiatives: Branding

By 1988, AGD saw the need to diversify its production of bulk edible oil. It was to be expected that a company that crushed and refined oilseeds would make a move into the retail market:

> The family wanted to keep one foot in the internal market as a safeguard in case the external market did badly. The retail market offered that opportunity. It was the opposite of what other companies were doing. Everybody wanted to export to avoid the turmoil of the internal market.[2]

Adrián Urquía Jr, the Director and CEO of the company, assumed the responsibility of preparing the launch of the new strategy.

> After one trip to the USA he [Adrián Urquía Jr] came to a Board meeting and opened a suitcase full of oil bottles. They were plastic bottles – a different concept to that used in Argentina back then, because the market leader used glass bottles. He also came up with the idea of non-cholesterol oil, which was a piece of luck because until then this was a dormant market.[3]

'Commercializing products with an extra value, achieving greater profitability and becoming more diversified were the outcomes of this strategy,' stated Roberto Urquía. 'Not putting all their eggs in one basket,'[4] as one Director said, was the strategy followed to stabilize the margins of the business.

In 1989 AGD launched the first pure sunflower oil to appear on the Argentinian market. Ketelhohn *et al.* (1998) pointed out that customers not only saw this product as healthier but also a good combination of relatively low cost price and perceived high quality, proving AGD's strategy of product innovation to be a successful one and achieving a high share of the market for brand name oils (see market share evolution in Figure 7.2).

AGD also took a step towards its entry into the massive consumer market by launching products related to the oil industry such as mayonnaise and juices based on soya and fruits. Figures 7.2 and 7.3 illustrate the sequence in which new products were launched and the market share obtained.

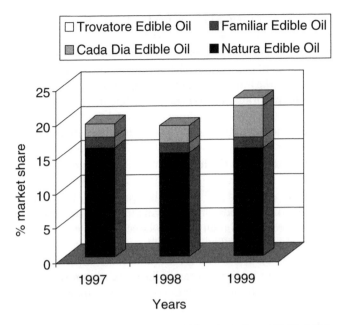

Figure 7.2   Market share for AGD's edible oil products 1997–1999

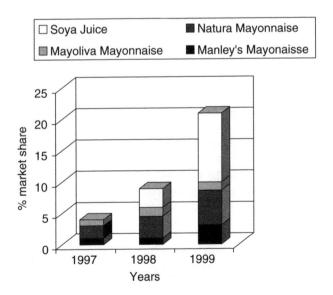

Figure 7.3   Market share for AGD's soya and mayonnaise products 1997–1999

Strategic Initiatives: Origination and the Logistics Chain

The success of AGD's entrance into the retail market made the Board and managers more confident about the future of the company. AGD also started to evaluate the implications of macroeconomic measures that caused inflation to fall and prices to stabilize. It became increasingly important to achieve cost-effectiveness. The company reacted promptly and started to attack the weakest part of its value chain: 'the origination' process and its logistics chain.

Origination is the name the industry uses for buying seeds, transporting and storing them. It is an activity which has always existed. AGD has always bought seeds, but its method of buying changed in the 1990s. Until then, the company had bought seeds from intermediaries or on the cereal stock market and stored them in silos (grain collecting stores) that were often owned by the same intermediaries from whom the company had bought the oilseeds. This way of doing business became the company's Achilles' heel: AGD was dependent upon the intermediaries to obtain the raw material it needed to process oil. In order to counter constant supply problems, as well as dealing with the new economic situation, the Board implemented a strategy that was to have an impact on the whole organization: they decided to move backwards in the chain of value to enable them to make available all the raw material needed. 'We are well aware of our company's history. In 1968 the company went bankrupt because we did not have the raw materials to supply the plant. We are not going to go through the same thing again. We have learnt our lesson.'[5] By 1999, the company had 22 grain collecting plants and two purchasing offices spread throughout the country.

The firm's strategy gave them two advantages: first, it did not have to pay commission to the agent at the stock market because it bought the raw material directly from the farmer: and second, it provided the company with a commodity backup, thus not leaving it heavily dependent on market prices. The outcome was what the company wanted: achieving efficiency by reducing costs.

The company saw that the logistics chain would have been incomplete without an adequate transportation system. Transport was also seen as critical for the business:

> Formerly the aim was to get the supplies needed for our processing facilities, but when you think that grinding a tonne of soya costs 12 or 13 dollars and transport between Tucumán and Rosario comes out at 14 dollars, you see that logistics are all-important in our business. And here is where you can achieve efficiency.[6]

In 1992 the company incorporated a fundamental link into its logistics chain: the Nuevo Central Argentina (NCA) railway which AGD operates.

With a 40 year concession, and in partnership with other groups, AGD controls the 4757 kilometres of track, linking storage facilities with industrial plants and the port, making connections possible with the rest of the country. Furthermore, this strategy was complemented by the facilities at the Terminal 6 port. In 1996, Terminal 6 became the biggest private port in the country.

> The company gained a real advantage in the sector with this strategy. I think we are ten years ahead of the other companies. The few national businesses that survived are trying to copy our strategy.[7]

Not only did this strategy help AGD become leaders in the industry, but it also allowed the company to incorporate new businesses and seize the opportunity in others. In 1993, following the strategy of making the very most of its logistics chain, the company moved into the purchase and export of cereals as an independent activity. In 1997, AGD sold one million tonnes of cereals worldwide and in 1999 one and a half million tonnes.

> The origination business made us broaden our perspectives at the same time. We started off buying only oilseeds, but to shut out possible competition from intermediaries we started to buy cereals too. That is how our Cereal Export Department came into being.[8]

The producer also required different services such as loans, agrochemicals, and seeds, so, in 1994, the company created the Agro-product Department, adding more businesses and services to the origination complex.

Generating the Process of Internal Change: Organizational and Structural Changes

Thinking out a new business structure

In 1995, once the new strategic initiatives were running successfully, the Board decided to implement a new structural design. The growth the company underwent over the period 1989–1995 plus the intense competition and changes within the industry made the Board reformulate the way the company should be organized.

The Board hired a group of consultants and started work on the most far-reaching and organizational changes in the firm's history. Behind such changes was a clear idea: 'We wanted a structural change which would enable the Board to have more time for planning strategies and spend less time on the operational side.'[9]

The document presented by the consultants is revealing in terms of highlighting the aims behind the changes in the structure: first, seeking ways to liberate the Board from operative tasks but at the same time allowing them to keep control of the operation; second, clarifying the different departments of the company and differentiating between operative (business units) and support areas: and lastly, the idea that the structure should clarify the relationships between the different departments, customers and suppliers.

The new structure brought a new concept into the organization: the idea of business units and support units. Until 1996 the structure had been a functional one in which all the departments were dependent on the Board, and the Directors played the role of Directors and Managers at the same time. The new concept of business units meant giving more responsibility to the managers of different units and also meant that the Board should start to delegate operational tasks.

Support areas were either reformulated or created from scratch such as the New Businesses unit and the Economic Studies unit. An economist with extensive experience in market studies was appointed to head the Economic Studies unit. The idea of setting up this new department was to consider the 'short, medium and long-term future of the company, to centralize the economic information that the Board received and to interpret environmental information for the Board.'[10]

The new structure meant that the different support units had to learn to offer services to the business units (that is, cereals and oilseeds, brand, peanuts and agriculture, and livestock business unit) rather than working according to what the Board required. The business units, on the other hand, had to be more efficient in the use of resources, coordinate their different activities to avoid duplication and restructure processes to attain more effectiveness (that is administrative processes in the different business units and production processes).

Communicating the changes in structure

In November 1996, the Board met the top and middle management of the company. Roberto Urquía gave a speech prepared by the Board and the consultants. Some paragraphs of the speech are enlightening in terms of defining the Board's aims for the future of the company. Firstly Urquía stressed the importance of the company's stance once the process of change had begun: 'AGD is an organization which, fortunately, is growing at the moment. The company is not in the critical position of some organizations in which re-organization is undertaken not in order to be more efficient, but to avoid collapse.'[11]

Customer focus was the reason given to justify the immediate need for change:

> In a phase of expansion like ours, we need to have a flexible organization and a flexible structure which allows us to adapt quickly to the needs of the customer

and the market. To achieve this we are thinking of giving more autonomy to the different areas to allow the businesses to develop better but within certain organizational guidelines, which will facilitate horizontal communication and allow the sectors to work together. This will be advantageous to the company and result in a better service for the customer.[12]

The Board also decided that a new area of human resources was needed to operationalize the changes. The HR manager's work also resulted in flattening the hierarchical levels of the company. From the six levels that existed in the 1996 structure, he streamlined down to the current three levels, eliminating the supervision level: 'One of the things that the Board wanted was for the managers to have more contact with the process. Having a top-heavy structure meant the middle managers had less of a hands-on approach towards the process.'[13]

Changes in the Management of the Company

A new generation of managers

The new businesses of the company and the need for better-prepared managers for running the business units opened the door to new managers with different skills and education. The profile of these new managers was stated in the speech given by the Board while launching the new organizational design of AGD:

We sought and want people who are not afraid of a challenge; who are oriented towards both internal and external customers; who have the capacity to work in a team and the ability to interrelate; who think analytically and strategically; who are enterprising and oriented towards action; and above all we are looking for people who would risk everything for the company.[14]

This was a challenge for a company used to low levels of employee turnover and a homogeneous culture. The running of the company's various departments required more sophisticated tools and those tools were brought to AGD by professionals who joined the organization over the 10-year period analysed.

With the new incorporations, we are looking for people with a more complete profile, not only professionally, but also with leadership and teamwork skills, things that we did not look for before, that were not prioritized. We had good managers, but we thought that we could be better than before and prepare for new challenges.[15]

(See the evolution over time of the profile required in different areas of AGD in Table 7.1.)

Table 7.1   Degrees requested and experience required for joining various departments over the period 1989–1999

Business units	1989	1999
Brands[a]	• University degree not required • Previous experience only needed in marketing or commercialization in the edible oil industry	• University degree is a pre-requisite • A minimum of 3 years' experience required for middle management positions • Previous experience in the food sector rather than edible oil industry is welcomed
Cereals and Oilseeds (origination, industrial, trading)	• Country people to deal with farmers • No higher education required • Technicians to work in the industrial complex • Internally trained people for trading	• A degree in agricultural engineering required to run the purchase offices and grain collecting plants • A degree in industrial engineering is required to work in top positions in the plants; group leaders must be technicians • Experienced traders with a university degree and previous experience in trading companies are required to fill these positions
Peanuts	• Technicians to work in the field • Technicians to operate the plant	• Engineers to operate the plant • Agricultural engineers to work in the fields
Agriculture and Livestock[b]	Not specified	• A degree in agricultural engineering needed for managerial positions

Notes:
[a] Includes brand and the fractional distillation area in the 1980s.
[b] Includes agriculture, pigs and agro-products areas in the 1980s.

Table 7.2   Average age of personnel in selected areas (taking into account the whole personnel of the department/area)

Areas of the company	1989 (Age-average)	1999 (Age-average)
Administration and IT	48	34
Finance	47	36
Brands	46	35
Origination	50	32
Peanuts	55	34
DH Plant	55	30

It was seen as important to professionalize the company so that it could face the challenges of the new context in Argentina. Nevertheless, there was a feeling of pride about the way the company was managed before the 1990s. This pride arose from the idea within the company that its managers were different from those of the MNC companies. In the opinion of different managers, the difference stemmed from the fact that managers at AGD were closer to the process, knew the area and its problems and had closer ties with the producers. As one manager said: 'If we need to use a Poncho,[16] we'll use it and if we have to dance at farmers' parties, we will. It is a different approach to those companies that send managers out in suits and ties.'[17]

Whereas the company had not set high standards as regards what it expected from its new employees in the 1980s, the 1990s were to see conditions change as it became much harder to join the firm (as indicated in Table 7.1). At the same time the demographic conditions of the company were also changing in that it was reducing the average age of its personnel. This last aspect was the outcome of the incorporation of younger personnel throughout the 1990s (see Table 7.2).

The challenge of having 'two generations of managers'

Probably one of the most important challenges, as the Board recognized, was dealing with the issue of having two generations fighting over the same power. The changes in the company structure and the possibility for a new generation of managers to work more freely under the new conditions caused conflict:

Around here, what happened was that before the process of change started, we had a few old leaders who were more in favour of the old system, more rigid, more for the establishment, less for teamwork. Now we have a group of young people who have come here and have been encouraged by the changes. They have had other ideas: to work as part of a group, to participate. This fact has generated conflict and strain sometimes.[18]

Nevertheless, AGD was able to handle the transitional stage first due to a good group of top managers 'aware of the future challenges'[19] and second, because of the company's decision to avoid sudden or large-scale replacements of managers, unless absolutely necessary. 'We think that our company was lucky because in most cases the old generation and the new get on well, the old one gave the new one experience and customer-oriented service and the new one gave the old one the administrative tools the senior managers lacked.'[20]

Control and planning processes

The 1990s also introduced new managerial concepts into the company. Both planning and control emerged as two different and complementary aspects that the managers of AGD started to learn and apply. The different areas of AGD at different levels started to formalize more what had been impossible in the 1980s.

The mechanisms of control and planning, nevertheless, were supposed to provide 'not only short term control but also long term vision.'[21] The company did not want to become more bureaucratic once the systems of control and planning were installed, nevertheless, these systems were necessary:

> Although we have grown as a company, we do not want to lose the virtue of being agile when it comes to decision making. It's important to avoid bureaucracy. Otherwise you end up accumulating things but not attributing any value to them. We need control and planning, we need more formalization, but not so much that we risk destroying the agility and promptness of our decision-making process that I would say we are proud of.[22]

The Board of Directors: Strategy and Family Alignment

Governing the company: structure and strategy

Until 1996, the year when AGD's founder died, Urquía's children had been working as company Directors. Soon after the first of his children started to work for the company in 1968, the Directors started to mould a profile that would shape the future of the Board. Adrián Jr was very keen on technology and marketing. He was the one that pushed for the launch of the new branded products and developed the retail market. Roberto was very committed to the industrial complex – that comprised more than 60 per cent of the company's turnover. He was the force behind the origination and plans for the logistics chain. Finally, Adriana, the youngest of the children was the last one to join the company. She liked the freedom that the very profitable Peanut area gave her and, at the same time, started to get involved in human resources.[23]

Adrián Urquía died in 1996. His children did not modify the way they were working. Adrián Jr took over as President because the company needed a President. Nevertheless there was a verbal agreement that the President would be *'primus inter pares'*.

The changes the company went through after 1996 made the Board rethink its function. The Directors wanted to 'think strategically and act in consequence;'[24] they did not want to get involved in the day-to-day operation. Once the business and support units were set up the Board divided its responsibilities: Adrián Jr would supervise the Brand business unit and the Purchasing unit; Roberto would control the Cereals and Oilseeds business unit, Administration and Information Technology, and Finance; and Adriana would be in charge of Peanuts and HR.

'While Roberto and Adrián are the strategists of the company, Adriana had masterminded the organizational changes AGD had gone through.'[25] It was Adriana who insisted on working in-depth on organizational issues once the consultants were hired. She saw the opportunity to speed up the organizational changes that were needed.

The Board was also working, pushed by Adriana, on a family protocol: 'If you don't plan, or you don't shape it [family protocol] when things are calm, afterwards it might cause a lot of problems. We have plenty of time. Adrián is still single, Roberto has two young daughters and my daughter is just a baby.'[26] The aim of the family protocol is to establish the pre-requisites family members had to fulfil to join the firm: 'It is really to stop loads of relatives joining in the future.'[27] Only the brightest and most committed to the company's work culture will be granted a place in the firm.

Strategic thinking and strategic decision-making

While the 1980s represented a period of economic turmoil in which strategic issues were set aside because of short-term problems related to the operational side of the business, the 1990s were seen as the opportunity to start focusing on strategy: 'In the 1980s there was so much time invested in the short term that you were not able to look to the medium and long-term.'[28]

In the 1990s the Directors wanted to focus on strategic issues. To do so, the Board started to prioritize strategic decisions over operational ones. The delegation process that began in the mid-1990s helped the Board to achieve this aim: 'The experience taught us to delegate, because in a family business this is not easy. We were starting to have a bottleneck situation. The bottleneck is the decision-making process that stops you moving forward.'[29]

The Board made a firm decision to distinguish between those decisions that had to have the Board's approval (considered by the Board to be strategic decisions) and operational decisions that did not need their intervention (see Table 7.3).

Table 7.3   Strategic decisions needing the Board's intervention

Areas	Strategic decisions
Brand	• Investments • Product images (control of advertising)
Origination	• Investments • Annual amount of money available for farmers' loans • Development of complementary activities such as production of materials, distribution of seeds and production of seeds

In 1998, with the launch of the new structure, more frequent meetings took place to inform the Board of aspects related to the business units and to allow them to control their operation.

In 1995 AGD hired a consultancy to start communicating the strategy down through the company, improving communication between the Board and the managers. In 1997 the company decided to start holding 'immersion days' to discuss the strategic directions of the company with the top managers of the different Business and Support Units.

The Directors explained these changes as a positive aspect that allowed them to focus on strategic matters: 'Focus on strategy needs the strategist to have time to think. We need time not to lose sight of what is going on outside the company. We want to see our colleagues, we want to watch the international companies to see what they are doing better than us.'[30]

The scale of the delegation process, however, gave some managers cause for complaint: 'I think that the Board still finds it hard to delegate'; 'there was a peak at that time of trying to delegate, and afterwards they went back to taking the reins.'[31] The same Directors felt that the delegation process was only half-complete:

> We have still not completed total delegation, but I would say that we have taken a big step forward. I spend much more time in meetings with different departments in the company than before. I am not concerned now about the Chicago stock market, whether it rises, sells or doesn't sell.[32]

The Unresolved Issues

There are two issues which the Board is very sensitive about. The first is the possibility of floating the company on the stock market; the second is the higher profile that the company needs in the internal market.

There is a general feeling of a lack of courage and audacity to float the business on the capital market. The Board is split over this topic. While

Roberto and Adriana want to move forward with this plan, Adrián Jr is not comfortable with the idea of opening up the company to shareholders. 'From an individual's point of view, I would have done it already, two years ago. This is a big advantage we are giving other companies by not capturing capital in the market. This is one area where I think we are lacking in audacity and decisiveness.'[33]

Adriana highlighted the limitations for growth as an outcome of not opening up the company to the stock market: 'We have projects and we do not work on them basically because we do not want to spoil the solvency equation of the company. If we were to open up to the capitals market, I think things would turn out better.'[34]

The other topic that has preoccupied the Board is the higher profile the company needed in the internal market. As this is a firm that used to export oil in bulk there was no need to cultivate an institutional image. However, this changed once AGD launched its branded products on the retail market. At that time the Board felt the need to encourage a higher profile to push its new products. Nevertheless, the company still has a low profile in Argentinian society. The products are not associated with the company. Everybody knows *Natura* oil, but few people realize who the company is behind it (Benechi, 1999).

Today you can offer 30 per cent of your company for sale and it makes no difference. I think that it would not even lose the family profile, that is the first point. Another point I think is important is that we are not keen on opening up the company because we are worried about the higher profile the company can achieve. We should not be scared of having a higher profile if this could considerably help our own brand products. When you are already in the retail market I think it is important that whatever product you pull out of your sleeve, you know that you have the company to fall back on, and we are weak in this respect.[35]

NOTES

1. Interview with Director of AGD.
2. Interview with Finance Manager.
3. Interview with Director AGD.
4. Interview with Director AGD.
5. Interview with Director and CEO.
6. Interview with Director AGD.
7. Interview with Director of AGD.
8. Interview with Director of AGD.
9. Interview with Director AGD.
10. Interview with Economic Studies Unit Manager.
11. Speech from the Board – November, 1996.
12. Speech from the Board – November, 1996.

13. Interview with HR Manager.
14. Speech from the Board – November, 1996.
15. Interview with Director AGD.
16. Poncho is a traditional outfit in the Argentine countryside.
17. Interview with HR Manager AGD.
18. Interview with Director AGD.
19. Interview with Director AGD.
20. Interview with Director AGD.
21. Interview with Manager of Origination area.
22. Interview with Director AGD.
23. By 1999, Adrián Urquía Jr was 58 years old, Roberto Urquía was 54 and Adriana Urquía, 38.
24. Interview with Director AGD.
25. Interview with HR Manager.
26. Interview with Director AGD.
27. Interview with Director AGD.
28. Interview with Director AGD.
29. Interview with Director AGD.
30. Interview with Director AGD.
31. Interview with HR Manager.
32. Interview with Director AGD.
33. Interview with Director AGD.
34. Interview with Director AGD.
35. Interview with Director AGD.

8. Case Study: St Martin

BRIEF OVERVIEW OF THE HISTORY OF ST MARTIN 1929–1999

In 1929, Juan and Raúl Martín set up what would become one of the most important companies in the edible oil industry in Argentina: St Martin.[1] Nowadays St Martin is considered an important crushing company in the edible oil industry and ranks high among the top exporters in Argentina in terms of the value of its exports.

The first generation tenure (1920–1973) was shaped by the work done by its two founders, Juan and Raúl St Martin. They saw the company reach many milestones, for example, when in 1943 the company first started processing oilseeds (mainly cotton seeds), or when in 1966 it incorporated solvent extraction, thus updating its production facilities and making them among the best in the world.

The third generation tenure started right after the death of its founders in 1973. Paul St Martin, grandson of Raúl, became President. The third generation bypassed the second generation and took control of the firm. The explanation for this was very straightforward:

> The foundational stage was very long. The founders had a grip on the business for a long time until they died. With 40 years running the business along with their children, when the time came to change the tenure, the second generation of family members were tired and preferred their children to be in charge.[2]
> (See stages of St Martin's history in Figure 8.1.)

This tenure witnessed the soya boom in the 1970s and 1980s. The boom in production and exports of soya in the 1970s made many companies in the edible oil industry shift their crushing production towards more profitable soya. And this is what St Martin did, but always maintaining the importance of the cotton activity. However, the problem of the cotton business was twofold: it was shrinking over time and necessitated heavy investments in infrastructure, thus preventing the company from investing heavily in fast growing markets such as soya crushing. In 1979 the company also entered the bottled edible oil market and attained, at that time, 14 per cent of the market share.

Although the Board initially held back while it decided whether it

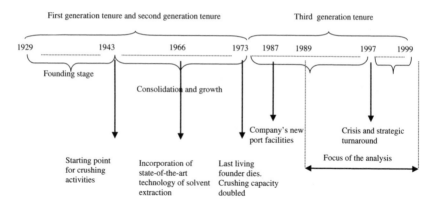

Figure 8.1   Chronology and stages in St Martin's history

should retain cotton ginning as its primary activity, the company invested in production and shipping facilities in the port that were completed by 1987. Ten years later, in 1997, these shipping facilities would become Port St Martin.

The year 1987 saw a turnaround in the company's activities. One result of the investments in crushing and shipping facilities, which allowed the company to start FOB exports,[3] was that turnover and crushing production doubled, thus becoming even more important than before.

St Martin, however, did not abandon investments in the cotton market. The investments in cotton ginning plants took off from 1985 onwards after the purchase of a ginning plant in the north of the country. During the 1980s and 1990s, St Martin advanced in the cotton business by incorporating four more plants. The deep involvement of the company in the cotton industry caused them to suffer when it faced the crisis which began in 1997.

The 1990s found a company that depended more and more on crushing activities but had heavy investments in a declining cotton industry. By the end of the decade it had increased its commitment to the cotton industry by integrating its activities from processing to spinning and weaving.

CHRONOLOGICAL AND ANALYTICAL TRACING OF KEY ELEMENTS OVER THE PERIOD 1989–1999

Markets and Products: The Pendulum Strategy 1989–1997

The 1990s brought major challenges for the industry as a whole: the opening up of the economy brought into the market the last competitors that were not already in the Argentine edible oil industry. Furthermore, a wave of mergers and acquisitions of local businesses was initiated because local companies found they were not large enough to compete. St Martin realized the importance of scaling up its plants to enable them to compete. However, decisions were taken regarding the scale of cotton plants rather than crushing plants:

> We had made a great effort in cotton processing in terms of attaining the right scale. However, the crushing activity, our main business, was demoted. Therefore, from 1997 to 1999 we invested a lot in increasing daily production. Nowadays both activities – cotton and crushing – produce 10 000 tonnes a day.[4]

From 1989 to 1997 St Martin invested a lot in cotton and port facilities. The crushing capacity was lagging behind its competitors who had already started to invest in updating technology and increase of scale:

> By 1995–1996 there was a strong consensus in the company that we did not have to invest in scaling up crushing capacity but use the idle capacity that existed in the market. We tried to use slack capacity and increase sales volume. We were also aggressive with our price policy, lowering our prices in the internal market for edible oils.[5]

Many interviewees stated the incoherence of this strategy, bearing in mind the importance of the crushing activity for the company and the declining cotton market: 'The Board was split into those that wanted to follow industrialization and processing cotton and those that preferred crushing of other oilseeds.'[6]

As another interviewee pointed out: 'The problem arose because St Martin started as a cotton processing company, so the senior members of the Board were reluctant to shift from that strategy although it was a loss-making strategy.'[7]

1979–1997: The failure of the brand strategy

In 1979 St Martin launched its edible oil on to the internal market. The edible oil launched was mixed oil. In a few years the company reached 14 per cent of the market share, an important slice of the market taking into consideration the predominance of companies such as Molinos. However, the company's market share, which reached its peak in 1981, had been falling over the period up until 1997 (see Figure 8.2). One manager explained this reduction in the market share:

> The problem was that St Martin could not consolidate its brand strategy. It was a pity because the company had taken up this strategy before many of today's

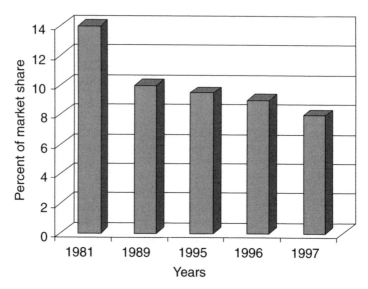

Figure 8.2   Market share of St Martin's branded edible oils 1979–1997

successful companies in the edible oil market. Had the company consolidated its brand strategy in the 1980s, today we would be leading this profitable market.[8]

Over the period 1979–1997 the company did not change the packaging or the type of oil sold, and therefore lagged behind more innovative brands that were introducing new packaging (such as PET bottles), or new types of edible oils (such as pure sunflower instead of mixed oil).

The company did not understand the customer. We just sold oil. The consequence was evident – we lost market share. This loss was considerable and difficult to recover because the market now is much more competitive than in the 1980s.[9]

1997: The company's strategic turnaround

In 1997 changes regarding the company's strategy were paramount. That year, due to weather problems, the production of cotton fell. Over this period many companies in the industry closed down and St Martin suffered as well because of its investments in the cotton industry. However, the company reacted swiftly and in 1997 realized that its tripartite strategy (cotton, crushing and branding) was over. It was the crushing activity that supported St Martin's heavy losses in the cotton industry.

Moreover, the branding strategy failed to secure substantial market share for St Martin's edible oils products, thus the whole commercial policy was at stake as well.

Table 8.1   Strategic objectives of St Martin since 1997

Strategic objectives	Obtained through
Focus on crushing and cotton ginning	• Investment in technology • Stable supply of raw material at competitive prices • Efficient logistics • Outsourcing (IT, transport, storage) • Competitive crushing costs through economies of scale, location of plants and technology • Multiseed production facilities • Solid financial structure
Invest to become a low cost and efficient provider in each market it participates in	• Investments in production facilities such as crushing plants and cotton ginning plants • Investments in port facilities
Maintain profitability through high production flexibility	• Crushing three different oilseeds (soybean, sunflower and cotton) at the plant (in the port)

In 1997 the Board agreed a new strategic focus that was described as follows:

> 1997 is a turning point for the company. A new image of the company has emerged. The Management of St Martin sees the company as an industrial group dedicated to crushing oilseeds and cotton ginning. By doing so it is seeking to achieve the highest standards of efficiency being a leading company in terms of both crushing capacity and technology. It does what it believes it is able to do best, performing an efficient role between the production of bulk commodities and international consumer markets. We are also of the opinion that the marketing function, in our particular case, is at present performed more efficiently and at a lower cost by the multinational trading companies with whom the company has developed very strong relationships over time. We have a strong focus within our company on our two core activities. Many services, not directly related to our core businesses, have therefore been outsourced.[10]

The strategic objectives of the company can be seen in Table 8.1.

The first decision, which was a product of the new strategic objectives the company defined, was that the factories in the north of the country that were used for crushing should be closed down and the crushing facilities located in the port area, thus saving money on logistics. Crushing scale was boosted by investments in technology. In 1999 the company crushed up to 10 000 tonnes of seed per day, the fourth largest company in terms of crushing capacity that year.

Crushing, became the most important business for St Martin through-out the ten year-period analysed. From 1997 onwards, St Martin would focus on crushing, and other activities besides crushing, such as production and direct exports, would no longer be a priority. St Martin would be an intermediary company buying oilseed from farmers and selling bulk oil to traders.[11]

The company also decided to make some investments in cotton ginning plants. Because of the crisis in the cotton industry caused by three years of floods, in 2000 St Martin bought a spinning and weaving mill, thus verti-cally integrating its activities in the cotton industry.

After 1997, the brand strategy was considered a marginal business:

> The policy our company decided to adopt was to carry on with the crushing business. There are great risks in the area of the diversification of products because it means you begin to compete with companies which are already present in the market. It would require huge investments in marketing and research into how we could best penetrate the market, and we simply could not afford that. We did not want to produce finished products such as soya milk and launch it on to the internal market. Our market is to export bulk products. The internal market is a marginal one.[12]

St Martin wanted to position itself as a low price, good quality brand. However this strategy was not the success the company was expecting. By 2000 the market share of brand products was 7 per cent, that means less than in 1997 when the company decided to change its branding strategy. Furthermore, market studies suggested that consumers' perception of St Martin's brands was that they were cheap and low quality products.

Organizational and Managerial Changes in St Martin 1989–1999

Neither the structure of the company nor the managerial team changed significantly over the ten year period analysed. The high level of centraliza-tion of decision making at the Board level and the reliance on family-members to cover managerial positions might explain the lack of changes.

> We did not see the need to change the structure. I think this is a trend in the industry. We do not think that changes in the structure would change much in the company. We have a centralized structure. Everything is decided at the cor-porate level. Remember that this is a family business with many shareholders, so we need to keep our eyes peeled.[13]

> There are only three managers that report back to the President. Our structure then is very flat at the corporate level, with all the characteristics of a family run business, having to deal with minor details.[14]

The structure of St Martin is still a functional one, with corporate areas that control its different plants or companies. The corporate structure consists of the Board of Directors and three Departments: Commercialization, Technology and Finance.

During the decade analysed the company has experienced no changes in its management team. The Directors of finance, technology and commercialization have not changed in recent years and few incorporations at the departmental level of the hierarchy have occurred.

> We have seen many companies in the industry that have gone through big changes and the incorporation of new managers. Those companies that did not go bankrupt had such a nightmare in terms of cultural clashes that they would have preferred not to change anything at all. I think this answers your question about the company's management.[15]

The main criteria for appointing managers did not change significantly over the period 1989–1999 (see Table 8.2):

> To be able to fill one of the managerial positions, you had to be a family member or forget it! There had been no change in this respect over the last ten years. On the contrary, new generations were pushing to enter the company and they didn't want to be part of the shop floor of course![16]

All the managerial positions in the company are given to family members, thus leaving little leeway for non-family members to gain access to important positions:

> If you work in St Martin you have to be aware that there is a limit to your professional career. That limit is the family. You cannot get access to the best posts. This company is good for trainees and administrative or shop floor employees. I would say that is also good for middle managers. But, bright people with ambition who are willing to succeed don't last long.[17]

Age and experience in the sector was a condition *sine qua non* for important posts as seen in Table 8.2. These selection criteria caused St Martin to become an elderly organization as indicated in Table 8.3, with low levels of staff turnover and with family members occupying managerial positions.

The fact that after 1997 St Martin decided that crushing and cotton ginning would be its most important activities also had an impact on the professionalization of the company. Neither activity needs a wide variety of skills. Technical skills are the most important requirement for understanding the problems of crushing and ginning. Cotton ginning, on the other hand, is a manpower intensive industry that requires staff with technical skills rather than professionals from different backgrounds.

Table 8.2 *Requirements for entering the different areas of the company over the period 1989–1999*

Areas of the company	1989	1999
Finance	• Family member for managerial positions	As in 1989
	• Accounting, Finance or Business studies degrees for intermediary positions	As in 1989
	• No specific requirement for administrative positions	Experience in edible oil and food processing industries
	• Experience in edible oil industry	As in 1989
Commercialisation	• Family member for managerial positions	As in 1989
	• Experience in branding in the industry	Experience in brokering
Technology	• Family member for managerial positions	As 1999
	• Technical or engineering studies	Engineering studies

Table 8.3 *Average age of personnel in the areas of the company (taking into account the whole personnel of the area)*

Areas of the company	1989 (Age average)	1999 (Age average)
Finance	48	57
Commercialisation	45	56
Technology	56	59

The company, also lacked an HR area. It had, however, two Personnel departments: one in the Port area and the other in the north of the country in the cotton ginning facilities:

> Why do we not have an HR department? Because we do not need it of course! Because all the most important managers are family members, all the problems are sorted out at the Board level. All other problems are sorted out by the heads of the different areas. The main aim of our personnel department is to hire shop floor employees and they also carry out administrative functions.[18]

While there were not many changes regarding structural or managerial issues, the governance of the company and family related issues have changed a lot, thus raising concerns over the future of the firm. The next section will discuss this aspect further.

Board of Directors: Governance, Strategy and Family

Corporate governance in St Martin

As time passes and more generations of family members have been incorporated into the company, the evolution of the governance in St Martin highlights two main issues: the interest of the shareholders and the best way of running the business effectively and efficiently.

When Juan and Raúl were in charge of the firm – from 1929 to 1973 – the governance of the company was simple. Raúl was the President and Juan the Vice-President and both ran the company together. There was no Board of Directors in the company until one of the founders died.

In the 1960s Raúl's children (the second generation) started work in the company and controlled the commercial, administrative and technical areas. The youngest of the male cousins – Juan's son – joined the company in the 1970s.

After the death of Raúl St Martin, his grandson Paul took over the Vice-presidency.[19] Later when Juan died, he was elected President by a general consensus of the shareholders. His cousin, on the other hand, was sworn in as Vice-President. All the Board members had executive roles as well. The President was therefore responsible for the commercial side of the business, the Vice President and one director for administration and finance, and another director was in charge of the technical area.

By 1976, and as a result of the selling of shares between family members, Juan's heirs held 40 per cent of the shares and Raúl's heirs held the remaining 60 per cent. Until 1980 the Board consisted of four members of the family.

By 1985 the third generation of family members was already working in the company and the first quarrels regarding the Board's arrangements flared up. The 1970s saw Raúl St Martin's children pass away. Plans to make the Board represent the whole family were left in tatters. For more than ten years the Board had been 'something for the books and auditing. The company was run by Paul and his cousin and the rest of the family did not participate at all.'[20]

A new Board arrangement was created when in 1990 the Board was restructured and the 75 shareholders were represented by ten directors: four directors were Juan's heirs and six Raúl's heirs. Only one Director – the Vice President – was a second-generation member, the rest were third generation family members.

The Board's arrangements are not perfect. But they are still better than nothing. Today more or less everybody feels represented in the company and we listen to everybody's suggestions regarding its future. However, this is far from perfect.[21]

New problems, however, are emerging among the fourth generation of family members who feel underestimated and dismissed:

The Board does not represent us [fourth generation], they do even not think about taking one of us on to the Board. We are more dynamic and entrepreneurial, open to what is happening in the sector and we are more determined to change things in the company.[22]

Strategy, delegation and control

The Board participates in everyday operations. Three of the Directors have an operational area under their responsibility. The heads of the commercial, finance and technology areas are Directors of the company; the President is deeply involved in the commercial area, and the Vice President in the administration. The rest of the Directors also have an operational responsibility in the different areas of the company.

Without the Board's agreement, nothing related to investments or spending can be processed. The Board started to centralize these decisions even more after 1997 when they saw that being cost-efficient was a crucial aspect for the company's survival.[23]

The Board therefore made all the decisions regarding investments in the company, such as buying cotton ginning plants, scaling up the crushing capacity, and hiring people. It also authorized all expenditure over US$500.

This concentration of power sometimes makes it hard to move forward:

On the one hand, I can understand that keeping costs down is a key issue, but on the other hand, you waste your time and decisions are delayed until the Board makes up their mind if they are going to let you go ahead with the spending. Why is the Director of the area not in charge of authorizing you to spend? Why should everything be concentrated at the Board level? Sometimes they [Directors] are involved in minor things and I do not think this should be the role of a Director, do you?[24]

Our Board meetings are exhausting. We sit around the table and first of all we discuss the different topics that range from important strategic decisions to buying paper for the photocopier. I think that this should change in the future so that we can have more time to think, analyse and work on important strategic matters.[25]

The control mechanisms of the company are based on personal control exercised by the members of the Board:

Sometimes I have to give three members of the Board the answer to the same question on the same day. It is quite a tiresome experience to deal with them. They think you want to rip them off or take their money. Their control is inquisitive rather than professional.[26]

Incomplete tasks

Two main issues concerned the Board regarding its governance. Both issues are considered to be 'hindering the company's potential for success and its ability to survive as a family business.'[27] The issues are the succession process and the role and entrance of family members.

Regarding the first issue – the succession process – the President is thinking of retiring but he is afraid that this will give rise to problems regarding the succession process.

> There are three candidates, natural candidates to replace me. They are the heads of the three departments of the company. Since I said that in five years I would bow out, wrangles have broken out and alliances have started to build up in the Board. This situation might destroy the harmony I have tried to establish since the enlargement of the Board was decided.[28]

Another important problem the company has to solve concerns the entrance of family members. The fourth generation has shown an interest in having a more active and dynamic role. However, the Board is still thinking about how to do this:

> We are thinking about writing down a family protocol that would help us to have the best family members in the company. This is crucial because family members are the managers of the company. There are 75 shareholders. In a few years there will be more than a hundred of us. A hundred shareholders would mean that the company was no longer viable.[29]

Challenges for the Future and Unresolved Issues

There are two issues that the company's managers have highlighted as important to the company's future: the first is the possibility of finding a partner as a way of injecting capital into the company. The second issue, which is related to the first, is finding ways for the company to grow.

The first issue was emphasized by many family members. There was a great concern among many managers that the market concentration in the industry would affect the viability of the company if St Martin does not acquire the right size to allow it to compete: 'The future shows that we are going to need to look for a partner, a buffer, with whom we can guide the company forward and weather the storm.'[30]

Having a partner was also seen as a way of sorting out financing problems. Furthermore, a partnership would accelerate decisions concerning the future of the family shareholders:

> With 75 shareholders, any partnership or alliance looks impossible. There would be resistance but I think in the end and after a long fight among family members some of them will get rid of their shares. The first step is to concentrate the shares in three or four family branches. To reduce the number of shareholders by a third or even more than that.[31]

The second issue is the current concern among several managers regarding future growth of the company. Many interviewees pointed out that this is the first issue to sort out because it is a process that can be managed by the company unlike finding a partner which is a long-term project that will depend on the company's market position.

The managers seemed to lack any clear vision as to where to start work to enable the company to grow faster. The concentration on the crushing industry and the low-margin profits that characterize it, affected St Martin's opportunities for investments in other areas. Furthermore, managers did not attempt to take risks, but waited for changes in the industry first, saw how leaders responded and after that made a decision:

> The processes of expansion have not been produced by strategic questions within the company, but by a movement that the whole industry has taken. So wait and see is our strategy.[32]

> Someone who thinks about how much his company is going to grow in two or three years will not get there. This is why you have to wait till the market shows you the ways to grow.[33]

Following the leaders and avoiding risks were stressed by other managers:

> I think that we are first of all going to see what Cargill, Dreyfuss and AGD have done. If we can compete we are going to copy the strategy, otherwise we will try to find a niche market that the big companies are not interested in and take advantage of that.[34]

NOTES

1. Some of the data (that is, names, dates among others) of the firm has been changed to preserve its anonymity.
2. Interview with Corporate Lawyer.
3. FOB exports are goods sold to a local or multinational company – generally large trading companies – which is then responsible for their distribution and re-location. CIF

export, on the other hand, is when the company that exports ships and distributes the merchandise on its own, thus dealing directly with end customers.

4. Interview with Head of Technology Department, Director of the Board and third generation family member.
5. Interview with Commercial Department Manager.
6. Interview with Commercial Department Staff and fourth generation family member.
7. Interview with Director of St Martin.
8. Interview Commercial Department Staff.
9. Interview with Commercial Department Staff and fourth generation family member.
10. Interview with Finance Director, Director of the Board and third generation family member.
11. Interview with Commercial Director, Director of the Board and third generation of family member.
12. Interview with Corporate Lawer in St Martin.
13. Interview with President.
14. Interview with Finance Director, Director of the Board and third generation family member.
15. Interview with President.
16. Interview with Personnel Department.
17. Interview with Personnel Department.
18. Interview with President.
19. Paul's father was already dead.
20. Interview with Corporation Lawyer.
21. Interview with Head of Technology Department, Director of the Board and third generation family member.
22. Interview with Commercial Department Staff and fourth generation family member.
23. Interview with Finance department staff.
24. Interview with Technology department staff.
25. Interview Operation and Director.
26. Interview with Finance department staff.
27. Interview with President.
28. Interview with President.
29. Interview with Finance Director, Director of the Board and third generation family member.
30. Interview Finance Director, Director of the Board and third generation family member.
31. Interview with Technology Department Director, Director of the Board and third generation family member.
32. Interview with Finance Director, Director of the Board and third generation family member.
33. Interview with Commercial Department, Director of the Board and third generation family member.
34. Interview with Finance Finance Department staff.

9. Concluding remarks on the transformation process of the firms analysed

It is beyond the scope of this book to discuss the different ways organizations can undertake organizational change. However, the fact that the four firms analysed underwent a process of transformation throughout the 1990s means that we need at least to understand the depth and scope of such a process. Moreover, writers in the field of organizational flexibility such as Volberda (1999) point out that adaptability can be achieved because flexible firms can transform when needed. For this reason, understanding how the firms in this study transformed also helps to shed light on their flexible capabilities (Volberda, 1996, 1999; Djelic and Ainamo, 1999).

It is therefore important to establish the basic differences between the concepts writers have used to explain change in organizations. Greenwood and Hinings (1996) differentiate between two aspects of organizational change. First, they distinguish between radical (or what we call transformational) and convergent change. It is radical not convergent change in which we are interested. Second, they draw a distinction between revolutionary and evolutionary change.

For Greenwood and Hinings (1996: 1024) radical change involves the transformation of the organization while convergent change 'is fine tuning the existing orientation'. Under great pressure from the competitive environment that characterized Argentina in the 1990s, indigenous firms needed to respond rapidly and transform the company's activities to be able to compete efficiently with MNCs (Toulán and Guillén, 1997; Guillén and Toulán, 1997; Volberda, 1999).

The pace of adjustment, on the other hand, defines revolutionary and evolutionary change. While revolutionary change occurs swiftly, evolutionary change happens gradually. In understanding the transformational process of organizations it is important to know whether change has evolved (Miller and Friesen, 1982) or has exploded on to the scene as a revolutionary transformation (Thomson and Millar, 2001; Tushman and Smith, 2001).

Questions also arise regarding the process of transformation undertaken in the four firms in our sample, for example, how did the firms under analysis tackle the challenge of transformation in their organizations? What were the main differences between flexible and less flexible firms? Did firms differ in terms of the speed of their transformation process, and if so, why? In the following pages we briefly examine the trajectories of transformation in both the flexible companies and the less flexible companies.

THE FLEXIBLE FIRMS: THE TRANSFORMATIONAL RENEWAL JOURNEY

The flexible firms in this research have transformed themselves through a process of organizational and strategic renewal. Thus far, the literature has analysed the implications of organizational and strategic renewal in organizations. Floyd and Lane (2000) depict renewal as an iterative process of beliefs, action and learning, with the purpose of aligning the organization and its strategy with changing environmental circumstances.

Volberda *et al.* (2001) have used the concept of transformational renewal to refer to those organizational transformations that are associated with significant unlearning, new ways of thinking and new mindsets, and different paths of technology. According to Volberda *et al.* (2001) a transformational renewal journey is characterized by periods of systemic exploration as the organization renews and changes its skills and competencies. For them, transformational renewal demands that the whole organization should be involved in radical changes at both the strategic and organizational level.

So, how did the flexible firms undertake their transformational journey? Both AGD and Sidus were able to undertake radical changes by renewing both their strategies and their organizations. The strategic renewal of the companies (that is, through their strategic initiatives) was accompanied by organizational renewal (that is, in terms of structural, managerial and governance changes) in order to align the whole organization and its strategy to the demands of the environment. Let us consider some examples of how both AGD and Sidus undertook their transformation process through organizational and strategic renewal.

Since 1986 AGD has introduced different strategic initiatives that have transformed not only the company but also the industry (Ketelhohn *et al.*, 1998). From being dependent on the crushing side of the business in 1989, AGD diversified and integrated its activities. Among the most important strategic initiatives in which AGD invested are the logistic investments in 1986, the launch of branded products in 1989 and farming investment in 1990.

But while exploring new strategies AGD was also able to go through broad organizational and managerial changes. By 1999, AGD had modified its functional structure to one based on business units. This structure provided a higher level of delegation and responsibility for the managerial team in running the company. The overriding intention behind the structural changes was to grant the Board more time to concentrate on strategic issues.

The new business AGD added during the 1980s was complemented in the early 1990s by the opening up of the firm to new managers with different educational backgrounds and experience. The governance structure of the company was also consolidated. The transition after the founder's death towards the second-generation tenure occurred smoothly and without problems. The Board had complementary roles in the process of transformation: Roberto and Adrián (Jr) Urquía masterminded the company's strategic change; Adriana Urquía was the one pushing for internal changes.

In the 1980s, Sidus began a series of strategic initiatives that transformed the company from a small nationally-owned laboratory to 'a health company.'[1] From the creation of the Biotechnology company in 1989 to the setting up of the Retail Business unit in 1999, Sidus diversified and integrated its activities both backwards and forwards throughout the value chain. This strategy had three outcomes: first, the company no longer depended on selling traditional pharmo-chemical products; second, it was a more efficient company that enjoyed economies of scale; and, finally, it became a company that was ahead of its competitors in terms of reaching different stages of the chain of value.

The strategic renewal of Sidus went hand in hand with a renewal of its organization. By the time Sidus launched its second strategic initiative in 1990 (that is, the distribution company) the firm had changed its functional structure to a divisional one. Each new venture of Sidus became an independent company. This new structure was designed to give the Board more time for strategic issues.

At the same time the company also experienced changes at the managerial level. The homogeneous culture of Sidus in the 1980s was transformed when the company started to diversify its activities. Professionals with different experience and from different backgrounds entered the company to run the different businesses Sidus had launched.

The case studies also illustrate the pace of change in AGD and Sidus. Although the changes in both companies were profound and transformational, the changes were neither dramatic nor revolutionary but continuous (Brown and Eisenhardt, 1997). Therefore, punctuated equilibrium explanations of the transformation of AGD and Sidus are not adequate to capture and explain such a process (see Tushman and Romanelli, 1985; Tushman and Smith, 2001). Our two flexible firms were quick to adapt to new changes by means of continuous explorative and simultaneous changes at different levels of the organization (that is, strategic and organizational changes).

The less flexible firms, however, display a different change journey. For reasons that we will explain, the companies were reluctant to change their strategies and the way they were organized although the context had already changed. In the next section, therefore, we analyse the way the transformation process was undertaken by both St Martin and DERSA.

THE LESS FLEXIBLE FIRMS: TRANSFORMATION THROUGH REVOLUTION

While the punctuated equilibrium model did not offer an adequate explanation of the change process in AGD and Sidus, the theory helps to answer an important question concerning the process of transformation in the less flexible firms: why was the transformation process at St Martin and DERSA revolutionary?

Tushman and Romanelli's (1985: 190) seminal paper on the punctuated equilibrium model of organizational change sheds light on the reasons for revolutionary changes in organizations. They state that resistance to change and inertia cause delay in aligning the organization to environmental requirements. Therefore, fundamental change 'occurs only via simultaneous and discontinuous interruption of on-going activities and interrelationships'.

Tushman and Romanelli (1985) also discuss conceptually the internal and external forces that resulted in the revolutionary transformation of firms. They mention as external forces the evolution of products in markets. As internal forces for fundamental change they point out that sustained low performance and/or a change in the balance of power may disrupt the organization. In another piece of research, Romanelli and Tushman (1994) report the results of their study of the causes of revolutionary transformation in 25 minicomputer producers in the USA. They suggest that revolutionary transformations were influenced by major changes in environmental conditions and successions of chief executive officers (CEOs).

The circumstances surounding the revolutionary transformation of St Martin and DERSA are similar to those described by Tushman and his associates. Both St Martin and DERSA were laggards in their own industries. For a long time both firms resisted any far-reaching changes. In St Martin, the Board's attachment to the tradition of cotton ginning delayed the decision to switch investments to the profitable activity of crushing. As one manager stated, the company 'was born and raised on it [cotton ginning]'.[2] Thus, St Martin's interest in that business was the result of conservatism regarding the activity that lay at the origin of the company and was not due to any consideration of the profitability of the cotton industry. Only after the performance crisis in 1997 did St Martin decide to shift its strategy and focus its activities on the crushing business. That sudden transformation was necessary to allow the firm's survival.

DERSA, on the other hand, had been influenced by its past success and the fact that the company had participated with its products in all the market niches. After years of bad commercial and financial decisions, the company modified its strategy to focus on the shrinking dermatology niche in which DERSA had a certain competitive advantage. The decision to transform, again, came late and in a revolutionary way. This happened after a new CEO took over in response to the critical situation that was threatening the survival of the company. In a few months the new CEO of DERSA replaced the top management team (that is, immediately dismissing 22 managers), shifted the strategy of the company (that is, towards a focus on dermatology) and started to change some key processes in the company (that is, new HR policies, IT investments). The newcomers, as Gersick (1991) states, facilitated the task of breaking up the old deep structure and reorienting the organization by removing sources of inertia and resistance to change.

Sull's study of adaptation and inertia in Firestone and Laura Ashley suggests that inertia and resistance to change are reinforced when firms resist transformation of their main activity and prefer to rely on old formulas that brought about their initial success (Firestone continued to produce bias tyres instead of shifting to the new radial technology. Laura Ashley did not move from its outdated designs and expensive manufacturing.) This, in turn, inhibits experimentation and organizational responsiveness to environmental shifts (Sull, 1999a, 1999b).

In delaying their transformations, DERSA and St Martin could not explore the most convenient alternatives (that is, in DERSA, to diversify into other niches such as paediatric medicine; in St Martin, to boost the brand strategy). Rather, the firms were pressed by the critical situation, and the selection of new strategies and organizational arrangements was made in a revolutionary way and according to one criterion: organizational survival.

We have explored the differences between the flexible and less flexible firms in terms of their transformational process. We have analysed how the flexible firms transformed by means of a process that included organizational and strategic renewal. We have also defined the process of transformation as continuous throughout time and occurring simultaneously at the strategic and organizational level. The less flexible firms, on the other hand, attempted a process of revolutionary transformation. These firms were slow to undertake the process of transformation that was eventually attained only in the late 1990s by means of a sudden change.

The continuous transformation experienced by the flexible firms involved a good deal of trial and error. These companies continuously explored new strategies and organizational arrangements. As the flexible firms changed what they were and what they offered through continuous transformation, they migrated into new strategic and competitive domains. As a result of this migration, they needed to regenerate competitive advantages relative to the new competitors they encountered in these domains. Rindova and Kotha's (2001) analysis of what they call 'continuous morphing' in two Internet firms shows that firms in a continuous state of transformation ('morphing') were able to regenerate competitive advantages when competitive conditions changed. Rindova and Kotha (2001) also highlight that dynamic capabilities (that is, determinants of organizational flexibility) facilitated continuous transformation in the companies they analysed (see also Marshak, 2004).

Conversely, the less flexible firms stressed exploitative activities and delayed any changes until a preponderance of evidence suggested that a major shake-up was necessary. Not only does the latter approach stifle experimentation, but action may also be delayed until time is too limited and resources are constrained.

The analysis of the transformation of the four firms is revealing in terms of the depth and scope of the changes undertaken. So far, however, we have not analysed what enabled the companies to transform and adapt so quickly in conditions of environmental turmoil that characterized Argentina in the 1990s. Therefore, questions arise as to what capabilities allowed flexible firms to engage effectively in the process of continuous transformation. What capabilities did the flexible firms have that helped them to be early adopters or first movers of strategies? Why were the less flexible firms laggards in their industry? Chapter 10 will introduce and analyse the determinants of organizational flexibility.

NOTES

1. Interview with CEO Sidus.
2. Interview with Finance Director St Martin.

10. Determinants of organizational flexibility

INTRODUCTION

In the last two chapters, we described the findings of our case studies of the transformation process in four firms: two of which were considered to be flexible and two less flexible companies. A number of themes were apparent in our data which highlighted a range of managerial, organizational and contextual factors related to the ability of the firms to adapt quickly under environmental pressure. These themes included the effect of new managers coming in from outside the industry, the firms' relationship with its industry peers, the nature of the decision-making process and the early adoption of strategies and organizational changes in the flexible firms.

Our review of the literature (see Chapter 2) indicated that research on the determinants of organizational flexibility and innovativeness and institutional embeddedness offer an insight into the explanation of patterns or mechanisms of adaptation. While the literature describes different organizational capabilities as enablers of transformation and adaptation, there is no mention of how the nature of the firm can affect the creation of those capabilities. Moreover, themes such as adaptation and flexibility have not even been the focal point of the literature of family businesses. The critical role of succession process in a family firm has eclipsed the study of other aspects of change and development in a family firm. Zahra and Sharma (2004) also raised the concern that the same issues have dominated the discourse in the field of family business research. In this case they mentioned succession, performance and governace of family firms.

We are dealing specifically with family-owned businesses. In Chapter 2 we analysed the main features of family firms (that is, the role of the founder, the professionalization of the firm and ownership issues) and how these characteristics can impact on the formation of the flexible capabilities necessary for them to adapt and transform under constantly changing environments.

The previous consideration leads us to raise the following questions: How did the family firms in this study build up the flexible capabilities needed to adapt under environmental pressure? How did the character and particular features of the family firms under study shape the determinants of organizational flexibility? Why were some firms able to achieve flexibility while others could not? The analysis of the determinants of organizational flexibility will seek to answer these questions.

The structure of the analysis is similar for the five determinants analysed: first we explain how the determinants are operationalized; second, we analyse and compare the highly flexible and less flexible firms in each industry (AGD and St Martin on the one hand, and Sidus and DERSA on the other). Finally, we present some patterns common to the flexible firms (Sidus and AGD) and the less flexible firms (St Martin and DERSA).

HETEROGENEITY OF THE DOMINANT COALITION

What it is understood by dominant coalition and what does heterogeneity of the dominant coalition mean? Hambrick (1989) states that the area of strategic leadership studies incorporates individual executives (CEOs), the top management team, or other governing bodies (a Board of Directors) as the subject of the analysis. The study uses a broad definition of the dominant coalition as the individuals responsible for determining a firm's direction (Wiersema and Bantel, 1992. See also Cyert and March (1963) for organizational coalition). This means that Directors of the companies and the top management team are included in the definition of dominant coalition used in this research. This broad definition of the dominant coalition derives from the fact that in family businesses the Directors of the company have a crucial role in executive decisions. Thus, to leave them out of the analysis would be to ignore the particularities of a family business as a special type of organization (Neubauer and Lank, 1998; Gersick *et al.*, 1997).

To understand what heterogeneity is, let us start by understanding what homogeneity means in terms of group dynamics. A homogeneous group is one whose members have a similar age, tenure and background and who may have been together for a long time. A homogeneous group is said to exert more influence on its members and produce greater conformity (Murray, 1989), contribute towards a firm's efficiency, and be more inclined to maintain the status quo (Hambrick and Mason, 1984). There would also be more solidarity among similar individuals, and more congruence in beliefs, giving rise to consensus in decision making (Wiersema and Bantel, 1992).

Heterogeneity in the top management team has the potential to enhance the adaptability and creativity of the group. The diversity of skills and backgrounds mean that heterogeneous groups are more adaptable (Murray, 1989).

Demographic heterogeneity may also lead to diversity in information sources and perspectives and more creativity and innovation in decision making (Wiersema and Bantel, 1992). Furthermore, the different, competing views in such heterogeneous teams may facilitate radical change (Webb and Pettigrew, 1999).

The study of the heterogeneity of the dominant coalition as a determinant of organizational flexibility is operationalized through the demographic studies tradition that analyses demographic variables to understand the characteristics of the management team in terms of their homogeneity and heterogeneity. In particular two empirical studies inform this analysis and the variables used here: first the research done by Bantel and Jackson (1989) in which the demographic features of the top management team in the banking industry are analysed (that is average age, organizational tenure, educational level and background); and second, Wiersema's and Bantel's (1992) study of 100 firms listed in Fortune 500, which uses similar variables to Bantel and Jackson (1989) and which sheds light on the relationship between a firm's diversity and strategic change.

To gain a holistic view of the features of the members of the dominant coalition, in this research we have analysed the following variables over three periods of time:[1] age, tenure in the company, tenure in the role, experience in the industry, experience in the industry and related industries, and finally, experience in other industries. We calculated the mean (average), standard deviation and ranges (maximum and minimum), for all the variables. Tables 10.1 and 10.3 and Figures 10.1 and 10.2 show the statistical analysis undertaken.

AGD and St Martin

In AGD the fall in the different variables is an indicator of the renewal of the number of professionals in the company. A closer look at the demographic analysis shows that the renewal of professionals in the early 1990s brought an increase in the variable 'years experience in other industries' (see Figure 10.1), thus producing a reduction in the average length of company tenure and industry experience between 1996 and 1990.

The case of St Martin, on the other hand, should be understood by reference to the changes the top management underwent during the 1990s. The sharp changes in the variables between 1989 and 1996 are the outcome of a reorganization of the Board of Directors when the third generation set up a new Board. Having a new generation of managers made all the indicators fall although to a lesser extent than in the case of AGD. The rise of the variables in 1999 is due to the fact that the top management team did not vary much and new managers did not have much experience in other

Table 10.1   Demographics of the dominant coalition team at AGD and
St Martin (Mean and Standard Deviation)

	Company	Average	1989	1996	1999
Mean (Average)					
Age	AGD	42.1	43	42.6	40.8
	St Martin	53.9	60.5	51	50.2
Tenure in company	AGD	11.6	12.3	11.8	10.6
	St Martin	21.1	27	17.1	19.1
Tenure in present role	AGD	7.8	10.8	7.1	5.4
	St Martin	12.7	15.5	9.9	12.7
Years experience in	AGD	13.6	15.9	13.9	10.9
industry (pharmaceuticals)	St Martin	22.6	30	18.1	19.8
Years experience in	AGD	14.6	18.7	14.2	10.9
industry and related industries[a]	St Martin	23.3	31	18.7	20.2
Years experience in	AGD	4.7	1.3	5.9	6.8
other industries[b]	St Martin	1	1.25	0.9	0.8
Standard deviation					
Age	AGD		10.5	6	6.4
	St Martin		10.8	5.4	7.6
Tenure in company	AGD		11.7	8.4	8.8
	St Martin		6.1	6.4	6.9
Tenure in present role	AGD		11	7.9	7.3
	St Martin		1.3	7.6	7.8
Experience in industry	AGD		10.3	7.2	8.7
	St Martin		9	5.9	7.1
Experience in industry	AGD		13.5	7	8.9
and related industry	St Martin		9.8	6.5	7.6
Experience other	AGD		1.7	3.4	3.7
industries	St Martin		1.5	1.5	1.2

Notes:
[a] Years experience in the industry and related industry refers to the number of years
working in a traditional pharmaceutical industry and related industries such as health
and biochemistry.
[b] Years experience in other industries refers to the number of years working in industries
other than pharmaceuticals.

industries. On the contrary, all of their work experience was in the edible
oil industry (see Figure 10.1).

What stands out in the analysis of the standard deviation in both AGD
and St Martin is the high dispersion AGD had in 1989 in variables such
as tenure in the company and role and experience in industry and related
industry, while in St Martin the standard deviation was lower. This difference

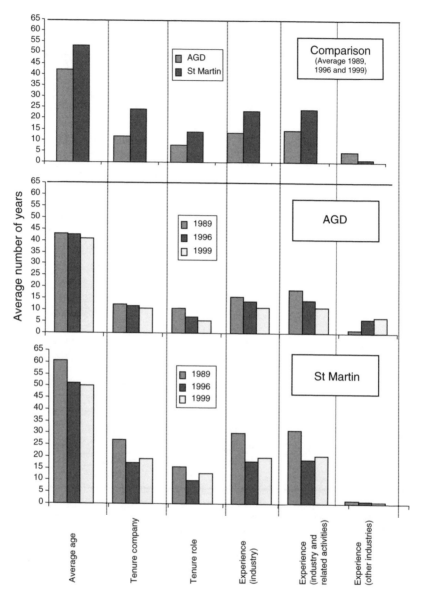

Figure 10.1   Dominant coalition demographics in AGD and St Martin
*   (average years)*

Table 10.2   Background experience of the dominant coalition in AGD and St Martin over the period 1989–1999

	1989	1999
Background experience/Areas of work experience	AGD: Edible Oil, Food, Cereals and Agriculture, Marketing, Accounting.	AGD: Edible Oil, Food, Public Sector, Commerce, Agriculture, Steel, Accountancy, Textiles, Auditing, Trading.
	St Martin: Edible Oil, Food Processing, Marketing, Agriculture, Engineers.	St Martin: Edible Oil, Food Processing, Cereals and Agriculture, Trading, Logistics, Engineers.
Formal education	AGD • 8% Postgraduate degrees • 50% University degrees • 50% Technical degrees St Martin • 25% University degrees • 75% Technical degrees	AGD • 40% Postgraduate degrees • 80% University degrees • 20% Technical degrees St Martin • 10% Postgraduate degrees • 50% University degrees • 40% Technical degrees • 10% No degrees

stemmed from the homogeneous management team in St Martin at that time (in terms of the variables analysed) and the diversity of managers' backgrounds in AGD (see Table 10.1).

People with different educational qualifications and work experience in non-traditional disciplines were hired in AGD whereas in St Martin this was not the case (see Table 10.2). In the case of AGD, new expertise was brought into the management team of the company mainly by outsiders and, to a lesser extent, from internal promotions of the younger generation of managers. Professionals from industries other than edible oil and food were hired, and others with a wide variety of experience in consultancy, textile and commercial activities were incorporated. However, these changes were not achieved randomly. It was a conscious decision on the part of the Board to confront the new wave of competition and economic

Table 10.3   Demographics of top management team at Sidus and DERSA (Mean and Standard Deviation)

	Company	Average	1989	1996	1999
Mean (Average)					
Age	Sidus	46.3	48.4	45.6	45
	DERSA	54.2	54	58.9	49.8
Tenure in company	Sidus	15	19	13.4	12.6
	DERSA	14.3	16.1	17.8	8.9
Tenure in present role	Sidus	7.9	13	5.4	5.2
	DERSA	10.7	11.2	14.3	6.7
Years experience in	Sidus	18.4	21.6	17.3	16.2
industry (pharmaceuticals)	DERSA	19.7	19.1	23.1	16.8
Years experience in	Sidus	19.7	23.8	18.1	17.3
industry and related	DERSA	23.4	23.8	28.1	18.7
industries[a]					
Years experience in	Sidus	5.2	0.8	7	7.8
other industries[b]	DERSA	2.9	2.4	3.2	3
Standard deviation					
Age	Sidus		3.3	9.1	10.3
	DERSA		10	11	9
Tenure in company	Sidus		5	10.4	11
	DERSA		9	8.5	5.6
Tenure in present role	Sidus		3.6	4.2	3.7
	DERSA		5	6.4	6.8
Experience in industry	Sidus		4.5	10.3	11.1
	DERSA		9.1	10.7	10.7
Experience in industry	Sidus		3.9	9.9	10.3
and related industry	DERSA		11.1	12.6	12.6
Experience other	Sidus		1.3	11.1	11.2
industries	DERSA		1.7	2.1	2.1

Notes:
[a] Years' experience in the industry and related industry refers to the number of years working in a traditional pharmaceutical industry and related industries such as health and biochemistry.
[b] Years' experience in other industries refers to the number of years working in industries other than pharmaceuticals.

openness. At AGD they stated: 'The Board is always open to what is happening elsewhere. A change in the contextual conditions triggered the hiring of new types of professionals. From nothing you will now find a group of professionals from different disciplines.'[2]

In St Martin, on the other hand, experience in the sector in which the company participates stands out as an important common factor among

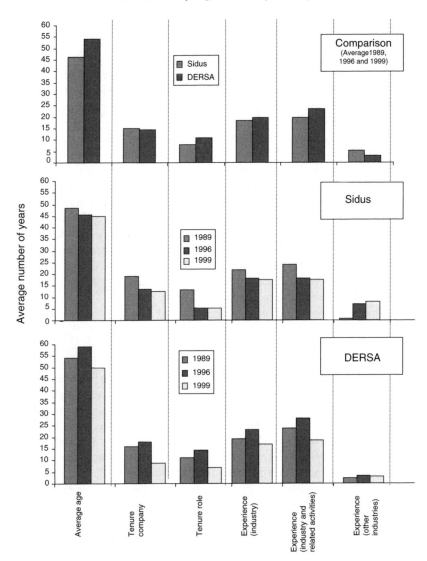

Figure 10.2   Dominant coalition demographics in Sidus and DERSA
(average years)

the top management team. Some of them show little or no experience outside the edible oil industry or food sector: 'We found that experts in the industry can make better decisions than other managers hired with different background experience. We are in the edible oil industry, so we do not need people with experience in the petrol or retail industry.'[3]

Sidus and DERSA

While AGD and St Martin presented dissimilarities in the variables analysed that were evident right from the beginning of the period of analysis, this was not the case with Sidus and DERSA. Prior to the 1990s, DERSA had low average levels in all of the variables except the average age if compared to Sidus (see Table 10.3)

A closer look at Table 10.3, however, shows that at Sidus all the variables analysed fell over time while in DERSA variables reached a peak in 1996 only to fall again in 1999 but always remaining higher than in Sidus.

By 1990, Sidus was a consolidated pharmaceutical company and running a biotechnology project successfully. By 1996, the company had incorporated new managers to run the new distribution business. In 1999 Sidus was a group of companies ranging from traditional pharmaceuticals and biotechnology to retail. These new strategic initiatives needed managerial skills to manage diverse businesses. New appointments are illustrated in the variable '(Experience in other industries)' in Figure 10.2. As can be seen, this variable began to rise in 1989.

The high dispersion indicated by the standard deviation found in Sidus in 1999 is the result of the business diversification undertaken by the company (see Table 10.3). This diversification meant the incorporation of new managers from backgrounds other than traditional pharmaceuticals (giving rise to the high dispersion in the variable '(Experience in other industries)', and with little experience in the pharmaceutical industry (hence, the high dispersion in the variable '(Experience in the industry' and 'tenure in company').

At DERSA, on the other hand, things were not so promising. The long tenure of Gali, the CEO (1981–1997), had a detrimental effect on the renewal of the top management team. Until 1997 there were few changes in DERSA's top management team. The sudden drop in all the variables in 1999 is a direct consequence of the reshuffle of the top team (see Figure 10.2). Twenty-two managers were dismissed when Michael Dufour became the new CEO in 1997. Most of the variables, however, showed a higher average compared to those found in Sidus in the same period of time (see Figure 10.2).

The new strategic initiatives Sidus undertook in the early 1980s and then again in the 1990s meant that the company needed new managerial skills. As a manager in Sidus stated: 'We knew that we needed more abilities and skills when setting up the new companies. That's why the new managers of the new companies of the group were not only very professional but younger than the average age in Sidus.'[4] Managers from different educational backgrounds and experience in fields such as marketing, consultancy, auditing and logistics were recruited (see Table 10.4). This renewal of

Table 10.4   Background experience of the dominant coalition in Sidus and DERSA over the period 1989–1999

	1989	1999
Background experience/Areas of work experience	Sidus: Pharmaceuticals, Biochemistry, Consultancy, Public Service (Health), Health	Sidus: Pharmaceuticals, Academia (research), Marketing, Logistics, Transport, Cereals and Agriculture, Finance, Consultancy, Auditing
	DERSA: Pharmaceutical, Chemistry, Biology, Marketing, Accounting	DERSA: Pharmaceutical, Chemistry, Finance, Marketing
Formal education	Sidus • 6% Postgraduate degrees • 67% University degrees • 33% Technical degrees DERSA • 54% University degrees • 31% Technical degrees • 15% No degrees	Sidus • 40% Postgraduate degrees • 80% University degrees • 20% Technical degrees DERSA • 11% Postgraduate degrees • 55% University degrees • 45% Technical degrees

the management team started earlier in Sidus than in DERSA, as shown in Figure 10.2 in the variable 'Experience (other industries)'.

Until 1997, 'age and experience in the industry'[5] was the most important factor in deciding who was appointed to DERSA's top team. This criterion made it difficult for new managers with diverse professional backgrounds to get into the company. By 1999, as shown in Figure 10.2, the new CEO could not reverse this tendency. The variable 'experience in other industries' has not changed from its level in 1996.

The Dynamics of the Dominant Coalition and Organizational Flexibility: The Cognitive Diversity of the Dominant Coalition

The literature on the top management teams and cognitive processes has signalled the importance of the cognitive diversity of the top managerial team

(Wiersema and Bantel, 1992; Hambrick and Mason, 1984). According to Hambrick and Mason's (1984) seminal paper on the role and influence of the top management team in organizations, a team of more heterogeneous managers interpret reality from a different cognitive base, with different visions and managerial perceptions. The result, for Hambrick and Mason, would be a decision-making process that would contain an array of innovative alternatives.

We found strong evidence to suggest that the most flexible companies in our study had broadened their cognitive bases, bringing new mental models into the firms over time. Two indicators illustrate the existing cognitive diversity in the most flexible firms: first, the capacity of the top managerial team to act; and second, the constructive conflict among the members of the management team. How these indicators influence the ability of an organization to be flexible and to adapt to market changes is described in the literature on cognitive processes and managerial elites.

Various theorists have suggested that different mental models in an organization might enhance the organizations' ability to adapt to change and to succeed enhancing the capacity for action (Greenwood and Hinings, 1996) or action orientation of an organization (Grinyer *et al.*, 1988). Greenwood and Hinings (1996: 1039) defined the capacity for action as 'the ability to manage the transition process from one template to another'. Capacity for action, according to Greenwood and Hinings, is the key to accomplishing radical change. This capacity for action will boost risk-taking behaviour. Three components are proposed as influencing a firm's capacity of action: first, the willingness of management to explore new strategic alternatives; second, the eagerness of the firms to take risks; and, finally, the keenness of the top team to confront difficult issues (Webb and Pettigrew, 1999; Greenwood and Hinings, 1996). In the light of these observations questions were asked about the capacity for action in the four firms under analysis.

There is also a rich array of research stating that a diverse cognitive base among the members of the management team might bring potential for conflict. However, the literature states that this conflict is valuable and essential 'for effective strategic choice' (Eisenhardt *et al.*, 1998: 142). To be constructive, this conflict should be issue-oriented rather than interpersonal (Eisenhardt, 1989b; Eisenhardt *et al.*, 1998) to sharpen the debate, create more options and energize the entire organization (Biggadike, 1998). A lack of cognitive diversity, on the other hand, will cause a group to have low conflict levels, thereby diminishing effectiveness and reducing its ability to offer alternatives (Eisenhardt *et al.*, 1998). The interviewees were therefore asked: were there different views as to what the organization was? Were there new ideas as to how to change the status quo? Did the CEO help to differentiate personal disagreement from disagreement on issues?

The use of visual mapping provides insight into the comparison between highly flexible and less flexible firms in terms of cognitive diversity over three periods of time: 1989, 1990–1995; and 1996–1999.

Figures 10.3 to 10.6 were created by coding the transcripts of each interview in the four companies under analysis according to the response the top management team provided to a range of questions that were indicative of the two components of the cognitive diversity of the dominant coalition: capacity to act and constructive conflict. Four responses were allowed – 'yes', 'no', 'it was increasingly changing or varied across the company' or 'no data' (n/d), when the manager was not able to give any answer because he/she lacked data or because he/she was not at the company in the period of time analysed. Responses were shaded according to whether the interviewees answered 'yes' (black shading), 'increasingly changing or varied across the company' (grey shading), or 'no' answer (no shading). The shadings are shown against the related question and under the interviewee's initials. An inter-coder reliability check gave a score of between 76 per cent and 81 per cent.[6]

The Capacity of the Top Management Team to Act

Sondergaard (2001) and Webb (1999) underline the importance of managerial intentionality as a way of explaining why some firms were able to respond more swiftly to market changes than others. With competitive pressures increasing in the different sectors after the opening up of the Argentinian economy early in the 1990s, a rapid adaptation to the new market was critical for the survival and success of the companies. However, as our analysis of the top management team's capacity to act shows, some firms were able to respond more rapidly than others.

Our interviewees in AGD stated the importance of the capacity for action by highlighting the significance of exploring different strategic alternatives over time (see Figure 10.3). AGD started to explore new fields before the 1990s. From 1990 onwards the company started to incorporate new businesses into its repertoire. Although originally a crushing company, AGD invested in transport, brands, farming, storage and soya sub-products – all this in a 12-year period (1986–1999).

Managers at ADG explained how this risk-taking attitude evolved over time:

> As a family business, AGD was not keen on taking risks, commercial risks. However, after the investments in our own brands, AGD started to pluck up courage and look at different possibilities in the market. Besides that, the incorporation of a new generation of managers helped AGD in this respect. They brought more ideas into the company and they were less worried about trying to innovate and less wary as well.[7]

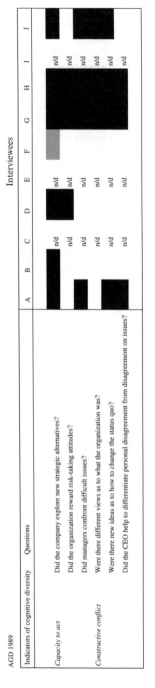

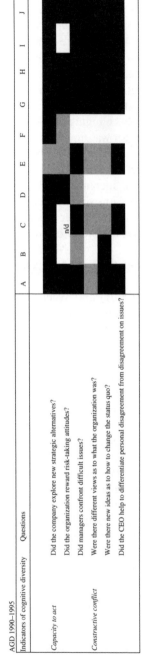

Figure 10.3   Indicators of cognitive diversity at AGD over time

132

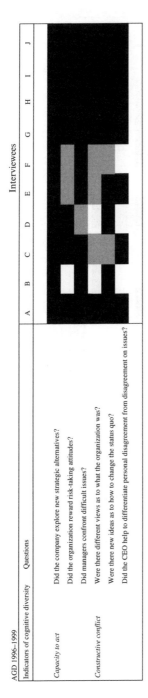

AGD 1996–1999

Interviewees

Indicators of cognitive diversity	Questions	A	B	C	D	E	F	G	H	I	J
Capacity to act	Did the company explore new strategic alternatives?										
	Did the organization reward risk-taking attitudes?										
	Did managers confront difficult issues?										
Constructive conflict	Were there different views as to what the organization was?										
	Were there new ideas as to how to change the status quo?										
	Did the CEO help to differentiate personal disagreement from disagreement on issues?										

Figure 10.3 (continued)

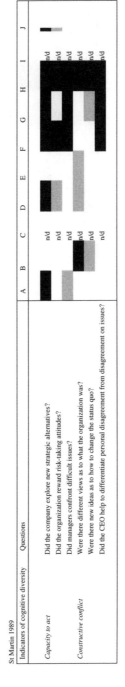

St Martin 1989

Indicators of cognitive diversity	Questions	A	B	C	D	E	F	G	H	I	J
Capacity to act	Did the company explore new strategic alternatives?			n/d						n/d	
	Did the organization reward risk-taking attitudes?			n/d						n/d	
	Did managers confront difficult issues?			n/d						n/d	
Constructive conflict	Were there different views as to what the organization was?			n/d						n/d	
	Were there new ideas as to how to change the status quo?			n/d							
	Did the CEO help to differentiate personal disagreement from disagreement on issues?									n/d	

Figure 10.4   Indicators of cognitive diversity in St Martin over time

St Martin 1990–1995

Interviewees

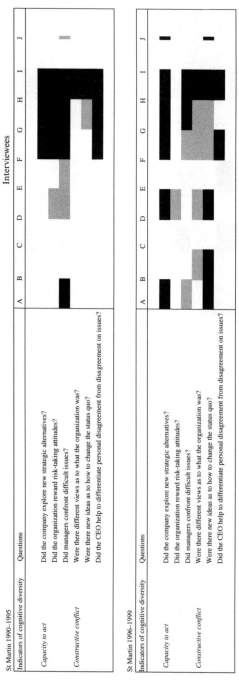

Indicators of cognitive diversity	Questions	A	B	C	D	E	F	G	H	I	J
Capacity to act	Did the company explore new strategic alternatives?										
	Did the organization reward risk-taking attitudes?										
	Did managers confront difficult issues?										
Constructive conflict	Were there different views as to what the organization was?										
	Were there new ideas as to how to change the status quo?										
	Did the CEO help to differentiate personal disagreement from disagreement on issues?										

St Martin 1996–1999

Indicators of cognitive diversity	Questions	A	B	C	D	E	F	G	H	I	J
Capacity to act	Did the company explore new strategic alternatives?										
	Did the organization reward risk-taking attitudes?										
	Did managers confront difficult issues?										
Constructive conflict	Were there different views as to what the organization was?										
	Were there new ideas as to how to change the status quo?										
	Did the CEO help to differentiate personal disagreement from disagreement on issues?										

Figure 10.4 (continued)

134

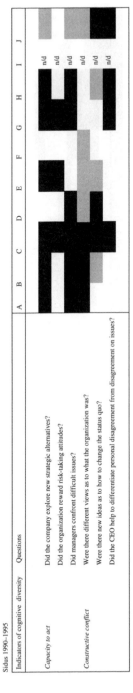

Figure 10.5   Indicators of cognitive diversity in Sidus over time

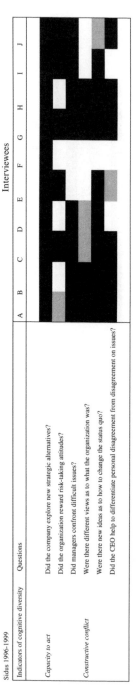

Sidus 1996-1999

Interviewees

Indicators of cognitive diversity	Questions	A	B	C	D	E	F	G	H	I	J
Capacity to act	Did the company explore new strategic alternatives?										
	Did the organization reward risk-taking attitudes?										
	Did managers confront difficult issues?										
Constructive conflict	Were there different views as to what the organization was?										
	Were there new ideas as to how to change the status quo?										
	Did the CEO help to differentiate personal disagreement from disagreement on issues?										

Figure 10.5 (continued)

DERSA 1989

Indicators of cognitive diversity	Questions	A	B	C	D	E	F	G	H	I	J
Capacity to act	Did the company explore new strategic alternatives?				n/d		n/d		n/d	n/d	n/d
	Did the organization reward risk-taking attitudes?				n/d		n/d		n/d	n/d	n/d
	Did managers confront difficult issues?				n/d		n/d		n/d	n/d	n/d
Constructive conflict	Were there different views as to what the organization was?				n/d		n/d		n/d	n/d	n/d
	Were there new ideas as to how to change the status quo?				n/d		n/d		n/d	n/d	n/d
	Did the CEO help to differentiate personal disagreement from disagreement on issues?				n/d		n/d		n/d	n/d	n/d

Figure 10.6 *Indicators of cognitive diversity in DERSA over time*

136

Interviewees

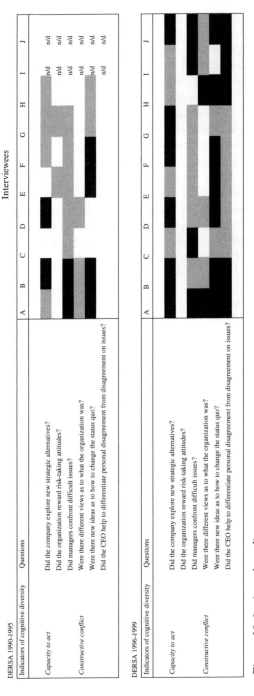

Figure 10.6 (continued)

137

St Martin presents a different case. Figure 10.4 shows how the interviewees perceived that their capacity to act was fading over time. The period 1990–1995 is indicative of a drop in the company's capacity to act and take risks. This is illustrated in Figure 10.4 by more negative answers to our questions regarding the capacity to act (no shading). This represents the interviewees perception of a low capacity for action compared with 1989. This period coincides with a lack of investment and exploration of new businesses. The period 1997–1999 is marked by the strategic reorientation of the company after many years of downturn.

After the strategic changes in 1997 there was a widespread feeling in the company that the capacity for action was damaged: '1997 was a watershed for the company in many respects. But one of the aspects that strikes me the most is our passivity. We preferred to avoid confronting problems.'[8]

The fact that St Martin relies on family members for its top managerial positions might be an explanation for the downturn in its capacity to act. As a manager and family member said:

> I believe that organizations need fresh blood and ideas. But we had been inviting family members into the company for as long as I could remember. This situation makes me remember something I studied about the Egyptian kings. They married their sisters. The result was that their heirs were so weak or so stupid that they could not govern. I am afraid that this situation will happen here. We need to open the company up to professional managers that will bring fresh ideas and action. Otherwise the Egyptian syndrome will affect us.[9]

The capacity for action in Sidus and DERSA also illustrates the influence of the cognitive diversity brought by new managers. As a product of the increasing managerial diversity in the company over time, Sidus presents a growing explorative attitude as well as major exposure of its managers to difficult situations. Figure 10.5 illustrates the incremental evolution of the firm's capacity for action (see where the black shading – indicating the presence of factors positively related to the development of the firm's capacity to act – has increased over time).

From the 1980s onwards the company pioneered the pharmaceutical sector, investing in diverse businesses such as biotechnology, distribution, OTC, retail and intermediary companies. It also started up the first strategic alliance in the industry, and it acquired a company.

> The new professionals were thought-provoking. The professionals that entered the company in this decade were different in that they were not afraid of changing the status quo, in fact they were very happy to change it.[10]

In DERSA, on the other hand, the capacity for action has been influenced by the absence of cognitive diversity in the company over time:

For many years the company lacked the managerial skills needed to confront the market changes. Managers were executors of orders. However, you needed a different type of manager, someone that could or would change things. We did not have this.[11]

However, the reshuffle of the managerial team in 1997 brought the winds of change to the company. The exploration of new alternatives was boosted by seeking new strategic alternatives for growth. Figure 10.6 shows that the exploration of new alternatives began to appear in the period 1996–1999 (coinciding with the reshuffle of the top team). However, the support for risk-taking actions was reduced over time as the company became financially more cautious and the focus on dermatology meant that fewer spare resources were available to try new alternatives (see in Figure 10.6 that none of our interviewees considered that DERSA had a risk-taking attitude in the period 1996–1999. This is indicated in the figure by a lack of shading).

The cognitive diversity of the most flexible firms enhanced their capacity for action as can be seen by the support for the exploration of new strategic alternatives, risk-taking attitudes, and the ability of the management team to face difficult situations. In the less flexible companies, however, the capacity for action was diminished (mainly in St Martin) by the lack of the new managerial capabilities needed to confront market changes.

The cognitive diversity found in the most flexible firms, however, made the management team more prone to disagreement. How this conflict evolved in both highly flexible and less flexible firms is the focus of the next section of this analysis.

Stimulating Constructive Conflict

Our interviewees in the flexible firms highlighted the importance of an increase in disagreements among the top management team. The increasing conflict was seen by the interviewees as providing flexible firms with more alternative views. The differences in this respect between AGD and St Martin are revealing.

Figures 10.3 and 10.4 show the differences between AGD and St Martin in the way the conflict (that is, constructive conflict) differed and varied over time. Figure 10.3 illustrates how different views of what the organization was and new ideas about how to change the company had followed the entrance of new managers in AGD (see how the black shading follows an incremental pattern). Figure 8.4, on the other hand, illustrates the lack of such a conflict in St Martin from 1989 to 1995 (that is, little or no black shading). Only during the period 1996–1999 did new ideas as to how to change the status quo begin to appear.

AGD encouraged its managers – both new and old – to interact more. However, the effect of this was more conflict: 'We thought that more inter-action would help managers to iron out differences. On the contrary these meetings sharpened the differences among them.'[12]

The diversity in the managerial team was, however, considered very posi-tive in the long run: 'Dissension flared up in the early 1990s and we thought it would delay decision-making. On the contrary, it made us think twice before launching ourselves into a new business, and be prudent but certain when we took a decision. It was like a brainstorming exercise.'[13]

St Martin, on the other hand, had seen a low level of conflict until 1997 when the strategy of the company changed. The low level of conflict had its consequence in terms of seeking new scenarios for the company: 'For a long time, the management of the company was too complacent and failed to offer alternatives.'[14]

On the other hand, interaction among the management team was too low: 'Everybody is too busy to meet. If you do not meet, you do not inter-act. And if you do not interact you do not exchange ideas, so you are not constructive.'[15]

The pharmaceutical firms present a similar perspective to that of the edible oil companies. As before, the amount of black shading shows when firms have had more or less constructive conflict. Figures 10.5 and 10.6 illustrate the contrasting patterns found between Sidus and DERSA: Sidus has emphasized constructive conflict in order to achieve a greater openness to alternative views; DERSA avoided conflict among its top team for most of the period analysed (see in Figure 10.6 the evolution of black and grey shading for 1989 and 1990–1995). A diversity of views only began to appear in the late 1990s after the new CEO took over and after the top manage-ment reshuffle took place.

Sidus managed the potential for conflict among the various managers by creating new companies. As the CEO of the company said: 'We interact a lot in meetings, but on a day-to-day basis we are in different companies, therefore allowing interpersonal animosity to subside.'[16]

The CEO is also conscious of the advantages and disadvantages of conflict among members of the management team: 'So, I reckon that you may lose time arguing but in the end we not only have different alternatives, but we also envision the future, as is the case with many of our initiatives.'[17]

The case of DERSA is one in which a powerful CEO impeded dissen-sion: 'Gali [the CEO until 1997] found conflict unpleasant. So he crushed it. None of the top team members at that time wanted to appear to be offending him, so they avoided conflict.'[18]

The changes in the top management team in DERSA from 1997 brought about new ideas as to what the company should be doing in order to grow.

The role of the CEO also changed: 'The new managerial team was open to dissent. I therefore acquired a different role. I not only had to think about the strategy but also make sure that dissension did not open up a chasm between managers.'[19]

Brief Remarks on the Differences Between Flexible and Less Flexible Firms

Our analysis of the demographics of the top management team and our interviews in the different companies revealed significant differences between highly flexible and less flexible firms. While in the highly flexible firms more heterogeneity prevailed among the top team, the less flexible firms presented a more compact and homogeneous managerial elite. We also revealed a second main difference between flexible and less flexible firms: the former are cognitively diverse compared with the latter. In addition to highlighting the contrasts suggested by our interviewees' comments, the coding of the interview transcripts also demonstrated the consistency of the findings (as shown in Figures 10.1 to 10.6).

Our discussion of the demographics of the dominant coalition in the firms shows that AGD and Sidus are more heterogeneous than DERSA and St Martin. AGD and Sidus appointed managers from outside the firm before the changes in the Argentinian economy had begun. AGD started to appoint executives from outside the firm earlier in the 1980s when the company made its first logistic investments. Sidus, on the other hand, did the same when the strategic alliance with Merck was forged. In addition, the inflow of managers with non-traditional backgrounds in edible oils (that is, in AGD) and pharmaceuticals (that is, in Sidus) reduced the degree to which the company was influenced by institutional pressures (this also links to another determinant of organizational flexibility – macroculture embeddedness). As a manager at AGD stated 'The variety of experience and backgrounds of our top team allowed us to leapfrog the competition because we were better prepared with more skills than them.'[20]

These appointments, together with internal promotion of young executives with different backgrounds and great potential, increased the diversity of views and cognitive mindsets among the top management team. That diversity of mental models generated a variety of interpretations of the firm and its environment. As Eisenhardt and Schoonhoven (1990) argue, the presence of divergent cognitive frameworks is essential in a turbulent environment. It granted AGD and Sidus a deeper understanding of the patterns of change that were occurring and allowed them to decide on the most appropriate actions to take or develop (that is, in both companies the different strategic initiatives). So, in the hypercompetitive environment in which the pharmaceutical and edible oil industries operated in the 1990s,

Sidus and AGD were better able to understand the new environment and act more quickly than the less flexible firms.

In contrast, in the less flexible firms the flow of outsiders into senior positions started either late in the 1990s (that is, in the case of DERSA, after 1997) or it did not start at all (that is, the case of St Martin in which the managerial positions are all occupied by family members). As a result, in both companies the top team in the 1990s was highly homogeneous both as regards its background and the way they saw the company and its environment. This homogeneity increased the degree to which the company was embedded in the industry macroculture. The lack of cognitive diversity that stemmed from the prevailing homogeneity in DERSA and St Martin's top team also made it difficult for the firms to interpret the signals from the environment and be proactive.

The finding of this determinant of organizational flexibility is also important in understanding strategic decision-making in organizations. Hickson *et al.* (1986) in analysing how decisions are made at the top of organizations question whether the management of the organization is more influential in decision making than those on the outside, such as trade unions and government departments. The cases of the flexible firms reveal the importance of those inside the firm in shaping decisions internally and even influencing decisions at the industry level. A great majority of decisions of this order arose from deliberate managerial strategies. On the other hand, the less flexible firms demonstrated how they were influenced by decisions taken by other actors such as industry leaders.

CENTRALIZATION AND FORMALIZATION OF THE DECISION-MAKING PROCESS

From our review of the literature on organizational flexibility and innovation, we would expect that the more formalized and centralized decision-making is, the less flexible an organization will be. However, high degrees of autonomy and laxity in control might constrain the implementation of innovation (Englehardt and Simmons, 2002; Damanpour, 1992) and strategies (Fredrickson, 1986).

Formalization reflects the emphasis on rules, procedures and control when carrying out organizational activities. Formalization is frequently measured by the presence of manuals, job description, procedures and mechanisms of control (Dastmalchian, 2001; Ng and Dastmalchian, 2001; Webb, 1999).

Centralization, on the other hand, reflects the extent to which decision-making autonomy is dispersed or concentrated. It is generally measured by the degree of participation of organizational members in decision-making (Webb, 1999; Damanpour, 1991).

To avoid misinterpretation, the interviewees were consistently informed how the concepts of centralization and formalization of decision-making were to be applied in this research. We also gave some examples of those concepts. In the light of these definitions, the interviewees were questioned about their perception of the levels of strategic and operational centralization and formalization in their companies throughout the period 1989–1999. For example, was strategic decision making (that is, strategic planning, strategic meetings) formalized? Were strategic decisions, such as investments and new strategic initiatives, taken mainly by the CEO or the Board?

The interviewees were also asked to assess the question according to degree: low, medium-low, medium, medium-high and high. The answers were coded on an ordinal scale starting from 1 (low) to 5 (high). An inter-coder reliability check gave a score of 87.5 per cent. Figures 10.7 and 10.8 demonstrate both the difference between the companies (AGD and St Martin; Sidus and DERSA) and the differences within each company between two periods of time, 1989–1999.

Organizational Flexibility and the Degree of Centralization and Formalization

AGD and St Martin

AGD showed lower levels of centralization (both strategic and operational) in 1999 than in 1989. However, strategic and operational formalization rose over the time analysed (see Figure 10.7).

In AGD, our interviewees stressed that the Board was more detached from operative decisions in 1999 than in 1989. 'In the 1980s the Board was involved directly in day-to-day operations. They were Executive Directors and Managers at the same time. Every decision taken at the operational level had to be agreed by one of them.'[21]

The organizational changes the company undertook in the 1990s – such as the changes in the structure from a functional to a business unit – were deliberately made in an attempt to change the role of the Board:

> The changes in the structure are a strong indicator of the Board's attitude regarding the operational side of the business. The change from a functional structure to a structure based on the business unit conveyed a message from the Board: 'look, the operation is your business, we are going to concentrate on the important matters'.[22]

However, strategic decisions were still highly centralised in the Board: 'The Directors were very clever: while they stood apart from the operation, they concentrated on strategic issues. They still have a strong grip on these issues.'[23]

The control mechanism grew over the ten years analysed. This is probably why managers' perceptions of the degree of formality over the period 1989–1999 also increased (see in Figure 10.7 the interviewees' mounting perception of AGD's level of formalization in 1999). In the 1980s there was an absence of control systems such as budget and planning. This low degree of formalization was the result of turbulence in the Argentinian economy, which prevented the company from working with control systems and planning. The 1990s drew attention to the necessity of updating and incorporating more formal mechanisms that did not entail, in the opinion of different managers, more bureaucracy.

> AGD is at a halfway point now: we do not have a hefty formalization process but some formalisation is required to succeed. We try to be flexible and to avoid bureaucracy. This is the most important thing to us.[24]

St Martin, on the other hand, presents a different picture (as seen in Figure 10.7). By 1999, centralization levels were still very high. Whereas formalization at the strategic level remained at low levels, the formalization of operative decisions increased substantially.

Regarding the high levels of centralization in the company, the interviewees pointed out that: 'Decisions in this company are centralised by the Board. They decide everything. You will not find an issue or decision in the company that has not been discussed by the Board.'[25]

Having Directors that also participate in the operation of the company caused decisions concerning the operation of St Martin to become highly centralized: 'Remember that they [Directors] are working on the operation of the company, so they know about day-to-day operations. They like to wander around and ask questions and decide about these issues.'[26]

Some managers and employees also complained about the high levels of formalization on a day-to day basis (see in Figure 10.7 how this variable rose over time). There is also a perception that after the enlargement of the Board early in the 1990s, the formal procedures increased:

> Decisions concerning investments are formalized. There are procedures you have to follow. However, in this company there is always a way of bypassing rules otherwise you would get stuck in bureaucratic paperwork. Things were better when the Board consisted of only four members of the family.[27]

Formalization at the strategic level showed a slight variation and remained at a low level compared to that of AGD. This low level of formalization at the strategic level may be explained by the lack of 'strategic

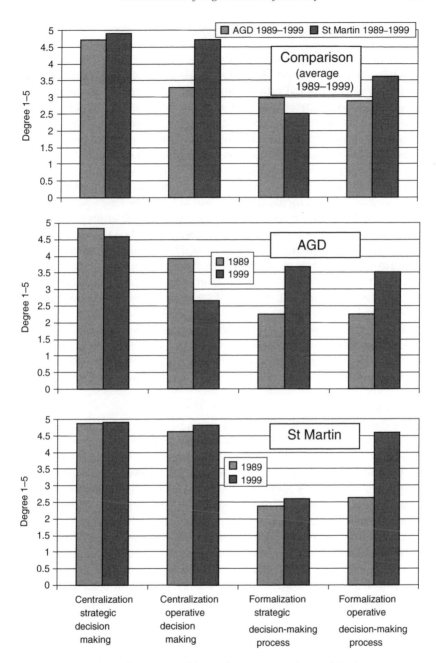

Figure 10.7   Centralization and formalization at AGD and St Martin 1989–1999

planning'[28], 'lack of strategic agenda'[29] or because of the size of the Board that 'prevents us from moving forward in strategic issues. Therefore our meetings are shallow and disorganized.'[30]

What stands out between AGD and St Martin is the differences between the levels of operational centralization and formalization (both strategic and operational). Operational formalization increased in both companies, but in St Martin the growth was much more marked than in AGD (see Figure 10.7). AGD's higher levels of formalization were balanced out by structural reforms and a delegation process that allowed them to achieve low levels of operational centralization. St Martin, on the other hand, did not change its structure and, by 1999, decision-making appeared to be even more concentrated at the Board level than in 1989. We have also shown the differences between the levels of formalization of the strategic decision-making process. St Martin's level was lower than AGD's over time (see Figure 10.7). The rise of this variable in AGD is due to the implementation of formal mechanisms at the Board level, such as strategic planning and strategic meetings. In St Martin, however, none of these mechanisms were applied, thus resulting in low levels of strategic formalization over time.

Finally, both companies present high levels of centralization at the strategic level. However, AGD shows a decreasing tendency while St Martin an increasing one (see Figure 10.7). These high levels should be understood in the context of these firms: both are family firms and the family maintains a strong grip on strategic issues (Poza, 1995).

Sidus and DERSA

Sidus' levels of centralization (strategic and operational) diminished over the period 1989–1999. Meanwhile, during the same period, levels of formalization (both strategic and operational) tended to increase (see Figure 10.8).

At Sidus, operational centralization decreased over time due to a re-shaping of the Board's activities. While in the 1980s the Board was 'everywhere', it now concentrates on strategic issues. Operational decentralization was boosted after the changes in the structure that split Sidus up into a group of companies. Since then, the different companies have gained autonomy of decision making. Each company has taken its own decisions and the Board has accepted this so long as these decisions have not been strategic ones.[31]

Centralization of strategic decision-making was still considered to be very high in 1999:

> The Board is reluctant to delegate those aspects that they consider strategic. They think about this, they make their own decisions and we acknowledge this after the decisions have been taken. . . . Of course they share their decisions with us, but these are their decisions, we are not participating in or formulating them.[32]

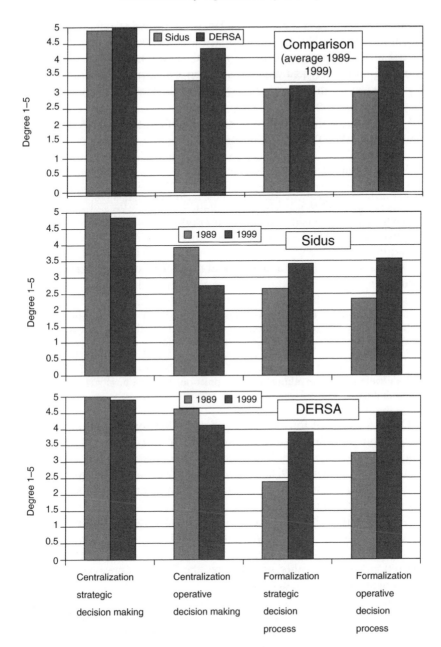

Figure 10.8 Centralization and formalization at Sidus and DERSA 1989–1999

Formalization was very low in the 1980s. At the end of the 1980s and the beginning of the 1990s the Sidus Board foresaw the importance of some sort of formal control mechanism to suit the new times. IT systems, budget control, productivity and indicators of performance appeared in different areas as a way of 'integrating and being more efficient and not with the idea of adding bureaucracy.'[33]

Changes in the outer context made the company standardize some procedures and add more formal mechanisms:

> With the regulations due to be implemented in 1995, the company had to be ready to face fierce competition. Informality and a relaxed attitude could have harmed the company. We have seen in the sector that companies with a lax attitude lost ground. We had to tighten controls, not because we wanted to do that, but because of the looming competition. Otherwise, we would be running a loss-making company.[34]

One manager outlined his ideas about the process of formalization in the company:

> I think everything that happened was a logical process in a family business. We [the managers] have more autonomy to decide; they [the Board] had a grip on strategy. Because the Board delegated the operation to their managers they also increased the control systems, otherwise how could they control whether what we were doing was right or wrong? How could they track several decisions that they were no longer taking? In their position, I would have strengthened the mechanism of control too.[35]

DERSA's levels of formalization and centralization of decision making, on the other hand, are marked by the change of the company's CEO. When Michael Dufour took over the post in 1997, operative centralization, which had been very high in 1989, had reduced slightly by 1999. The levels of both operative and strategic formalization, however, increased notably from 1989–1999 (see Figure 10.8).

Centralization – both operative and strategic – was considered too high by far, as was the interference of the Board in running the operation: 'Everything concerning the company, from hiring a shop floor employee to the retirement of another one requires the Board's approval, as do any investments made in the department.'[36]

It was not only the number of control mechanisms that had increased the perception of high levels of formalization in DERSA (as shown in Figure 10.8), but also the administrative procedures that were set up by the new CEO after years of disorder and corruption. These procedures were seen as both a burden and as producing 'decision-stiffness'.[37] 'For a project to be approved it has to have fourteen signatures!'[38]

The most conspicuous differences between Sidus and DERSA, however, are the differences at the level of operative centralization and operative formalization. The delegation process Sidus started in the 1990s allowed the company to achieve higher levels of operative decentralization. This process was accompanied by changes in the structure from a functional to a divisional one. These changes helped to compensate for the rise in the levels of formalization in the company.

At DERSA, on the other hand, the high levels of operative centralization in the late 1980s had lessened in 1999 but were still very high compared with those in Sidus. Formalization was still very high in 1999, both strategically and operationally. These levels of formalization are the outcome of stringent controls and administrative processes.

Comments on the Pattern Found in the Highly Flexible and less Flexible Firms

Our discussion of the variation over time of the degrees of formalization and centralization clearly indicates that they influenced the flexibility each organization had to adapt under circumstances of turbulence and uncertainty. The individual effect of either centralization or formalization was difficult to establish because in our case studies a change in one degree resulted in a change in the other. So, how have the flexible firms balanced out the effects of different levels of centralization and formalization? What form did the process take in the less flexible firms?

In the flexible firms we found three common patterns in the way they have managed centralization and formalization processes: firstly, both AGD and Sidus had centralized strategic decision making while the operation of the business was delegated to the managers; second, both firms underwent deep structural reforms; and finally, the formalization levels had increased over time in both firms.

Our analysis of the centralization process both at AGD's and Sidus highlighted the high level of strategic centralization and the low level of operative centralization of decision making. In both firms, the Board delegated the operation of the business to the managers while the Board itself concentrated on strategic issues. The reduction of operational centralization increased the autonomy of business managers and with it their freedom to act and be flexible. In so doing, the firms believed that new strategic initiatives would be encouraged and implemented quickly.

The interviewees also stressed the importance of the structural changes throughout the 1990s. For the Boards of both AGD and Sidus, changes in the structure of the firms were essential in helping them to delegate and dedicate their premium time to strategic issues.

The changes in the structure helped AGD and Sidus mitigate the possible harmful consequences of the upsurge of formalization. The business units at AGD and the new companies or divisions at Sidus had fewer layers thus facilitating communication and fast responsiveness. AGD's and Sidus' new way of organizing is more horizontal and organized across functional core processes. Thus, hierarchy is vanishing and teamwork is becoming the cornerstone of these organizations. In AGD they claimed that 'We built a flatter structure which was an advantage we had over our competitors. Our flat structure gave the managers more autonomy, and we were very flexible and adapted quickly.'[39] As Pettigrew (1999) and Pettigrew and Fenton (2000) state, new ways of organizing are required to improve flexibility, creativity and companies' capacity to react.

The levels of formalization – strategic and operational – found at AGD and Sidus went surprisingly against the results found in the literature on organizational innovativeness and flexibility that state that low levels of centralization and formalization of decision making are required to boost innovativeness and creativity in an organization (Nicholson *et al.*, 1990; Damanpour, 1991; Overholt, 1997).

There are two reasons why we found higher levels of formalization in AGD and Sidus. The first reason is related to the changes in the economy over the period 1989–1999, and the second is associated with the control mechanisms the Board needed.

First, the 1980s were very hectic in terms of economic and political turmoil, and therefore the companies could not plan or strategise in advance. In 1989 alone, inflation reached approximately 5000 per cent. Speculation was more important than production and budget control. Hence, informal procedures were needed to enable companies to respond quickly to the changes in the environment.

The 1990s, on the other hand, brought economic stability but difficult times for the companies in terms of competitiveness. More formal procedures and a less relaxed attitude were needed. Long-term thinking replaced the attitude of rushing into short-term matters. Deregulation opened the country up to foreign investors and helped create competitive and efficient companies. More control and planning appeared as a way of being cost-efficient. If decision making had become too decentralized and informal, organizational flexibility might also have suffered. As an interviewee in Sidus pointed out 'the 1990s meant the search for efficiency, and attaining efficiency meant having more formality.'[40]

Adler's theoretical studies on different types of formalization (Adler, 1996, Adler, 1999) highlight that whether the impact of formalization is positive or negative (enabling or coercive formalization) on employees' attitudes is a function of whether that formalization enables them to master their tasks or impedes them from doing so. The evidence provided by both AGD and Sidus illustrates that the incorporation of formal mechanisms in the 1990s was enabling rather than coercive.

The second explanation is related to the control mechanisms the Board needed. While delegation of operational matters started in 1990, the Board also increased control mechanisms so as to be able to monitor their managers. In family businesses characterized by strong leadership, this might be considered a normal process (Ward, 1987; Aronoff and Ward, 1997).

Regarding the less flexible firms – St Martin and DERSA – the main similarities lay in the high levels of centralization and formalization of decision making over time.

Levels of strategic and operative centralization were higher in DERSA and St Martin than in their fellow flexible firms. However, it is important to note that in DERSA operative centralization has tended to decrease while in St Martin it has increased. This different tendency over time may be explained by the internal changes the new CEO in DERSA was trying to implement (in terms of more delegation of the operation to the new top team) after the reshuffle of the top management team in 1997.

The high level of centralization in both St Martin and DERSA, as increases the probability that cognitive limitations of the top management will constrain the 'comprehensiveness of the strategic process' (Fredrickson 1986: 284). Our interviewees have been clear about the lack of fresh ideas or lack of strategic orientation in both St Martin and DERSA.

Formalization, on the other hand, also presents its differences. Formalization at the operation level was higher in both DERSA and St Martin than in the highly flexible companies and was increasing over time. In St Martin, one interviewee indicated: 'The level of bureaucracy in this company stifles our decision-making process. We suppressed any incentive our managers might have had to innovate.'[41]

Conversely, the formalization of the strategic decision-making process varied in both companies: St Martin showed low levels of formalization (even lower than AGD) and DERSA saw this level soar over the period 1989–1999. The differences between the companies stem from the ways strategy is formulated and implemented. DERSA's high level of strategic formalization was the outcome of the implementation of strategic planning and control. St Martin's low level, on the other hand, was the result of informality and lack of strategic planning.

The results of the findings about the determinant centralization and formalization in decision making are important for those that have emphasized the relationship between structure and size of the organization. Child (1984) highlights the concern of the impact of large organization on organizational structure. The larger an organization is, states Child, the more likely it is that a centralized approach to control will generate top management overload. One of the most difficult transitions for a young firm, according to Child, is when the CEO, who may be the founder, has to hand over some of the reins to subordinates. Pugh *et al.* (1975) also consider large size to influence structural complexity that sets up pressures for delegation.

The findings in the flexible and less flexible firms, however, showed a different pattern where the large flexible firms were able to mitigate the harmful consequences of an upsurge of formalization and the less flexible firms (that were smaller in size) could not.

We have seen then how the flexible firms balanced out the effects of different levels of centralization and formalization. The less flexible firms were not able to balance the levels of centralization and formalization needed over different periods of time. The overlaying of more centralization and formalization in DERSA and St Martin in the 1990s increased the negative influence on organizational flexibility. We will return to the conflicting advantages of high and low levels of formality and centralization later in Chapter 11.

LOW MACROCULTURE EMBEDDEDNESS

Another factor identified by this study as a determinant of organizational flexibility is the extent to which the companies analysed are embedded in their sectoral macroculture. This factor reflects the institutional pressures exerted upon an organization and may affect the speed with which it can adopt new strategies.

From our inductive analysis, two factors emerged as indicating the degree to which the companies under analysis were embedded in their macroculture: the perceived similarity and dissimilarity to other firms in the industry and the degree of connectedness to other firms in the industry.

Institutional theory describes how these factors influence the degree of embeddedness within the industry macroculture. The higher the perceived similarity to others in the industry, the more likely it is that firms will accept the prevailing norms and become more institutionalized in that industry (Greenwood and Hinings, 1996). On the other hand, the degree of connectedness refers to interpersonal contacts between executives in the same industry (Gnyawali and Ravindranath, 2001; Dacin *et al.*, 1999; DiMaggio and Powell, 1983). Frequent contacts promote the awareness of the practices and values of an industry (Webb and Pettigrew, 1999).

To understand the perceived similarity/dissimilarity to their macroculture, interviewees were asked about which company or companies were used by them for benchmarking. Similarly, to understand the levels of connectedness, the interviewees were asked whether their company supported any professional association in the industry and, if so, which professional association they supported. Questions were asked regarding two specific years: 1989 and 1999.

Answers for each question were displayed in a table and different percentage scores calculated as shown in Tables 10.5 to 10.11. An inter-coder reliability check gave a reliability score between 85 and 90 per cent.

AGD and St Martin

The interviewees at AGD and St Martin were consistent in their description of the extent to which these two factors were present in their companies. Tables 10.5 to 10.8 demonstrate the different perceptions in both firms regarding the level of similarity/dissimilarity and connectedness with the industry macroculture. While the level of embeddedness of AGD in the macroculture of the edible oil industry declined over the period 1989–1999 (that is, demonstrated through benchmarking outside the industry as illustrated in Table 10.5, and low level of contact in professional associations as shown in Table 10.7), St Martin's embeddedness was more manifest as illustrated by the evolution of its benchmark within the edible oil industry (Table 10.6) and its high level contact with the professional associations (Table 10.8).

At the end of the 1980s, AGD's benchmark was mainly against indigenous businesses that participated in the edible oil industry and also against some MNCs (see Table 10.5). However, this benchmark started to change by the time the company launched its first strategic initiative (1989–1990). Molinos, a food and edible oil company, was then used as the benchmark.

The process of benchmarking before launching the first strategic initiative illustrates the way the company's benchmark has changed over time: 'We have our own strategies. We look inside and outside the country to see what we can to do to differentiate ourselves from the rest, not to see how

Table 10.5   Level of similarity/dissimilarity within the industry: benchmarking at AGD

With whom is the company benchmarking?	1989 (%)	1999 (%)
Benchmarking with indigenous edible oil companies	61	7
Benchmarking with multinational edible oil companies	44	27
Benchmarking with food-processing companies	0	67

*Table 10.6   Level of similarity/dissimilarity within the industry:
          benchmarking at St Martin*

With whom is the company benchmarking?	1989 (%)	1999 (%)
Benchmarking with indigenous edible oil companies	73	87
Benchmarking with multinational edible oil companies	33	33
Benchmarking with food-processing companies	7	0

we can copy them.'[42] This was the thinking behind the way the brands were introduced by AGD. First of all Adrián Urquía Jr went abroad to see what other companies were doing. The Board also analysed the competitors within the internal market, although none of the companies in direct competition with AGD were the focus of the benchmarking: 'The first comparison we made was with big companies such as Molinos. It would have been nonsense to compare ourselves with other direct competitors. We would have remained a medium sized company.'[43]

The diversification process AGD underwent over the period 1989–1999 caused the company's benchmark to change over time. Today's benchmarks are with Bestfood, an American food company, and Arcor, a regional food company (based in Argentina) (see Table 10.5). 'Now, as a company, we do not have only edible oil products but other products such as mayonnaise and soya milk. So we no longer consider edible oil companies to be our ideal parallel, but food companies.'[44]

St Martin, on the other hand, has seen a different pattern regarding its benchmark. In the 1970s and 1980s managers claim that the company liked to benchmark against companies such as Cargill and Dreyfus – both of them MNC companies. The company was a growing one that had 'aspirations of becoming a leader.'[45] However, the critical 1990s caused the company's choice of benchmark to shift dramatically. The strategy of the company evidently favoured concentration on crushing and cotton ginning as a niche market, thus the benchmark leaned towards crusher companies. The clarification of the strategy in 1997 fixed the benchmark on nationally-owned crushing companies. Since then, the company's perceived similarity within the edible oil industry has grown even more (see Table 10.6).

> We'd like to compare ourselves with other nationally-owned businesses. It is impossible to benchmark with multinational companies. They have resources

Table 10.7   Degree of connectedness in the industry: AGD's support for participation in professional associations

Support for Participation in Professional Associations	1989 (%)	1999 (%)
Yes. Participation in professional associations is actively supported by the company	80	47
No. Participation in professional associations is not actively supported by the company	20	53

Table 10.8   Degree of connectedness in the industry: St Martin's support for participation in professional associations

Support for Participation in Professional Associations	1989 (%)	1999 (%)
Yes. Participation in professional associations is actively supported by the company	64	79
No. Participation in professional associations is not actively supported by the company	36	21

that we do not have; they have worldwide experience that we do not have. Multinationals have different objectives in mind. Copying them would have been disastrous for us.[46]

Compared with St Martin, AGD also demonstrates a lower level of connectedness in the industry over time. This can be seen in AGD's declining participation in the professional association as seen in Table 10.7. The company maintains passive participation in CIARA. Table 10.7 shows how the support of professional associations was trimmed down from 80 per cent in 1989 to 47 per cent in 1999.

St Martin, on the other hand, has seen its level of connectedness increase over the period 1989–1999 (see Table 10.8). The perceived similarity of the company with its industry counterparts grew after its strategic orientation changed.

The high level of connectedness in St Martin made industry associations the most important source of information for the managers of the company. Such frequent interaction with the professional bodies of an industry, as Webb and Pettigrew (1999) point out, reinforces the values and norms of the sector in the firm. The interviews with some managers of the company are revealing in this sense:

> I personally participate in CIARA [professional association]. Meeting other colleagues in the industry helped me to acquire information about what the trends are and what they are doing and whether what we are doing follows that path or not.[47]

Sidus and DERSA

Tables 10.9 to 10.12 and our interview data demonstrate that the level of embeddedness of Sidus in the macroculture of the pharmaceutical industry declined over the period 1989–1999 (see Table 10.9 and 10.11). In contrast to Sidus, DERSA was deeply embedded in the macroculture of the industry (see Tables 10.10 and 10.12).

In contrast to the benchmarks that Sidus used in the 1980s, which were with indigenous companies such as Roemmers and Bagó, its current benchmark lies outside the Argentinian market (see Table 10.9). In 1999 Sidus targeted health companies in the biotechnological market – such as Genetech and Amgen (both American companies) – as the focus of its benchmarking activities.

The evolution of the benchmark is related to the image of the company its members had. Early in the 1980s the company saw itself as a small national company and benchmarked accordingly. However, by the time the biotechnology initiative and the strategic alliance with Merck (in 1988) took off, the paradigm had changed:

> In the early 1980s we saw ourselves as part of the national market, we were a tiny company in the industry. We compared ourselves to other competitors in the market. Today, our models are outside the Argentinian market. We have the most important biotechnological company in the region, so why should we be

Table 10.9   Level of similarity/dissimilarity within the industry: benchmarking at Sidus

With whom is the company benchmarking?	1989 (%)	1999 (%)
Benchmarking with indigenous pharmaceutical companies	87	9
Benchmarking with multinational pharmaceutical companies	20	39
Benchmarking with biotechnology or health companies	7	52

Table 10.10   Level of similarity/dissimilarity within the industry:
benchmarking at DERSA

With whom is the company benchmarking?	1989 (%)	1999 (%)
Benchmarking with indigenous pharmaceutical companies	91	63
Benchmarking with multinational pharmaceutical companies	18	37
Benchmarking with biotechnology or health companies	0	9

compared with a national laboratory? We look at companies such as Genetech or Amgen.[48]

DERSA, on the other hand, saw important changes in its benchmark over time. Most respondents stated that from the 1980s to 1996 the benchmarking was against nationally owned companies (see Table 10.10). The appointment of a new CEO in 1997 caused the benchmark to start to change. Today's benchmarking is mainly against national companies. However, multinational laboratories running their businesses in Argentina have also been incorporated into the company's benchmark (see Table 10.10).

In the 1980s and 1990s as well, we tried to copy the behaviour of other laboratories, with the risk of incurring the loss of the company's vision and the potential it could have. In the economic conditions of the 1980s, I can understand this. Copying what other players in the sector were doing reduced the risk. That was our benchmark before.[49]

From 1997 onwards the company broadened its benchmark. National and MNC companies were then the subjects of comparison:

We wanted our managers to have a broad picture of the sector. We came from a company in which the benchmark was simple: we had to follow the leader. Now, if you ask the different managers, they have more companies they want to imitate or follow. However, we still have to work on that. We are still imbued with the old culture of benchmarking.[50]

Regarding the level of connectedness, Sidus saw changes in its level early in the 1980s. Since breaking away from the professional association of the industry in 1988, the level of connectedness has diminished substantially, as seen in Table 10.11. Since then, its support for professional bodies has continued to fall until it reached the low levels of 1999.

*Table 10.11   Degree of connectedness in the industry: Sidus' support for
participation in professional associations*

Support for Participation in Professional Associations	1989 (%)	1999 (%)
Yes. Participation in professional associations is actively supported by the company	40	27
No. Participation in professional associations is not actively supported by the company	60	73

*Table 10.12   Degree of connectedness in the industry: DERSA's support
for participation in professional associations*

Support for Participation in Professional Associations	1989 (%)	1999 (%)
Yes. Participation in professional associations is actively supported by the company	53	73
No. Participation in professional associations is not actively supported by the company	47	27

After breaking from the most important professional association, Sidus joined a low profile professional body that operated among small and medium size laboratories.

DERSA, on the other hand, saw an increasing level of connectedness between 1989 and 1999 (see Table 10.12). After re-defining the strategy in 1997, the new CEO encouraged participation in the different activities prepared by the professional association or other chambers in the different areas.

> Each manager participates in meetings in different chambers. I try to go on a monthly basis to the meetings. This is a way of keeping in touch with sectoral trends and changes.[51]

The Impact of the Company's Embeddedness on the Speed with which it can Adopt Strategies

One of the consequences of the level of macroculture embeddedness of the firms analysed in this book is their freedom to make strategic moves and become either early adopters of strategies or laggards. Institutional theory states that over time firms tend to adopt a particular strategy that will become increasingly institutionalized within the framework of the industry (Abrahamson and Fombrun, 1994). To be early movers or first adopters of strategies, firms must try to avoid the pressures exerted by the environment (Dacin *et al.*, 1999, 2002; Oliver 1991, 1992). Therefore, those firms which are less embedded in their macroculture may succeed in their attempt to adopt new strategies more rapidly (Greenwood and Hinings, 1996; Sharma, 2000).

Perceived turmoil encourages companies to try explorative activities such as diversifying, broadening the boundaries of the sector, making alliances, and investing more in R&D, among others. The coevolutionary approach of Lewin *et al.* (1999) states that in periods of disorder, companies are keener to intensify exploratory activities.

What were the strategic responses of the companies under study? How did macroculture embeddedness influence this response? By tracking the strategic initiatives of the four companies – as shown in Figures 10.9 and 10.10 we were able to visualize the early adoption of strategies and follower behaviour.[52]

Figures 10.9 and 10.10 show the main difference between highly flexible and less flexible firms in terms of their adoption of strategies. AGD, for example was an early adopter of strategies compared with St Martin. AGD disrupted the edible oil industry by integrating all its activities, from farming to selling products in supermarkets. None of its competitors followed this strategy, a fact which demonstrates that AGD operates outside institutional norms. In many cases – such as investments in transport, farming and storing capacity – AGD was a first mover in the edible oil industry and its competitors were followers.

By contrast, St Martin was only an early adopter in terms of branding strategy. However, this strategy failed and needed to be re-launched in 1997, nine years after AGD had released its own successful brands. The figure also shows that AGD was keener to explore different strategies that St Martin did not eventually want to adopt.

The differences between Sidus and DERSA are also noticeable (see Figure 10.10). Of eight strategic initiatives undertaken by Sidus, only two were adopted by DERSA. Sidus' weak ties with its macroculture can be seen in the company's investments in biotechnology and the integration of its businesses far beyond the wholesaler channel by acquiring a pharmaceutical retail chain. None of the company's competitors used similar strategies. Sidus was also a first mover in strategies that were later followed by its competitors, such as the acquisition of pharmaceutical companies (Manzone, 2000).

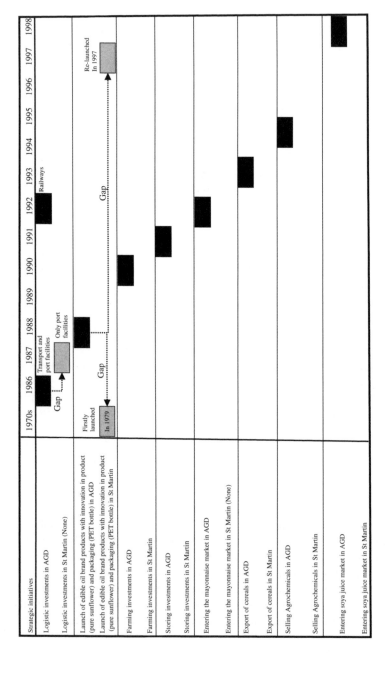

Figure 10.9   Early adoption of strategies in AGD and St Martin

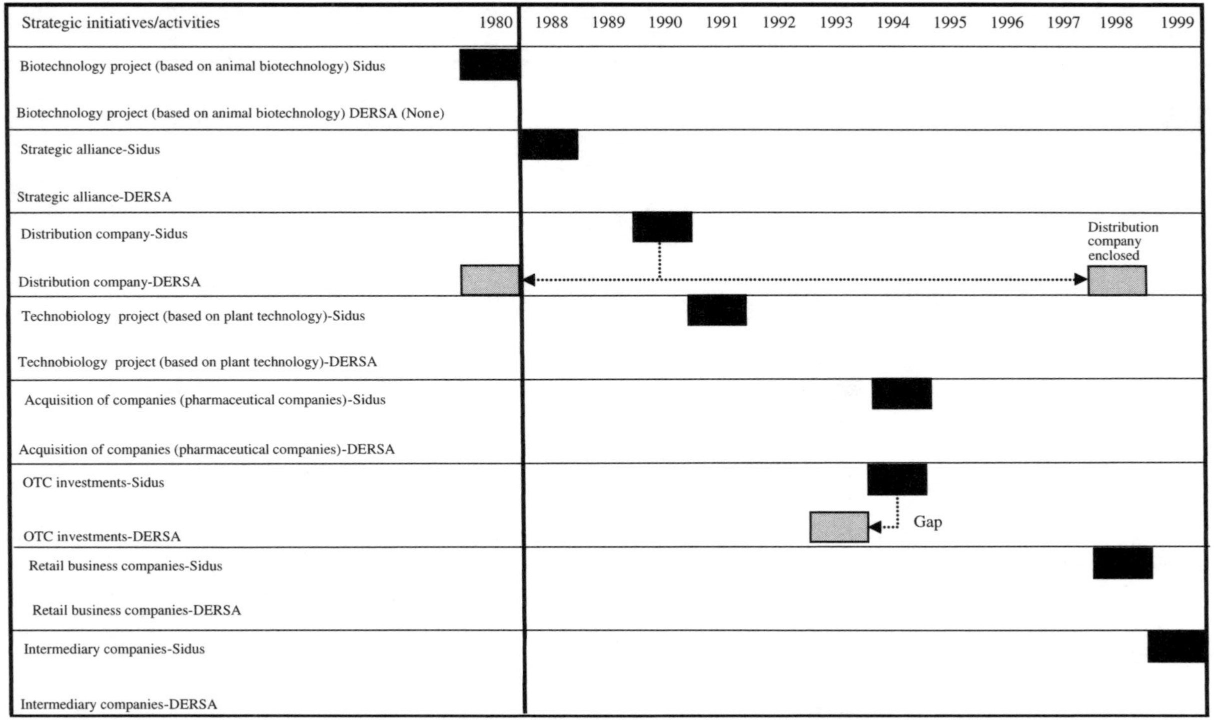

Figure 10.10   Early adoption of strategies in Sidus and DERSA

Remarks on the Differences between Highly Flexible Firms and Less Flexible Firms

From the previous analysis the differences between highly flexible and less flexible firms are self-evident: AGD and Sidus – both highly flexible companies – demonstrate a degree of 'disembeddedness', that is, a low degree of embeddedness (Dacin *et al.*, 1999: 341). On the contrary, the less flexible firms illustrate a higher level of embeddedness in the industry macroculture.

This notion of low embeddedness, or 'disembeddedness,' relies on intentional action by AGD and Sidus to step back from institutional frameworks of cognition, culture and the social structure of inter-actor relations. This was indicated by the perceived high levels of dissimilarity and low levels of connectedness in both companies. St Martin and DERSA, on the other hand, demonstrated high levels of perceived similarity and connectedness over time (see Tables 10.5 to 10.12). The strategic content and speed, and cognitive activities of the firms are revealing of the differences between flexible and less flexible firms in terms of their level of embeddedness.

These comments and our previous discussion indicate that because of their high level of embeddedness in the industry macroculture, DERSA and St Martin faced considerable institutional pressure to conform. This in turn had a negative effect upon the strategic content and speed of the companies. In the case of AGD and Sidus, the fact that they increasingly distanced themselves from other Argentinian competitors meant that institutional pressures to conform to the norms of the edible oil and pharmaceutical industries were much weaker. As a result, the industry macroculture had little effect upon the firms' selection of their strategies.

The flexible companies in this study adapted by exploring new competitive advantages but moving rapidly from one advantage to another, from one series of short-lived actions to another, thereby disrupting the market place). The most flexible companies in this study showed what Tushman and Anderson (1986) and Anderson and Tushman (1990) called competence-destroying discontinuities instead of competence-enhancing discontinuities. Evidence was offered to confirm that the most flexible firms disrupted their industry with new competence-disrupting discontinuities (that is, AGD through strengthening its logistic chain and through launching its branding strategy; Sidus through its biotechnological initiative and through its retail strategy).

In Figures 10.9 and 10.10 it is possible to observe that there is a short lag between the different strategic initiatives launched by the firms. The short lag between initiatives was a way of achieving competitive advantage over other companies in the industry. In periods of environmental turmoil in which advantages are eroded rapidly this might be considered an offensive rather than a defensive strategy (D'Aveni, 1994).

DERSA and St Martin, on the other hand, did not show any of the patterns evidenced by AGD and Sidus. On the contrary, their strategic initiatives were isomorphic with the predominant strategies in the sector. The institutional pressures these firms had to conform to and the high level of similarity to other companies in their sector meant that it was very difficult for them to achieve non-isomorphic behaviour such as that found in AGD and Sidus.

As in the findings in the literature on organizational embeddedness, we have also identified other major sources of pressure on institutionalized norms from cognitive practices that may have influenced the strategic and organizational responses of the flexible and less flexible firms (Oliver, 1992; Dacin *et al.*, 2002).

The study of the cognitive mechanisms of the organization is concerned with the way the frameworks of meaning affect individual and corporate actors as they interpret and make sense of their world (Dutton and Dukerich, 1991). With a more heterogeneous management team, the flexible firms had the possibility of a broader cognitive range that helped them to act fast and take risks (such as the strategic initiatives undertaken by the flexible firms). The less flexible firms, however, with a more compacted and homogeneous top team with background experiences mainly in the edible oil and pharmaceutical industries, were constrained by institutional pressures and thus their strategies were isomorphic with the rest of the industry.

ANTICIPATING CHANGES IN THE INDUSTRY: ENVIRONMENTAL SCANNING

In introducing their model of organizations as interpretative systems, Daft and Weick (1984) assert that the capacity to interpret is a key element that distinguishes human organization from others. To achieve a deep interpretative capability, scanning the environment is a fundamental activity for the organization. Scanning, then, can be considered both the starting point of the interpretation process in an organization (Daft and Weick, 1984: 286) and the starting point of the decision making process (Mintzberg *et al.*, 1976).

So why is it important for a flexible company to be aware of the mechanism of scanning the environment? In an attempt to provide an insight into the relationship between the strategic sensemaking process (that is, scanning, interpretation and action) and organizational performance in 156 hospitals, Thomas *et al.* (1993) argue that when managers implement a mechanism to increase information use by scanning the environment, they increase the likelihood of interpreting issues quickly and will sense the controllability of the process. Companies are thus able to respond more swiftly to any environmental threat or opportunity. The idea of fast response capacity is reinforced by Pettigrew and Whipp's (1991) detailed study on the ability of UK firms to manage strategic change. They emphasize that companies that can absorb signals and mobilize resources from the environment will be more proactive and able to deliver successful changes. Thus, scanning may represent a dynamic capability for the firm (Eisenhardt and Martin, 2000).

From the inductive analysis, two indicators emerged as factors illustrating the importance of environmental scanning in the companies analysed. Under conditions of intense competition in the period 1989–1999, firms sought new sources of information and set up both formal and informal mechanisms for scanning the environment.

The literature on environmental scanning describes the extent to which the two indicators found may help companies to interpret and anticipate market changes. Daft *et al.*'s (1988) empirical research on the scanning behaviour of 50 CEOs emphasizes the importance of using different sources of information to prevent managers from forming their impressions on the basis of narrow environment data. They state the importance of scanning both the task or operational environment (that is, customers, suppliers, competitors and technology) and the general environment (that is, economy, politics, social and cultural matters and regulations).

Pettigrew and Whipp (1991), on the other hand, recognize that environmental scanning happens across the organization. They also argue that it is highly dangerous to assume that a single specialist can alone achieve an adequate interpretation of the outer context. Therefore, formal structures for scanning the environment are not only not enough, but they are also dangerous as they can lead the organization to inadequate interpretations. Informal ways of scanning are also necessary.

The use of visual mappings helped to simplify and visualize the results of the analysis (see Figures 10.11 and 10.12).

Environmental Scanning and Organizational Flexibility

AGD and St Martin

AGD and St Martin sought new sources of information throughout the 1990s. AGD, however, procured information from different sources, unlike St Martin in which the scanning behaviour was more erratic as evidenced by the opinion of the interviewees (and illustrated in Figure 10.11).

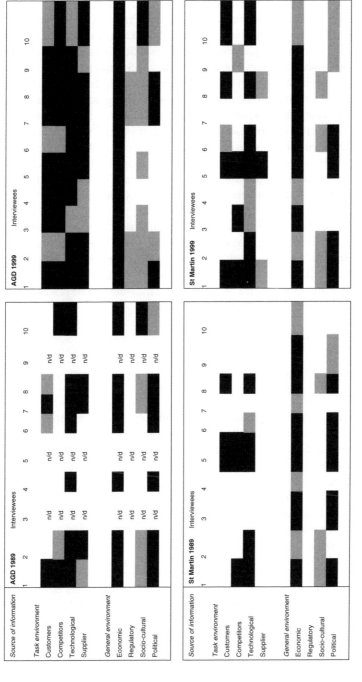

Figure 10.11 Sources of information at AGD and St Martin over the period 1989–1999

Figure 10.11 shows our interviewees in AGD laid considerable importance on scanning the environment. However, Figure 10.11 shows a variation over time: while in the 1980s the company stressed the scanning of the general environment, in the 1990s the greatest effort was made in scanning the task environment (see in Figure 10.11 the black shading representing the extensive scanning activity in the task environment in the 1990s).

In the 1980s AGD stressed the scanning of the general environment – mainly macroeconomic issues – and in the task environment only gathered data from the crushing industry and 'somehow' found information about the edible oil industry. During the course of the 1990s this situation changed: 'We are not only aware of what is happening in the edible oil industry, but also in the food industry, and we have stronger relationships with customers and suppliers. They are also key elements in sensing the environment.'[53]

The idea of 'being open to what is happening outside the organisation'[54] is an integral part of the Board's day-to-day work: 'thinking strategically means that you have to be aware of what is going on not only in your company, but also in the rest of the industry and the country.'[55] Adrián Urquía Jr stated that the idea of scrutinizing the outer-context was not new, but had always been in the spirit of the Board:

> We learnt from the founder always to be ready to listen, to be aware of what others were doing. The difference now is that with the new contextual reality, this is more organized and our agenda is full of activities to enable us to look into this reality. . . . this openness allowed us to take advantage of market opportunities as in the case of our branding strategy.[56]

St Martin presented a different scanning behaviour compared with that of AGD. Our interviewees described the extent to which their scanning behaviour had changed over time. Figure 10.11 demonstrates that in the 1980s the company was mainly scanning the general environment. The task environment was not tackled as a priority. Only in the 1990s, as Figure 10.11 illustrates, was there more stress on scanning the task environment, albeit to in a lesser extent than AGD. Some managers blamed the problems they experienced during the 1990s on the company's failure to pay attention to the outer context:

> In the 1980s and 1990s we could not anticipate the changes in the market for edible oils, the importance of scaling up our crushing capacity and the consequences of the economy opening up in Argentina. I would not say we failed, but we did not perform as well as other companies did.[57]

Differences between both AGD and St Martin also arose in terms of the formal and informal mechanisms the companies had for scanning the environment. First, AGD used both more formal and informal mechanisms than St Martin. Second, from 1989 to 1999 AGD had increased its informal mechanisms compared with St Martin.

The emergence of formal and informal mechanisms of scanning in AGD reveal the ways in which the company supported the scanning behaviour it wanted from its managers and employees. AGD set up an Economic Studies Unit as a means of channelling macroeconomic and sectoral information to the Board and managers.

> Setting up this unit gave us a means of channelling the information from the environment, and secondly, it formed part of an organizational effort to emphasize the importance of being open to the outside world. Of course this is a process that takes years. Setting up this unit was the outcome of a whole philosophy.[58]

The importance of scanning the environment in AGD was reinforced by informal mechanisms at different levels of the organization. The Board supported different levels of contacts with colleagues from other companies in different industries, trips abroad to visit other companies and institutions, and internal meetings between different levels of employees and experts in different fields.

St Martin did not have a formal structure for scanning and while informal mechanisms were developed over the period 1989–1999 they were still not enough for some managers:

> They've got everything [Directors], we have nothing. If you do not have information, you make the wrong decisions. This is an issue here. The management do not bother to share the information they have to help us in our work. I do not think they do this on purpose, I think it is more to do with the culture of the organization: 'we family members make decisions, so you do not need to bother about it'.[59]

Middle managers and employees therefore keep themselves informed through publications issued by the professional associations and industry reports the company buys for specific reasons, such as those related to the branding market. Visits to suppliers in the country and abroad are some of the informal mechanisms used in St Martin.

Sidus and DERSA

Our interviewees in Sidus and DERSA, as shown in Figure 10.12, were consistent in their descriptions of the extent to which the scanning behaviour of the firms has changed over time. The opening up of the industry to competition in the early 1990s boosted scanning activities in Sidus and, to a lesser extent, in DERSA. While both companies saw changes in their scanning behaviour and structures, the main differences need to be stated.

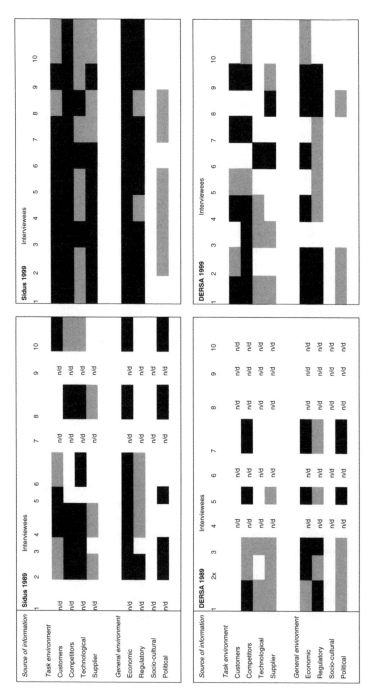

Figure 10.12   Sources of information in Sidus and DERSA over the period 1989–1999

In the 1980s the most important scanning activity in Sidus sought to understand the national economy and competitors' moves in the pharmaceutical industry. However, by the 1990s new scanning interests in customers, suppliers and competitors emerged, as the increase of the black shading in Figure 10.12 shows.

The transformation of the company from a simple national laboratory in the 1980s to a major health company in the 1990s was considered as having an impact on the assessment of the environment:

> Over this period [from the 1980s to the 1990s] you could imagine that we went through stages in which more information was needed from different sectors like biotechnology and new relationships were built. Gathering this information was vital for seizing opportunities in the market.[60]

DERSA, on the other hand, showed a different pattern of scanning behaviour. Based on our interviews in the company, Figure 10.12 displays the low level of scanning activity in the 1980s and the rise in this activity in the 1990s albeit to a lesser extent than in Sidus (see evolution of black shading in Figure 10.12).

The low level of scanning activity in the 1980s was the result of the concentration of decision-making power in the hands of the CEO, as many interviewees suggested. The 1990s required a different approach and this was brought into the company by the new CEO, Michael Dufour. The company's focus on its customers rather than the wholesaler chain (one of the main changes after 1997) made DERSA start to scan more and look at different sources of information.

Both Sidus and DERSA also diverge regarding the way formal and informal mechanisms of scanning were used. Sidus not only used more mechanism of scanning (that is, formal and informal) but also increased the number of informal mechanisms over time.

Informal and formal structures of scanning became much more widely used in Sidus over the period analysed. Three areas were created: legal and regulatory analysis; sectoral; and macroeconomic analysis to keep the Board and managers abreast of the latest changes in the sector and in national economy. The information produced by the legal and regulatory area was widely disseminated throughout the company to keep employees informed of recent changes in legal and regulatory systems.

Informal mechanisms supported the scanning structure of the company. Internal workshops were a widespread practice at different levels of the company and formed an arena in which relevant aspects of the national economy or sectoral trends were discussed. Also employees from different levels of the structure had access to a wide variety of publications including retail reports, and sectoral and macroeconomic reports, among others.

The scanning mechanisms in DERSA, on the other hand, evolved over time. From the 1980s up to 1996 managers in DERSA only had access to sectoral reports. Contact with Gali, the CEO, was sporadic, thus preventing managers from discussing sectoral and company strategies with him.

Michael Dufour – the new CEO – started to have meetings with the different managers and sought to convey those factors in the environment that would affect the company in general and each manager's particular area: 'I try to analyse with the different areas the impact of the macro-policies on the company and on their department. This is important for us because we used to have a blinkered view of what was going on outside.'[61]

What stands out in Sidus and DERSA as a similarity in their scanning behaviour is the fact that the scanning of the general environment was considered critical in both companies. Figure 10.12 shows the relevance of the scanning of the general environment over time. Being a regulated industry in the 1980s and in a process of deregulation in the 1990s might explain this behaviour (Grabowsky *et al.*, 1978). The increased scanning of the 'regulatory' source of information in the 1990s is also noticeable. This occurred after the regulations of the industry were loosened, opening up new opportunities in the industry.

Environmental Scanning in the Most Flexible Firms and in the Less Flexible Firms

What are the similarities and differences between the scanning behaviour of the flexible and less flexible firms? And what has influenced that behaviour?

In the flexible companies we found three common patterns in the way they scanned the environment: first, both AGD and Sidus created formal and informal structures of scanning; secondly, both companies attempted to create an external openness and orientation; and, finally, the scanning behaviour of both companies was boosted by the new mental models that prevailed during the 1990s.

Regarding the first aspect, AGD and Sidus tried to limit the ambiguity of the environment by setting up information-processing structures (Thomas *et al.*, 1993) and informal mechanisms of scanning (Pettigrew and Whipp, 1991). AGD set up the Economic Analysis Unit and Sidus convened three units to keep the company abreast of the macroeconomic situation, the sector, and legal and regulatory changes.

The second aspect – external openness and orientation – was also seen as a common factor in both AGD and Sidus. Externally oriented companies are more able to sense competitors' moves (Thomas *et al.*, 1993) and perceive themselves as more capable of implementing competitive responses than internally focused firms. Managers in these firms are also more confident at creating a fit between the organization and the environment by using environmental scanning (Smith *et al.*, 1991; Barr and Huff, 1997).

It was essential for AGD and Sidus to scan the environment to become externally oriented:

> From the foundation of the company, the founders were aware of the impor-tance of understanding what was going on outside the company. We were never a self-absorbed company. We were always aware of the importance of being externally oriented . . . Every employee is aware of the importance of having an open mind and catching all they can from the sector, competitors and customers. This is our constant message to them.[62]

> Watching what was going on outside the company, and observing the trends and changes in the competition was the only way of succeeding we found. This [external orientation] helped us to seize the opportunity while others [competi-tors] were more concerned with domestic problems.[63]

The third common aspect we found in AGD and Sidus was the influence of the new mental models on their scanning behaviour. While analysing the heterogeneity of the dominant coalition as a determinant of organizational flexibility, we flagged the importance of the cognitive diversity or diversity of mental models in the dominant coalition. These new mental models helped managers to sense signals from the outer context and it also helped them to make sense of those signals.

> The fact that we have changed the profile of our management over the last 10 years to suit the requirements of the Argentinian environment, also swayed our decision-making process. Managers are fully aware of what is happening in the external context through our department of economic studies and their own information, reports and contacts. We have internal meetings or workshops – a word that is trendy now – to clarify and share information and make decisions accordingly.[64]

> Before, we [the Board] made decisions by relying on common sense. Today things are different. The new professionals come better prepared and are very quick off the draw. That is better because it accelerates our response.[65]

Regarding the less flexible firms – St Martin and DERSA – the main sim-ilarities lay in the lack of a formal structure for scanning and the impor-tance of scanning the general environment instead of the task environment during the 1980s.

Neither St Martin nor DERSA have formal structures for scanning. There are different reasons for this lack of formal structure. In St Martin they claimed that there was no formal structure because there was no need or because the main scanning activity fell to the Board of Directors. In DERSA, on the other hand, they are more hesitant regarding the usefulness of such a structure: 'We are not a big enough company to afford an area fully dedicated to assessing the context. We found, however, that companies in the sector are setting up these structures. We have still not made up our mind about the best route to follow.'[66]

In the 1980s both companies also highlighted the importance of scanning the general environment. This attitude has changed since 1990 and the focus of the scanning behaviour has been placed firmly on the task environment (see Figures 10.11 and 10.12). The lack of support in the 1980s for task scanning in the companies had harmful consequences for business, as can be seen in the opinion of the interviewees:

> The problems we have are the result of not caring much about our customers' taste and our competitors' moves. Now there is an awareness that the customer is the king and our competitors are there to watch them and care about what they are doing.[67]

> We were a closed company. The result in St Martin was clear: the crisis in 1997, low profitability and a low level of professionalism in the company.[68]

The highly flexible firms in this research sought new sources of information much more actively and applied a rich array of formal and informal mechanisms for scanning the environment. The less flexible firms had a less well organized approach to environmental scanning. The outcome of the scanning behaviour was self-evident: flexible firms anticipated changes in the sector and seized opportunities while the less flexible firms simply could not.

A STRONG ORGANIZATIONAL IDENTITY

Why does the concept of organizational identity emerge as important in understanding how flexible firms adapt? And what are the main features of the concept of organizational identity?

Albert and Whetten (1985) characterize organizational identity as a concept with three dimensions: first, what is considered central to the organization; second, what makes the organization distinctive; and finally, what is perceived by members to be an enduring or continuing feature linking the present of the organization with its past. At the heart of this definition are core values that make organizations act or react in a particular way and the lenses through which managers interpret organization level issues.

We preferred to use the concept of values rather than culture or organizational culture because the former is more sharply demarcated than the latter facilitating organizational analysis (Alvesson, 1987). While culture is more preoccupied with limited organizational meanings, symbols and beliefs (Pettigrew, 1979), values are central aspects of the organization and more enduring as well (Albert and Whetten, 1985).

Therefore, how can a firm's identity enhance or harm organizational flexibility? Some writers on organizational identity emphasize that because organizational identity is composed of values that are enduring and deeply ingrained, it is likely to provide a natural inertial force (Stimpert *et al.*, 1998; Reger *et al.*, 1994) and cause resistance to change (Dutton and Dukerich, 1991).

On the other hand, among those favouring the idea of organizational identity as a source of both organizational continuity and change are Collins and Porras (2000). In their examination of 18 long-lasting firms, which they term 'visionary firms', they concluded that visionary companies are those that can articulate a core ideology. Through these core values, companies have a clear identity, lending the organization strategic continuity and precision. For Collins and Porras, strategies change as market conditions change, but core values remain intact in a visionary company.

The questions that emerge from this are: what type of organizational identity do the companies under analysis have? And how did their organizational identities – through their set of core values – promote or constrain their organizational flexibility?

Due to the central role of core values within the concept of organizational identity, we tried to operationalize this determinant through one activity: ideological coaching over successive generations. Ideological coaching, a term previously used by Collins and Porras (1991, 2000), is the anchor that makes it possible for the values of previous generations to be passed on, accepted and used by successive generations.

How this factor influences the identity of an organization and its ability to change is described by the literature on organizational identity. The analysis of the evolution of company values over successive generations seems more appropriate when seeking to determine whether or not the firms are conservative about their values and how this influences their organizational identity (Collins and Porras, 2000), and whether those values acted as enablers of organizational flexibility or as constraining factors (Volberda, 1999).

To undertake the analysis of ideological coaching over successive generations, we used different types of written material (that is, speeches, letters) from which we attempted to obtain organizational values. For each company, a set of values was indicated. At AGD, values such as constant learning, an agile decision making process, and innovation, were identified as values that had been rooted in the company since the first generation tenure of family

members. Some quotations from the documents analysed are indicative of
the values the companies uphold over time:

> Our father always preached that you should learn from your experience. We are
> under pressure to make a decision [about investing in origination]. We have to
> learn from the lessons of the past. In 1968 we nearly went bankrupt because we
> had not realized the importance of having adequate stocks of raw material.
> This is an opportunity to move forwards and still learn as the founder
> said.[69] (Quotation indicative of constant learning as a value in the current
> generation.)

> We do not want to lose something that we have been cultivating since my father
> created this company. This is to make decisions fast, without bureaucratic struc-
> tures that hinder the decision process. With these changes we want to ensure fast
> resposiveness.[70] (Quotation indicative of agile decision making process as a
> share value over time.)

> Our father always says that we have to be quick as a rabbit to take on competi-
> tors. This can be only achieved throught creating and innovating. Natura is the
> example of this. This is our first step towards leading the market.[71] (Quotation
> indicative of innovativeness as a share value over time.)

At Sidus, values such as risk taking and innovation were found to be
ingrained in the two generations of family members. Again, some quotations from documents currently used by the firm are indicative of the existence of such values:

> The founders took a great risk while trying to set up the basis of this company.
> They always stated that this is the only way to achieve things. But risks, as you
> know from the history of the company, also imply sacrifices.[72] (Quotation indi-
> cating risk taking as a share value over time.)

> We are pioneers: we were innovative in our research, we diversified, always trusting
> the country and its human potential. Over 60 years we privileged and invested in
> the development of science [. . .] Our growth is based on a solid base of infra-
> structure, technology and innovation.[73] (Quotation indicative of innovation as a
> share value over time.)

> Infrastructure, technology and innovation, are what made this possible. This
> new methodology is the latest in the process of genetic engeneering. We
> achieved this because of our commitment to innovation and creating solu-
> tions like this one.[74] (Quotation indicative of innovation as a value in the
> current generation.)

St Martin and DERSA, on the other hand, differ from AGD and Sidus
in this respect. We could not find strong evidence to support the existence

of many shared values over time. What we found, however, is an indication of rejection of values sustained in previous generations. In St Martin we found some evidence indicating that values such as innovation and being ahead of competitors that were considered important in previous generations of family owners were abandoned by the current generation as the following quotations indicate:

> When I was a child my grandfather told me about a company of dreams. We had products on the shelves of the supermarkets, our brand name sounded in customers' heads and we took care of details. We were an innovative company in the market.[75] (Quotation indicative of innovation as a value in the previous generations.)

> The worst thing for me is that innovation is not at the heart of the company's values. On the contrary, innovation implies risks and we hate that. Innovation implies investment in research and development of products, and we cannot afford that. Finally, innovation implies managerial capabilities that we do not have.[76] (Quotation indicative of innovation as a value not shared by the current generation.)

> What strikes me, and you can consider this a change in values or ideas, is that we were winners, or we felt as if we were winners. Now we feel like survivors. This is a big change because if you think you are a winner, you will try to succeed and lead, but if you believe you are struggling to survive, you will never lead, you are a follower, whichever way you look at it.[77] (Quotation indicating that 'being ahead of competitors' is not a value shared between the previous and current generation.)

The case of DERSA is similar to that of St Martin where risk taking is now rejected while it seems that in previous generations risk taking was considered critical to succeed. The following quotations show this apparent difference:

> As pioneer, Jean Dufour had the capacity to merge a good idea and the courage to take the risk of starting with this company. Without this entrepreneurial and risk-taking spirit, this company would not have been possible.[78] (Quotation indicating risk-taking as a value in previous generations.)

> We cannot afford to take risks. We would like people with stamina to try new things but under a controlled process. Therefore, we can attempt new things but only after we have thought a lot about it.[79] (Quotation indicating that risk taking is not a value shared between the previous and current generations.)

How did the firms under study build up their identity over time? And, most importantly, how did the identity of the organization affect the possibilities the organization had for changing and thereby its flexibility?

We start by explaining how the core values we previously indicated helped the flexible firms to build up a strong identity, unlike the less flexible firms.

Ideological Coaching from Previous Generations to the Current One

The core values that shape organizational identity did not emerge out of the blue, but it took time to form a consistent set of beliefs that moulded the identity of the organizations. The role of leadership in tackling this task proved to be important in the most flexible firms, and lack of leadership or problems of leadership proved to be critical in this respect in the less flexible firms.

In introducing his conceptual framework to understand the creation and change of organizational culture, Gagliardi (1986) states that in the early phases of an organization, it is the leader who sets up the core values and beliefs of an organization. Over the life span of an organization, a series of formal structures will be created, and rules and procedures will replace the active role of the leader. The leader's role would then be important but not as critical as in the first stages of the organization.

In AGD and Sidus many interviewees conveyed the critical role played by their founders in setting up the organization's values and aims:

> Through our identity we convey what we are and what we want to be. We follow the way marked out by the founders, and we have a commitment to those values and that way of doing things they first established.[80]

> What my father did is immeasurable. From nothing he set up what today is a leading company in its sector. His commitment and ideals remain today. His ideals are vivid and jog our memory about the right things to do.[81]

But leader's beliefs are not enough. Argyris (1992) asserts that success tends to consolidate the commitment and the set of beliefs an organization has. What happened with AGD and Sidus was that the success of the business shifted the rational agreement members of the companies had with the leader's beliefs towards a concentration on identifying with those beliefs. This is why, in our opinion, the process of identification started in both companies. Both companies developed consistent actions over time to build up their organizational identity. AGD and Sidus asserted the validity of their faith in innovation even when they faced threats and criticism from the external environment (Sidus with its deal with Merck, and AGD with its investments in the origination area); both companies made long-term investments even if the economic situation was bad (Sidus in biotechnology and AGD in brands).

The lack of success in both St Martin and DERSA, on the other hand, harmed the commitment to the companies' set of beliefs. DERSA disinvested and, for a long time, many of the market launches were not successful. After the new CEO took over, releases of products were called off for two years. 'We were a shrinking company. In a shrinking company nobody cares about the ship, but about their lives. You need to find a lifeboat rather than commit yourself to a sinking company.'[82]

St Martin was careless regarding the innovativeness that characterized the company in the 1970s and put aside the branding strategy. The company no longer aspired to be a leader of the market – as previous generations had pleaded – and instead became a laggard.

Our findings in the flexible and less flexible firms are important in understanding the relationship between strategy and leadership. The leaders in the flexible firms were an important element in strategy formation. Viewing leaders as historical figures and 'tenants of time and context' (Leavy and Wilson, 1994) made us emphasize on the challenges the leaders faced during their tenures at the top rather than on personal attributes. Strategy in the four firms was informed by the organizational history and the organization leaders. Raff (2000) shows how the founders' vision and values in two book retailers in the USA have influenced what the company became and the strategies they followed. Kimberly (1979) and Pettigrew (1979) empirically demonstrated the critical role of the leaders of the organizations analysed (that is, the founders of the organizations) in shaping the organizations' strategies and set of beliefs. Similarly, this book demonstrates how the founders' values and beliefs helped the organizations to cope with the demands of the new environment through implementing new strategic initiatives (that is, biotechnological project in Sidus, branding in AGD) (Kimberly, 1979).

Briefly, by ensuring that their values remained largely unchanged throughout different generations, the flexible firms forged a very strong identity, unlike the less flexible firms in which the organization's core values changed over time. The role of the founders in creating a set of beliefs (that is, values) and in consolidating the people's commitment to those values allowed the companies to achieve a strong organizational identity.

The indoctrination of one generation by the previous one may, however, prove to be a critical element in forging organizational identity and most importantly, we need to understand how the firms (that is, flexible and less flexible) coped with the transformation needed to be able to survive. Also how did the strong identity found in the flexible firms encourage change rather than impede it?

Change and Identity in the Flexible and Less Flexible Firms

The main difference between highly flexible and less flexible firms is in the way their identity – through their organizational values – helped them to change or trapped them in inertial forces.

However deeply-rooted, the strong identities of both AGD and Sidus did not trap them in the rigidity of inertial forces. On the contrary, both companies were able to change quickly and smoothly without affecting their organizational core values. So how were AGD and Sidus able to cope with the relationship between strong identity and change? And why did St Martin and DERSA fail over time to undertake substantial transformations?

Barney *et al.* (1998) suggest that organizational identity is likely to be a source of competitive advantage when the environment is stable and homogeneity is high. Otherwise, identity is likely to be a source of competitive disadvantage. However, when the identity includes ideals favouring change, innovation and risk taking, identity may not be a factor causing resistance to change.

Both AGD and Sidus incorporated values related to innovation and change (in AGD values such as agile decision making, and innovation; in Sidus values such as innovation and risk taking). The incorporation of these values enabled them to undertake major transformations without damaging their core identities and yet avoiding resistance to change (Barney *et al.*, 1998).

St Martin and DERSA, on the other hand, rejected those values from a previous generation that emphasized change or transformation. St Martin, for example, rejected the value of innovativeness. DERSA, conversely, dismissed the value of risk taking that had been emphasised by previous generations.

Based on their theoretical analysis of organisational identity and change in turbulent environments, Gustafson and Reger (1995) distinguish two parts of an identity: the intangible attributes that are central and enduring – the core values – and the substantive attributes of organizational identity. Examples of those substantive attributes are products, strategies, and geographic scope, among others. In times of turmoil, when organizations need to adapt to new environmental circumstances, the substantive parts change while the intangible parts remain unchanged. For Gustafson and Reger the outcome of this process is organizations that embrace change while simultaneously maintaining a sense of stability by using their sense of identity as a psychological anchor.

The strong sense of identity gave the most flexible companies the organizational anchor they needed to be able to move forward and change (Gustafson and Reger, 1995; Calori *et al.*, 2000). By maintaining core values but changing their strategies, products and processes, AGD and Sidus managed to transform themselves without creating internal turmoil. The interviews are revealing in this respect:

> Over the 1990s the company has changed a lot. However, if you ask an employee whether they have felt the changes, they would say that they had not noticed internal turmoil. They did not feel threatened by the changes. I do not know how or why this has happened. However, if you compared our business now and ten years ago, you would think we were a different company. [. . .] Regarding the process of transformation we went through, I would say that we did well in terms of avoiding internal chaos, but we were probably lucky enough to avoid these problems or we built some capabilities over time without noticing their effects in the long term.[83]

At Sidus, they stated:

> One amazing aspect of this company is that over the last decade or over the last 13 years, Sidus has shifted its strategy completely but we still have the spirit of the old times, even similar traditions and stories. We did not lose the thread that links us with our past, although we look to the future – a wise combination that was fostered by the founders and their children.[84]

We have therefore underlined the critical role of identity in the process of change. Both AGD and Sidus were conservative about their core values but dynamic at the same time. This dynamism is represented by organizational values that were enablers of change and transformation. The strong identity found at Sidus and AGD did not imply, as some writers in the field of organizational identity state, an inertial force impeding change and transformation. On the contrary, the companies' strong organizational identity enhanced their organizational flexibility by providing the anchor they needed to change, try new things and take risks.

THE INTERCONNECTION BETWEEN THE DETERMINANTS OF ORGANIZATIONAL FLEXIBILITY

So far, we have considered the different determinants of flexibility individually, and have not addressed the linkages between them. The evidence provided suggests that there is an interconnection between the five determinants of organizational flexibility, which facilitated the rapid adaptation in the flexible firms analysed.

We argue that the five determinants we have analysed individually in previous pages form an interconnected model that enhances our understanding of the way flexible firms have successfully adapted in conditions of environmental turmoil. This model is not a prescriptive one. On the contrary, it has emerged from the interplay of the initial theoretical framework and the empirical research undertaken in the four companies as shown in Chapters 7–9. We are not claiming that this model could be used as an instruction manual to enable a firm to achieve flexibility. Instead, we would like to offer 'a representation of the mechanism by which the phenomenon under study operates' (Pettigrew and Whipp, 1991: 270).

The issue of interconnection between different organizational elements is critical for this study. No single factor can provide an answer as to how a firm managed change to achieve competitive success. Rather, the explanation of change and competitive success is to be found in the interconnection of the five factors.

Figure 10.13 illustrates the existent interrelation between different determinants of organizational flexibility as revealed by the evidence provided in this chapter. This relationship is shown through dotted lines. The lines represent a qualitative interpretation and do not imply a quantitative relationship. An explanation of those interrelations follows.

The inflow of new managers with diverse experience background in the 1980s and early 1990s helped both AGD and Sidus to reduce the influence of institutional pressures. The heterogeneous top team had different

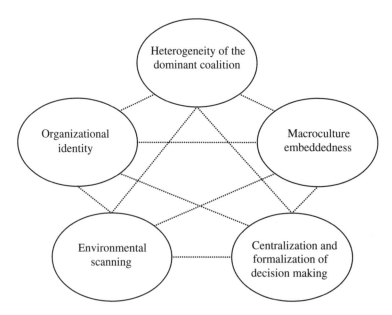

Figure 10.13   Interconnection of determinants of organizational flexibility

cognitive frameworks that also helped the firms both to sense the signals from the environment and broadened their capacity for interpretation. As a result, both AGD and Sidus explored new strategic initiatives and became either early adopters or first movers of strategies (that is, Sidus in biotechnology and retail in the pharmaceutical industry; AGD in branding and logistics in the edible oil industry).

The importance of the low level of macroculture embeddedness of AGD and Sidus (that is, through the low level of connectedness and similarity in their industries) has been demonstrated by the fact that both firms were able to move rapidly and anticipate other competitors' moves. The 'disembeddedness' of AGD and Sidus from their macroculture was facilitated, first, by, mechanism of scanning (that is, formal and informal mechanisms as previously analysed) and, second, by managers who came from industries other than those in which the firms participated.

The low levels of centralization and formalization demonstrated by the flexible firms, on the other hand, increased the possibilities the top team had for interacting more (that is, the constructive conflict we have analysed in this chapter), participating in decision making (that is, through the process of delegation started by the Boards of both Sidus and AGD in the 1990s), and speeding up the responses of both firms when needed (that is, the strategic initiatives of the flexible firms).

Scanning the environment in the flexible firms not only became a critical factor for anticipating competitors' actions (that is, through the firms' formal and informal mechanism) but also influenced other determinants of organizational flexibility. Being open to the signals of the environment influenced the firms' ability to notice the importance of new managerial skills early in the 1990s as a competitive advantage (that is, both firms had incorporated new managers throughout the late 1980s early 1990s). Similarly, scanning has also been important in the firms' decisions to rearrange their structure and initiate a delegation process to allow greater participation of the business managers in operative decisions and allow the Boards of AGD and Sidus to perform a strategic role in the firms.

Finally, the strong organizational identity of AGD and Sidus represented by their set of core values impacted on the rest of the determinants. By supporting values related to change and innovation (such as a risk-taking attitude and innovation in Sidus, and agile decision making and innovation in AGD), the firms were able to avoid isomorphic behaviour in their industries. The same set of values enabled the firms to achieve external openness in an attempt to find new opportunities and maintain the competitive advantages that made them successful at adapting quickly. AGD's and Sidus' set of beliefs also made it necessary for managers to realize those values. Finally, the values also necessitated organizational arrangements to enact those values. The changes in structure and delegation process implemented in AGD and Sidus were the fruit of the companies' values of innovation and change.

The five determinants of organizational flexibility interconnected and complemented each other in a way that allowed the flexible firms to adapt rapidly under environmental turmoil, to move fast and first in their industries (that is, through their strategic initiatives) and to cope with political and economical changes (that is, changes in regulations and government policies).

The less flexible firms, on the other hand, were laggards in their industries. They were not able to adapt rapidly under environmental uncertainty and they were lagging behind the flexible firms (that is, losing market share, lack of strategic initiatives). The less flexible firms were affected by what Whittington and Pettigrew (2003) called 'a complementarities trap'. This happens when firms persist with what once fitted the organization best, making it difficult for an organization to change and adapt to new contextual challenges.

DERSA was trapped in an old formula of success: the idea that they should participate successfully in the different market niches of the pharmaceutical industry. DERSA toyed with different niches for a long time and overlooked the dermatological niche in which the firm had a competitive advantage. St Martin, on the other hand, became trapped in the low-profit business of cotton ginning because it was part of the business the company started with. St Martin did not invest in its brand strategy that was proving to be more profitable than cotton ginning and crushing. Both firms became stuck in the modes of thinking and working that brought them their initial success. When business conditions change, their once winning formulas instead bring failure (Sull, 1999a, 1999b).

The absence of determinants of organizational flexibility (most notably in St Martin) may have encouraged St Martin and DERSA to stick to the old complementary system that no longer worked in the 1990s. Neither DERSA nor St Martin could envision a new system to replace the old one. Instead, they kept the same strategic frames that blinkered their vision, preventing managers from noticing new options and opportunities. This process led both DERSA and St Martin to achieve high levels of inertia, making adaptation a difficult process. What saved the companies from succumbing was mainly the fact that either the markets were willing to buy the firms' products (that is, the case of St Martin) or the internal changes in the company saved it from a downward spiral of more inflexibility (that is, the case of DERSA after the replacement of the CEO) (see Figure 10.14).

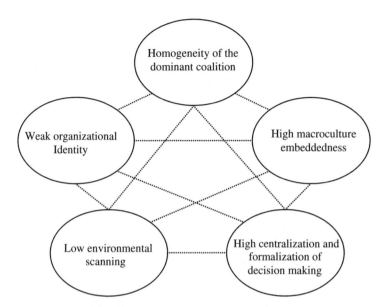

*Figure 10.14   The downward spiral of flexibility: interconnection of
determinants of organizational flexibility in the less
flexible firms*

NOTES

1. The three periods of time are: 1989, the starting point of the analysis; 1996, the year
    before the radical changes happened in the less flexible companies and; 1999, the end of
    our period of analysis.
2. Interview with HR Manager AGD.
3. Interview with President of St Martin.
4. Interview with Executive Director of Retail Businesses.
5. Interview with Logistic Manager in DERSA.
6. The reliability score was calculated by the researcher re-coding three interview tran-
    scripts for the sets of questions asked as influencing the cognitive diversity of the dom-
    inant coalition of the firms under analysis. The re-coding was then compared with the
    original coding and the percentage score calculated according to Huberman and Miles
    (1994) formulae: reliability = number of agreements/total of agreements + disagree-
    ments.
7. Interview with Finance Manager AGD.
8. Interview with Finance Manager in St Martin.
9. Interview with Commercial department staff and fourth generation family members in
    St Martin.
10. Interview with HR manager in Sidus.
11. Interview with CEO DERSA.
12. Interview with Director AGD.
13. Interview with Director AGD.
14. Interview with Finance Manager in St Martin.

15. Interview with Finance Manager in St Martin.
16. Interview with CEO Sidus.
17. Interview with CEO Sidus.
18. Interview with CEO DERSA.
19. Interview with CEO DERSA.
20. Interview with HR Manager in AGD.
21. Interview Finance Manager AGD.
22. Interview Finance Manager AGD.
23. Interview HR Manager AGD.
24. Interview with Director AGD.
25. Interview with Commercial Department staff in St Martin.
26. Interview with Commercial Department Director, Director of the Board and third generation family member.
27. Interview Personnel Department staff in St Martin.
28. Interview with Finance Director, St Martin.
29. Interview with Technology Department Director.
30. Interview with Commercial Director.
31. Interview with CEO Sidus.
32. Interview with Finance Manager Sidus.
33. Interview HR Manager Sidus.
34. Interview Finance Manager Sidus.
35. Interview Executive Director of BioSidus.
36. Interview with Logistic Manager in DERSA.
37. Interview with Ethical Marketing Products Manager in DERSA.
38. Interview with Ethical Marketing Products Manager in DERSA.
39. Interview with HR Manager in AGD.
40. Interview with HR Manager in Sidus.
41. Interview with Commercial Department staff and fourth generation family member in St Martin.
42. Interview with HR Manager, AGD.
43. Interview with Director AGD.
44. Interview with Director AGD.
45. Interview with Corporate lawyer in St Martin.
46. Interview with Vice President St Martin.
47. Interview with Commercial Department Director, Director of the Board and third generation family member in St. Martin.
48. Interview with CEO Sidus.
49. Interview with OTC Manager DERSA.
50. Interview with CEO DERSA.
51. Interview with OTC Marketing Product Manager in DERSA.
52. The most important strategic initiatives between 1989 and 1999 were tracked in Figure 10.9 and Figure 10.10. The strategic initiatives of the most flexible firms are shown in black shading and the ones corresponding to the less flexible firm are shown in grey. The appropriate shading is shown under the year that the strategic initiative was launched. The existent gap – if there was any – between the launch in one company and the other is highlighted with an arrow.
53. Interview with Director AGD.
54. Interview with Director AGD.
55. Interview Director-CEO AGD.
56. Interview Director-CEO AGD.
57. Interview with Finance and Administration Manager, AGD.
58. Interview with -Economic Studies Manager in AGD.
59. Interview with Commercial Department Manager in St Martin.
60. Interview with CEO of Sidus.
61. Interview with CEO DERSA.
62. Interview with Director in AGD.

63. Interview with family member and Executive Director of Retail Businesses in Sidus.
64. Interview with Director of AGD.
65. Interview with CEO of Sidus.
66. Interview with CEO DERSA.
67. Interview with Promotion and Sales Manager DERSA.
68. Interview with Commercial department manager.
69. Speech given by the CEO to managers in June, 1990.
70. Speech from the Board November, 1996.
71. Speech given by Board member to managers and employees in 1989.
72. Speech given by CEO in the 'Executive Programme for Sidus Managers' 6/7 December, 2000.
73. Article in 'Argentime' Magazine. Number 5, year 1998, page 123.
74. Speech given by CEO at the launch of a genetic therapy in a joint venture with Fundacion Favaloro. May, 2000
75. Interview with Commercial Department staff and fourth generation member in St Martin.
76. Interview with Commercial Department staff and fourth generation member in St Martin.
77. Interview with Corporate lawyer St Martin.
78. Speech given by Émile Dufour in anniversary of the company in Argentina.
79. Speech given by CEO to the in the year 2000.
80. Interview with CEO Sidus.
81. Interview with Director AGD.
82. Interview with CEO DERSA.
83. Interview with AGD Director.
84. Interview with HR Manager Sidus.

11. Conclusions

This book examines the process of organizational adaptation and the competitiveness of firms in an emerging economy. The study is set in the Argentinian context of the 1990s when a combination of economic and political change triggered a transformation in the competitive context of indigenous family firms. Two highly flexible firms and two less flexible firms were studied from the pharmaceutical and edible oil industries and longitudinal data were used to explore the determinants of organizational flexibility in those organisations.

This perspective raised a number of important issues regarding the content and process of being flexible and the determinants of organizational flexibility. Recognition of this gap in the literature prompted the development of three researchable questions:

- Do some firms display more flexibility than others in competitive circumstances?
- Why are some firms able to display more flexibility?
- And how do they do it?

In this final chapter we return to our research questions and draw together the results of our case study findings and analysis. We will also discuss the contributions this research has made to the study of flexibility, adaptation and change theory. We also identify the contributions to both the literature and practices of family firms and the literature on the influence of national differences as shapers of the organizational action of firms. Finally, we describe the limitations of our work and suggest recommendations for further research, both to address these limitations and to exploit the utility of the research method developed during this study.

FINDINGS AND CONTRIBUTIONS OF THIS STUDY

In Chapters 1 and 2 we stressed the importance of organizational flexibility as a way firms have of adapting under high levels of competitive pressure. We have also described our two main criticisms of research into adaptation – the extreme views in adaptation theory (that is, contingency theory, population ecology) and the single level of analysis in some research on organizational adaptiveness. We argued that organizational adaptation and therefore flexibility is the interplay between inner and outer context, a dynamic process in which elements of both managerial choice and environmental influence coexist. Thus, deterministic and voluntaristic positions are rejected. Regarding the single level of analysis predominant in some research into adaptation, we propose a multilevel approach to understanding organizational flexibility. As yet, there are few multilevel analyses of organizational flexibility. If we recognize the dynamic and multilevel character of organizational flexibility then it is possible to raise a number of important questions concerning the process and character of a firm's flexibility over time and the factors that influence such a process. This study took up the challenge of exploring these dynamic issues regarding organizational flexibility.

Our research questions also encouraged us to address two critical aspects of the methodology (see Methodological Appendix). First that data collection had to be longitudinal. Second, although the firm level of analysis was the focus of our interest, we also needed to investigate the phenomena at the industry level. Our choice of multiple levels of analysis therefore required the use of multiple research methods.

In Chapter 3, we examined the national business environment (NBE) and the elements that may have influenced a firm's development in an economy characterized by turmoil. These factors were the role of the state, the role of financial institutions and the role of national culture. We demonstrated how the different elements of the NBE impacted on the constitution of indigenous firms. We first underlined the role of the state as critical in deciding the different types of firms that predominate over time (that is, indigenous firms, multinationals, national holdings) (Whitley, 2000; Kosacoff, 2000). Second, we stressed the role of financial institutions as determining the way firms funded their growth (that is, through bank loans or own savings) (Zysman, 1983). Finally, the role of national culture was considered crucial in influencing a firm's governance structure, the ways in which people deal with each other and with other organizations, and the patterns of work organization and control (Hofstede, 1991; Whitley, 2000).

In Chapters 4 to 10 we turned our attention to our second and third researchable questions: why are some firms able to display more flexibility? And how do they do it? In essence, what factors will determine whether a firm is flexible? The four comparative case studies presented in Chapters 6–8 revealed the transformation trajectories of the flexible and less flexible firms. In the course of the case studies we were able to see how the flexible firms renewed their strategies and organizational arrangements in a process of continuous change. The less flexible firms, on the other hand, followed a different transformational trajectory characterized by attempts of revolutionary change (see Chapter 9).

Our comparative case studies of the four firms identified five interrelated factors as determining a firm's flexibility: characteristics of the dominant coalition; the degree of formalization and centralization of decision making; embeddedness within the industry macroculture; environmental scanning; and organisational identity (see Chapter 10).

Our findings demonstrate that none of the determinants identified on its own promotes organizational flexibility. It is, however, the interrelation of the five determinants that causes firms to be more flexible.

Implications of Our Framework and Findings for the Interpretation of the Current Argentinian Context

We have already discussed the empirical evidence this study provides for the understanding of the determinants of organizational flexibility and their importance in the adaptation of a firm in highly changeable contexts. We have not only revealed what determines whether an organization is flexible (Chapter 9) but have also identified a set of indicators to identify flexible firms (see Methodological Appendix).

The critical socio-economic situation that began in Argentina at the end of 2001 gave the researcher an opportunity to witness directly the way flexible and less flexible firms adapted in a rapidly changing environment. The way in which the crisis has begun to affect the firms in this study also confirms the appropriateness of the sample we have chosen to use: all four firms have begun to show patterns of behaviour previously identified in this study. AGD and Sidus have adapted quickly, whereas St Martin and DERSA were sluggish in their response. Let us comment briefly on the way flexible and less flexible firms were adapting to the economic situation that was emerging by the end of 2001.

From 1998 Argentina began to enter and suffer a long recession. As a consequence of that recession, and the resultant fiscal and debt burden the economy had almost ground to a halt by the end of 2001. The chain of payments between consumers, businesses and suppliers had broken down, and people were prevented from using their bank savings. Moreover, after a decade in which the peso was fixed by law at parity with the dollar the government allowed the peso to float on the open market (*The Economist*, 2 March 2002).

How did the flexible and less flexible firms in this research confront such an unpredictable and changeable situation? The case of the edible oil industry is illustrative of the way the strategies elaborated by the firms in the 1990s helped them to make decisions according to the market needs a decade later. AGD's diversification strategies helped them to avoid making huge losses. Since 2000, AGD has focused its efforts on exporting branded or elaborated products (that is, soya milk, soya sub-products, and mayonnaise, among others) to avoid tax retentions from the government for products sold in bulk.[1] The brands for the internal market continued but with a higher price (due to the devaluation of the peso). Market share was stable and showed no signs of losing ground in the edible oil market. In addition, AGD's efficient logistics chain helped the company to be cost efficient.[2]

St Martin's focus on exporting bulk products was not rewarded by the new economic plan. A 10 per cent retention tax was levied on exports of bulk products. Cotton ginning exports had to compete with lower prices from other developing countries and the internal sales of those products stagnated. In a deep economic crisis, St Martin's inexpensive edible oil brand however was doing well and increasing its market share. It is important to remember, however, that the company had cast off such a strategy in the past and the brand strategy was a marginal one. Therefore, the company could not counteract the effect of the losses the firm suffered in the main businesses.[3]

When, as a result of the economic crisis, the pharmaceutical industry was running short of basic products, Sidus' biotechnological project was the good sign on the horizon. Through reinforcing exports of biotechnological products, Sidus invested the result of the exports into supplying their own pharmacies with pharmaceutical products. It was an exception among the shortages that affected the whole industry:[4] 'This is a bad time for the country and the industry, but we have also seen an opportunity in trying not to betray our customers. They can find products in our pharmacies. The economic situation will see some pharmaceutical firms struggling for survival, and we are going to gain terrain in the market.'[5] In spite of the crisis, Sidus also decided to make a percentage of BioSidus public. The sell-off will provide Sidus with the money to continue to invest in a market that 'will become even more concentrated after the collapse of some of the remaining national firms'.[6]

Finally, the case of DERSA is not so promising. The decision to focus on skin care is backfiring on the company. In the current economic situation, skin care is not seen to be an essential product, so sales have dropped. The company is running short of imported products. All these factors are worsening the financial situation of DERSA. In March 2002 there was a drop of 16 per cent in sales compared with the same period the year before. DERSA's response to the crisis was to postpone investments and to cut costs including salaries.

The flexible firms have adapted quickly to the new economic situation. Furthermore, the diversification strategy initiated in the 1990s gave Sidus and AGD flexibility to adapt a decade later. On the contrary, the focused strategy of the less flexible firms only provided them with short-term solutions, but in the longer term, these have turned out to be traps because such a focused strategy has impeded the firms' ability to adapt. The 2001/2002 crisis in the Argentinian economy confirmed Khanna and Palepu's (1997) assertion that focused strategies may be inadequate for emerging markets.

ORGANIZATIONAL FLEXIBILITY

Throughout this book we have further developed the term 'organizational flexibility' to refer to the repertoire of organizational and managerial capabilities that allow organizations to adapt quickly under conditions of environmental change. The term organizational flexibility has previously been used to refer to the means firms have for limiting the impact of environmental change on the organization (Ansoff, 1988). In Ansoff's words, the aim of organizational flexibility is to provide the firm with a buffer to protect the organization from disturbances so that uncertainty will be reduced. However, the passive connotation of the idea of organizational flexibility as used by Ansoff does not result in fundamental changes to the organization.

We have demonstrated the significance of a much more active interpretation of organizational flexibility than that offered by Ansoff (1988). The active interpretation includes factors that made the flexible firms analysed highly responsive to environmental change, allowing them to adjust their strategy and organization quickly to exploit changes in their environments. Flexible firms were able to respond successfully to sudden environmental changes and able to build up new organizational capabilities (that is, flexible capabilities) if required.

Flexible organizations do not just respond quickly to change in the environment, they also proactively influence that environment and force others to match their moves. AGD's and Sidus' strategic initiatives have changed the map of competition in their industries as they became first movers or early adopters of strategies, while other companies attempted to imitate the strategies adopted by Sidus and AGD in their respective industries.

In the case of the flexible firms analysed in this book, organizational flexibility also involved adaptation to environmental turmoil across the organization and at different levels within the organization, namely the strategic, organizational and managerial levels. Both AGD and Sidus have simultaneously changed their strategic orientation (that is, both firms invested backwards and forwards in the chain of value of their respective industries), while transforming their organizations (that is, introducing new managerial skills, and working on new organizational practices such as enhancing the delegation process, developing more professional management and a structure that stresses operational autonomy).

FURTHER CONTRIBUTIONS OF THIS RESEARCH

This study makes a number of contributions to the study of organizational adaptation and organizational flexibility. These are mainly methodological and empirical, but this research also contributes to the theoretical debate about a number of related analytical issues. These include an understanding of how the character and specific nature of family firms shaped the determinants of organizational flexibility; and also understanding of the role of national differences in the ways firms organize and act.

Organizational Flexibility Process

Is flexibility an intended or emergent process? This is another question that this book helps to answer. McKinley and Scherer (2000) distinguish between intended and emergent actions. The former is the goal towards which the action is destined; the latter is the outcome of an action that the actor is not expecting. This is an important differentiation that can shed light on the process of being flexible.

In contrast to what some writers in the field of organizational flexibility have argued (see Volberda, 1999), there is clear evidence in the case studies to show that the flexible firms were building organizational flexibility as an intended process instead of just an emergent one. The intentionality of the process triggers questions about what the antecedents and origins of the process of being flexible are, and whether the building of organizational flexibility is a long-term process. To understand the trajectory of building organizational flexibility in these companies, we need to draw upon the five determinants of organizational flexibility we analysed in Chapter 10, and in particular we need to understand not only how many determinants the firms had, but also when they had them.

Sidus' process of building flexibility is revealing as far as the intentionality of such a process is concerned. The firm showed low macroculture embeddedness early in the 1980s when it decided to follow a different strategic orientation, that is, investment in biotechnology. The company decision to withdraw from the professional association of the industry in 1988 was an intentional action that confirmed Sidus' objective of differentiating itself from the rest of the firms of the industry.

Similarly it was a deliberate action on Sidus' part to become more decentralized and to enhance the scanning activities of the organization.

As early as 1989 Sidus recognized the importance of splitting the Group into different companies thereby emphasizing a decentralization process to avoid bureaucracy in a company that was growing very fast. We also provided evidence of how Sidus, in a calculated move, enhanced its scanning behaviour by creating three areas which aimed to look at the context surrounding the company: regulation and legal analysis, sectoral analysis (both areas created in 1990), and macroeconomic analysis (set up in 1997).

The heterogeneity of the dominant coalition at Sidus can be considered both an emergent and intentional process. When the company set up its biotechnological venture, it opened up the doors of the Group to new professionals with a different educational profile, experience and background. The cultural gap between Instituto Sidus and the new professionals was an unexpected result of the changes. However, after this first experience with a new profile of managers and employees, the company deliberately attempted to achieve high levels of professionalism in all its new ventures by hiring professionals with diverse backgrounds. This was also used as a way of putting pressure on the more resistant management of Instituto Sidus to make them change.

Similarly, AGD reveals a trajectory of building organizational flexibility that underlines its intentionality. AGD's low macroculture embeddedness goes back to the 1980s when the company launched its first strategic initiative – branding. The intentionality of the process was asserted by some members of the Board when saying, 'copying what others in the sector are doing is a loser's strategy. If you want to be in the forefront, you have to leap forwards, outside sectoral boundaries, and this is what we did. You need to have your body in the sector but your head outside it.'[7] Some investments that allowed AGD to become a strong, vertically integrated company, however, were the consequence of opportunities such as the grain export business that became an important business in its own right.

It was also a purposeful action on AGD's part to boost the levels of autonomy and scanning in the organization. To avoid problems with the upsurge of formalization needed after the opening up of the economy early in the 1990s, AGD favoured and reinforced operational autonomy through the creation of business units with more freedom to act. Regarding the scanning of the organization, the Directors of the firm pointed out the fact that being open to what the context had to say was a constant fact in the Board's day-to-day work. AGD's scanning behaviour was intentionally boosted when the firm, in 1996, set up the economic studies unit with the main purpose of scanning the environment.

Like Sidus, in AGD the heterogeneity of the dominant coalition can be considered both an emergent and intentional process. When AGD began its logistic investments in 1986 and its branding strategy in 1989, the company received a flow of new managers and professionals who ran the new businesses. However, as many in the company believe, AGD did not expect this process to be a challenge for the company. The company confronted some startling problems stemming from the wave of new professionals combined with the old generation of managers. The intentionality of the process can be seen when in 1996 the Board deliberately implemented a strategy of professionalizing and diversifying its management team.

Regarding the determinant related to the strong organizational identity in both AGD and Sidus, the analysis of the case studies indicated that the current generation of family members in both companies have intentionally forged their identity around the values of previous generations. We suggested in Chapter 10 that Sidus and AGD deliberately wanted to preserve the values of previous generations as a way of giving the company an anchor to try new things and change yet, at the same time, avoid organizational chaos.

The experiences of both Sidus and AGD demonstrate that intentionality in building organizational flexibility matters. As such, creating organizational flexibility is not a short-term process but a long one in which firms build up the capabilities that will form the determinants of organizational flexibility. The trajectory process, however, may differ in each company. On the one hand, Sidus built up its flexible capabilities between the early 1980s and early 1990s, while in AGD that process lasted longer. The main reason for this difference lies with the different sectoral realities in which the firms were embedded. Sidus, unlike AGD, was in an industry unaccustomed to competitive pressures of the deregulated market. Therefore, Sidus needed to build up its flexible capabilities more quickly than AGD.

Contributions to Adaptation and Change Theories

Our research has also provided empirical evidence which can contribute to the long-standing debate within the organizational and management literature – that of continuous versus revolutionary transformation, and that of environmental determinism versus strategic choice.

We have already shown in Chapter 9 how the flexible firms undertook transformations that involved continuous change, while the less flexible firms displayed a more revolutionary attempt at transformation. The outcome of the transformation process in the flexible firms does not conform to the pattern portrayed in the literature on adaptation and change which explains transformations as processes that include long periods of stability or convergence and short periods of revolutionary change (Tushman and Romanelli, 1985; Tushman and Smith, 2001; Benner and Tushman, 2001). The most flexible firms have shown continuous change rather than stable equilibrium positions punctuated by sudden change.

Our study also contributes empirical evidence to the debate between environmental determinism and strategic choice. We have seen how deterministic and voluntaristic approaches have influenced the field of organizational adaptation (Chapter 2). However, we reject purely deterministic theories in which adaptation and thus flexibility are reactive capacities of the organization (that is, contingency theory), or even more radical approaches in which the power of the environment is such that organizational adaptation is impossible (that is, population ecologists). Additionally, we claim that voluntaristic approaches that rely entirely on the power of managerial enactment and choice are also false (that is, strategic choice).

Our findings suggest that these polar positions are empirically untenable. In line with the contextualist approach proposed by Pettigrew (1985) and Pettigrew and Whipp (1991) we view adaptation as a dynamic concept and the result of a fusion of managerial choice and the pressures imposed by the internal and external contexts in which firms operate. In this context, flexibility is a set of organizational capabilities (that is, managerial and organizational) allowing the firms to adapt fast in conditions of environmental turmoil.

Contributions in the Field of Family Businesses

Our study has also contributed to the understanding of the transformation, adaptation and flexibility of family firms. Ward (1987) and Gersick *et al.* (1997) have highlighted the lack of research into transformation and change in family firms. In the most important journal in the field of family firms (*Family Business Review*) less than 4 per cent of the articles published between 1988 and 1997 addressed the issue of change and development (Dyer and Sanchez, 1998).

But most importantly, this book highlights the way the character of family firms has influenced and shaped the determinants of organizational flexibility. At the beginning of Chapter 10 we introduced three main issues affecting the organizational flexibility of family firms, namely: the life cycle of the family firms and the role of the founder; control systems and professionalization of the management team; and, ownership issues. The first two issues have shaped different aspects of the determinants of organizational flexibility analysed in this book.

The role of the founder had a great impact on the way the identity of the flexible firms developed. We pointed out that the flexible firms in this research, unlike the less flexible firms, had a strong identity based on a set of core values shared with previous generations. The strong identity found in the flexible firms is contrary to some organizational studies that assert that a strong identity can hamper the ability to see important changes in the market (Ouchi, 1981). Burgelman (1983), for example, underlines the importance of a strong organizational identity in helping the organization to preserve order. However, Burgelman also warns that a strong identity may impede organizational change. The flexible family firms analysed in this book, however, managed to maintain an identity containing values that facilitated and motivated change.

The life cycle of the firm and the mechanisms of control applied in our family firms impacted on the determinant 'centralization and formalization of the decision-making process'. The evidence provided by AGD and Sidus confirms the conclusions of the literature on family firms: both firms became more autonomous in their operation and also more formalized in later stages of life (see evidence in Chapter 10, and also Moores and Mula, 2000). The decisions of the companies to give more autonomy to the managers meant that more formalization and control was necessary to keep the family abreast of operations. The less flexible firms followed a different pattern: both St Martin and DERSA had increased formalization and centralization of decision making over time, therefore taking a more hands-on approach towards the running of the company. The evidence by flexible and less flexible firms revealed a pattern different from that found in studies of non-family firms that have widely accepted that low levels of centralization and formalization foster innovativeness and flexibility in organizations (Volberda, 1996, 1999; Bahrami, 1992; Damanpour, 1991, 1992). The evidence provided by our case studies indicates a different process inside family firms.

Finally, the degree of professionalization of the top team in the family firms had an important influence on the demographic characteristics of the firms analysed. The literature on family firms has suggested that professionalization of the management team is a critical issue in the middle or late stages of their organizational development. Failure to professionalize might have devastating consequences for the survival and success of the firms (Ward, 1987). The earlier professionalization of Sidus and AGD helped them to build a more heterogeneous top team. By contrast, the lack of incorporation of a professional management with different background experience, and the fact that the less flexible firms relied upon family members to fill top jobs shaped the existent homogeneity found in DERSA and St Martin. The long-term consequences were evident in the firms: the heterogeneous firms had more cognitive diversity that helped them to take risks and boosted their capacity to act. Meanwhile, the homogeneous firms revealed some of the cognitive limitations that restricted the top team capacity for action.

The Influence of the National Business Environment (NBE) as a Shaper of Organizational Action in the Firms

This book also contributes to our understanding of the different ways the NBE impinges on a firm's ability to adapt and change. While there have been some attempts to address this issue (Khanna and Palepu, 2000; Hoskisson *et al.*, 2000; Lewin *et al.*, 2002) there is still a large gap in our understanding of how institutional factors affect management practices, innovation processes, creativity and flexibility in organizations.

In presenting a combined approach to which institutional and cultural elements were gathered together, we were able to examine the context in which the firms have to operate from a multidimensional viewpoint. Such an analysis makes it possible to begin to answer the following questions: what are the institutions that can help us to understand the evolution of indigenous firms? How have these institutions shaped the development of the national enterprise? And finally, what elements of the national culture influence the managerial behaviour of the firms and their ability to change and adapt?

The two institutions analysed – the role of the state and the role of financial institutions – clarifies the institutional influence of the emergence, development and demise of indigenous businesses. The role of the state in the economy was significant in shaping the levels of centralization and formalization of decision making found in the firms. With the sudden opening up of the economy early in the 1990s flexible firms became more formalized and less centralized as far as the operations were concerned to confront the efficiency required in a market that stabilized (in terms of macroeconomic indicators) and became more competitive (after the opening up of the economy to international competition). This implied an approach that differed from that used in the 1980s in which flexible firms were less formalized and more centralized to be able to confront a closed but highly unstable market.

The scanning behaviour of the firms was also influenced by the changes in the economy. After the opening up of the economy, flexible firms, and to a lesser extent the less flexible firms, started to scan more of the environment to understand competitors' moves and customers' needs.

The sudden opening up of the economy fostered by the Argentinian state also impacted on the strategies of the flexible firms. To be able to compete in an open economy, the flexible firms needed to integrate their businesses because of the lack of reliable suppliers. New business strategies and long-term planning were necessary to confront the new competitive landscape.

Elements of the national culture also shed light on the implications for organizational action. Linking the results of our analysis (Chapter 10), and the cultural elements analysed in Chapter 3, produces some revealing results regarding the way flexible and less flexible firms behave.

In Chapter 3 we described how four elements of national culture as stated by Hofstede (1980, 1991) may have impacted on the way firms organized themselves and changed. Hofstede stated that Argentina would be a country with high power distance, high uncertainty avoidance, collectivism and masculinity. The less flexible firms confirmed the patterns we found when trying to link the four elements of analysis of the national culture as suggested by Hofstede and the ways firms organized themselves in the Argentinian case (that is, high levels of centralization and formalization, resistance to change among others).

Most interesting is the case of the flexible firms that did not comply with some of the factors of our analysis of national culture. Sidus and AGD behaved counter culturally *vis-à-vis* the predictions of national culture. It seems that in these companies a local organizational effect overrode the effects of the national culture. This was demonstrated by the fact that the flexible firms decentralized decision-making, took risks and undertook organizational change.

There is still a question to tackle: that is, whether organizational action in flexible firms is shaped only by elements of the national culture or, as Whittington and Mayer (2000) argued, by convergence based on efficiency. The results of our research make it difficult to answer such a question. More research comparing flexible firms in different countries will facilitate the understanding of whether flexible firms converge towards adapting structural and process routines associated with greater flexibility, or whether prevalent management practices reflect specific national state configurations as determined by cultural factors.

LIMITATIONS AND SUGGESTIONS FOR FURTHER RESEARCH

Our findings are based on a comparative case study of polar types: two flexible and two less flexible firms in two industries – pharmaceuticals and edible oils. Consequently there must be questions as to the extent to which these findings are applicable to other contexts. Because the extent to which our findings are supported by elements of the literature on organizational flexibility, organizational innovativeness and institutional embeddedness, some level of generalizability can be claimed. However, the originality of this work within the adaptation literature cannot be claimed until further research into other industries is carried out. This is a critical issue which needs to be resolved before we can claim generalizability of the findings.

The use of a particular set of indicators to select flexible firms and the selection of the determinants of organizational flexibility as categories of analysis may also have limited the findings of this research. Further research needs to show whether a selection of other indicators would produce similar results and also whether other determinants can shed light on the way firms can achieve flexibility.

As discussed earlier, the selection of the determinants of organizational flexibility as categories of analysis may also have limited the findings of our research. We have not analysed three important issues that may have had an influence on the organizational flexibility of the firms researched: leadership, technology and the role of HRM.

Although we have addressed the issue of leadership while analysing the strong organizational identity determinant, we have not tackled such an important topic directly. Leadership style can clarify issues such as the potential for a participative or delegative culture, the planning approach of the organization and the management attitude (Volberda, 1999). However, our analysis of the dominant coalition, organizational identity and transformation of the firms is a proxy analysis of leadership effects. Instead of isolating it out, we picked up its effects in different ways.

In this book one issue emerged as central to our understanding of governance and leadership in family firms and their influence on organizational flexibility. This aspect is related to the corporate governance of family firms.

The family is the most important component of the governance structure in most family firms. Hence, power is normally concentrated at Board level. None of the companies investigated have intermediary structures such as an executive committee. But how can a different corporate structure enhance organizational flexibility? Can, for example, executive committees help to boost the flexibility of a firm? Neubauer and Lank (1998) emphasize that less concentration of power in the Board and the presence of intermediary structures in family firms might facilitate the participation of managers and younger family members in strategic decisions. On the other hand a corporate structure that incorporates intermediary structures may offer the Board alternative views and therefore enhance its capacity to act. Consequently, a less centralized corporate structure may offer some insight into other ways flexibility can be achieved at the top level of the firm.

The four companies analysed in this book do not offer insight into the benefits of intermediary arrangements in corporate structure. As Figure 11.1 shows, the concentration of power at the Board level in the firms analysed meant a lack of intermediary structures between the Board and managers. Moreover, the Boards in the four firms are exclusively made up of family members. In the Boards there were no part-time members, non-executive

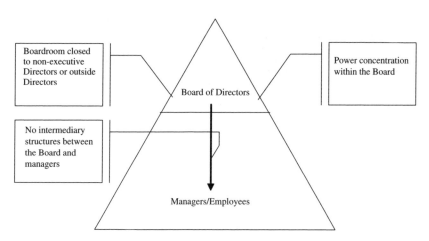

Figure 11.1 Power concentration and corporate governance structure in the firms analysed

members or outside Directors. This is another element of the Board composition that Neubauer and Lank (1998) consider a key issue in family firms. They suggest that in family firms part-time or executive directors can act as knowledgeable outsiders who can potentially offset the management's shortcomings and can also give and test new ideas. Outsiders offering alternative views to the Board, then, may influence family firms' flexibility. More research analysing flexible firms with different corporate structures may shed light on the way the firms' capacity for action may be boosted and organizational flexibility enhanced.

We introduced Chapter 1 with a quote by D'Aveni (1994) in which he warned researchers and practitioners about the complexity of the business world. In the same essay D'Aveni predicts that hypercompetitive environments will favour organizations that are able to be flexible and to adapt quickly to change. Throughout this book we have developed theoretically and empirically what determines whether an organization is flexible. However, our study is still a limited contribution to the understanding of organizational flexibility. More research needs to be done in a field the importance of which has been recognized for the survival and future success of organizations, but which, to date, has been characterized by scarce research.

NOTES

1. The retention tax was 10 per cent for agriculture exports and 5 per cent to industrialized products.

2. Interview with Director AGD in December 2001.
3. Interview with Financial Director in St Martin in March 2002.
4. La Nacion Newspaper. 27/06/2002, sección Economía.
5. Interview with family member and Executive Director of Retail Businesses.
6. Interview with family member and Executive Director of Retail Businesses.
7. Interview with Director AGD.

Methodological Appendix

INTRODUCTION

Two methodological issues are central to any research study, what to research? and how to research? (Guba and Lincoln, 1994). The first of these questions was addressed in Chapter 2, which culminated in the statement of our research questions. A further issue is analysed in this appendix: how should the research be carried out? The questions that we raised at the end of Chapter 2 aim to guide and support the empirical analysis of determinants of organizational flexibility. In stating the questions we also underline the research strategy and design adopted in this research. We conducted the study in two main stages. The first one was the sectoral level of analysis and the second one – the focus of our analysis – the firm level.

The first research question – do some firms display more flexibility than others in competitive circumstances? – involved both selecting the most appropriate industries to be analysed and discovering the most suitable firms for the analysis. Regarding the selection of the industries, a common denominator throughout the 1990s was the competitive pressure that affected different industries across different sectors after the opening up of the economy to foreign competition. The general level of foreign direct investment was therefore the main factor in the selection of the industries in this study. However, different industries may differ in terms of their degree of regulation which may considerably moderate competitive pressure in a sector (Smith *et al.*, 1991). Exploring the differences between firms in extreme sectoral situations (that is, regulated sectors and sectors in transition to deregulation) can shed light on different ways of handling institutional pressure. We therefore selected the pharmaceutical industry (that is, in process of deregulation) and the edible oil industry (a deregulated industry).

Moreover, a series of indicators was created to rank the different companies in the two industries according to their organizational flexibility. The indicators highlighted a group of flexible and less flexible companies from which the firms studied in this research were chosen: two flexible and two less flexible firms from both industries.

The second stage of our research – the firm level of analysis – aimed to answer the other two broad research questions we have: why are some firms able to display more flexibility? And how they do it? This stage implied a deeper level of analysis using comparative case studies to explore the content, context and process of transformational change in the firms identified at the first stage (Pettigrew, 1990; Eisenhardt, 1989a; Pettigrew *et al.*, 1992). In so doing, we started to give shape and scope to the determinants of organizational flexibility.

The depth of the analysis needed to understand the different determinants of organizational flexibility, on the other hand, also necessitated a different approach in which multiple methods – both qualitative and quantitative – were applied. These methods were backed up by the specific literatures supporting each determinant. These methods are indicated later in this appendix and their operationalization explained in Chapter 10.

Multimethod Analysis

We needed to combine qualitative and quantitative research to help us to understand macro and micro levels of the phenomena analysed. Quantitative analysis was more suitable for the investigation of macro phenomena in our research (such as the use of indicators at the sectoral level of analysis to discover flexible firms) as well as micro level ones (such as the analysis of some of the determinants of organizational flexibility). Qualitative analysis was better suited to penetrating the meaning of micro phenomena (such as the stories presented in our case studies that illustrate the meaning actors attribute to the structural environment).

Different methods were selected to analyse the determinants of organizational flexibility. Each method was drawn from the empirical literature on each determinant. For example, demographic analysis was used to analyse the heterogeneity of the dominant coalition; coding analysis for centralization and formalization of decision making, low macroculture embeddedness and environmental scanning. Significance tests were used for heterogeneity of the dominant coalition and centralization and formalization of decision making. Finally, discourse analysis was used to understand the identity of the organization.

Table A1 briefly shows the different methods used in analysing the determinants of flexibility and their sources. The operationalization of the different methods is explained in detail in Chapter 11 where the different determinants of organizational flexibility are also analysed.

Given the broad questions with which we started, it would have been unrealistic to expect one method to satisfy all the requirements. Not only was the explanation of the firm level features that cause the phenomena deemed important in the research, but so was the identification of the phenomena at the sectoral level. We have therefore tried to find flexible and less

Table A1 Determinants and methods of analysis used

Determinant	Data sources and method/s	Sources
Heterogeneity of the dominant coalition	• Demographic analysis (quantitative variables and qualitative indicators) • Significance test • Use of qualitative data obtained from the fieldwork	Hambrick and Mason, 1984; Wiersema and Bantel, 1992; Bantel and Jackson, 1989; Murray, 1989; Webb, 1999; Hambrick, 1989
Low centralization and formalization of decision making	• Coding analysis • Significance test • Use of qualitative data obtained from the fieldwork	Webb and Pettigrew (1999); Webb, 1999
Low macroculture embeddedness	• Coding analysis • Tracking strategic initiatives • Use of qualitative data obtained from the fieldwork	Webb and Pettigrew, 1999; Damanpour, 1991
Environmental scanning	• Coding analysis • Use of qualitative data obtained from the fieldwork	Daft *et al.*, 1988; Beal, 2000; Choo, 1999; Pettigrew and Whipp, 1991
A strong organizational identity	• Analysis of speeches, discourses and letters.	Collins and Porras, 2000; Webb *et al.*, 1966; Lee, 2000; Hardy, 2001

flexible firms. Moreover, we have also tried to reveal what determines whether a firm is flexible.

Multimethod Analysis

A multiple level of analysis was required to show how firms shape their organizational flexibility. Understanding the transformation of the firms from a multilevel perspective sheds light on the historical, organizational and economic roots from which it emerged (Pettigrew and Whipp, 1991). Pettigrew (1985), however, points out that because phenomena are studied in the context of interconnected levels of analysis, the researcher must clearly delineate these levels. These levels of analysis are explained below.

In order to be aware of the business system in which firms run their business it is important to recognize those factors (that is, institutional or cultural) that either restrict or support businesses in a particular country. In his examination of organizations from both a postmodern and new organizational economics position, Clark (2000) states the importance of the study of national factors. Institutionalist (Whitley, 2000) and culturalist approaches (Hofstede, 1991) also stress the importance of studying national contexts because nations shape organizational action. In the particular case of Argentina, the process of the opening up of the economy to foreign competition, the privatization programme and political reform were fundamental factors that disrupted the national business environment during the 1990s (see Chapter 3).

The sectoral level, on the other hand, has an immediate impact on the organizational life and performance of the companies (Pettigrew, 1990; McGahan and Porter, 1997). In the case of the industries analysed in this research, edible oils and pharmaceuticals were affected by a process of deregulation that either impinged on the companies directly (such as the pharmaceutical industry) or indirectly (in the case of the edible oil industry).

Finally, the firm level of analysis – the main unit of analysis in this research – allowed us to further our understanding of organizational flexibility by looking at the transformation companies underwent (see Chapters 4–9).

Different levels of analysis also make it possible to answer different questions and reveal different causal factors. Examination of the outer context (that is, the national, sector and industry levels of analysis) raises questions

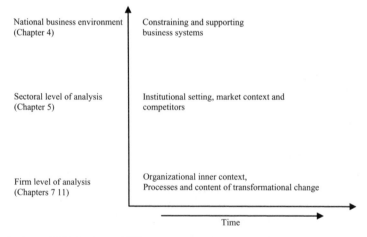

Source: Pettigrew, 1990; Pettigrew, 1992.

Figure A1   Multiple level of analysis in this research

about how high levels of competitiveness may affect the capacity of firms to adapt, transform and achieve flexibility. Similarly, levels of regulation may explain whether organizational flexibility is influenced by intermediary agents. The inner context, on the other hand, will reveal the process of transformation within the firm. The analysis of different internal processes such as managerial, structural and cultural transformations may shed light on the determinants of organizational flexibility (Volberda, 1996, 1999; Djelic and Ainamo, 1999).

SECTORAL LEVEL OF ANALYSIS

Sector Sample Selection

The pharmaceutical and edible oil industries were both chosen as sites of this research primarily as a result of the strong competitive pressures to which these industries were subject during the 1990s. The level of competition they faced during this period is indicated by the general level of foreign direct investment (FDI) and the degree of regulation (CEP, 1998).

The impact of FDI on the host economy was widely analysed in the literature on multinationals: (Hood and Young, 1979; Helleiner, 1990; Porter, 1990; Jenkins, 1991; Dunning, 1993, 1997; Jones, 1996 among others). Dunning (1993) points out that FDI can contribute as a creator and organizer of technological capacity, as an upgrader of human resources and the general welfare state. Competition might rise if FDI goes to a sector with the aim of enhancing it with innovative activities and capabilities.

However, FDI can also harm indigenous businesses. Porter (1990) demonstrates how foreign companies have driven out local car manufacturers in the British car industry. Sectoral concentration might be another outcome of FDI flowing into a sector (Evans, 1976a, 1976b; Blomstrom, 1986; Cho, 1989; Aswicahyono *et al.*, 1995).

The Argentinian economy received substantial levels of foreign investment which changed the internal dynamic of both the pharmaceutical and edible oil industries in terms of the new companies entering the industry and the levels of competition and efficiency (Helleiner, 1990; Dunning, 1993). In the 1990s, Argentina became the destination for the second largest amount of FDI in Latin America after Mexico (Toulán and Guillén, 1997). The food and pharmaceutical sectors are among those that received most FDI in the country (see Table A2). Other sectors which received a high level of FDI – such as communication (whose inward investments were more than a quarter of total FDI in the period 1990–1998), banking and

Table A2　Ranking of inward investment per sector 1990–1998

Industry	Inward investment (%)[d]
Communication[a]	25.62
Banking and financial services[b]	16.60
Food and beverages	12.03
TV[a]	11.58
Chemistry and pharmaceuticals	11.06
Telephone[a]	10.82
Commerce	7.37
Petrol[c]	5.31
Cellulose and paper	3.70
Automotive	3.50

Notes:

[a]　No indigenous businesses among the 20 largest companies in terms of turnover.

[b]　Only one indigenous bank among the 20 largest companies in terms of turnover.

[c]　This does not include the acquisition in 2000 by Repsol of YPF (the Argentinian Petrol Company).

[d]　The percentage takes into account the process of merger undertaken by MNCs. However, the inflow of foreign investment coming from the privatization process was not taken into consideration because it was mainly directed towards state owned businesses.

Source:　CEP (1998).

TV – were rejected because survival rates of indigenous businesses were too low, thus making comparison very difficult if not impossible (see Table A2).

The level of regulation of the industries, on the other hand, illustrates how regulatory agencies act to mediate competitive pressures, thereby protecting the firms from competition and market forces. As the environment in which companies operate becomes more deregulated, it provides them with greater freedom to transform their organization by adapting to environmental changes. Thus, the level of regulation in an industry can shape the demands for organizational flexibility in a firm (Grabowsky *et al.*, 1978; Mahon and Murray, 1981; Smith and Grimm, 1987). With this in mind, two industries, one regulated but in transition towards deregulation (pharmaceuticals) and one deregulated (edible oils–within the food sector) were selected.

Indicators to Identify Flexible and Less Flexible Firms

Having decided on the most suitable industries for the analysis, it was also necessary to build a set of indicators to identify the companies in the different industries according to their level of organizational flexibility. We focused our analysis on indigenous family-owned businesses following two criteria: first we wanted to analyse firms in which the process of trans-

Table A3 *Indicators of organizational flexibility in the pharmaceutical and edible oil industries*

General indicator	Customized indicators used in the pharmaceutical industry	Customized indicators used in the edible oil industry	Sources
Product innovation (innovation capacity)	Product innovation in traditional pharmaceutical products Product innovation in non-traditional pharmaceutical products	Product innovation (branding)	Eisenhardt and Tabrizi, 1995; Brown and Eisenhardt, 1997; Jonsson, 2000
Collaboration and partner-ships	Collaboration and partnerships with local competitors of foreign players	Collaboration and partnerships with local competitors of foreign players	Bahrami, 1992; Liebeskind *et al.*, 1996; Regner, 2000; Birkinshaw, 2000; Pettigrew and Fenton, 2000
International-ization	Internationalization	Internationalization	Aaker and Mascarenhas, 1984
Diversification	Diversification	Diversification	Ansoff, 1988; Webb and Pettigrew, 1999

formation was clearly observable, as in the case of family-owned firms in the 1990s; and second, we also wanted to control some of the possible sources of variation in our analysis by having a homogeneous sample of firms such as family-owned firms.

Relying on a single indicator to select the companies for a comparative study can be problematic. Problems arise because of the different nature of the industries in which companies operate, making it difficult to generalize the use of an indicator for different industries. In the light of this argument, this research adopted a combined approach in which a set of indicators deriving from the literature on organizational innovativeness and flexibility were chosen. The indicators selected were: product innovation; collaboration and partnerships; and internationalization and diversification (see Table A3).

A list of indigenous family-owned companies among the first 20 firms in the pharmaceutical and edible oil industries was compiled and ranked so as to reflect the organizational flexibility according to the indicators shown in Table A3. The indicators revealing organizational flexibility were measured as high, medium and low, and the companies were ranked accordingly.

FIRM LEVEL OF ANALYSIS

Comparative and Longitudinal Case Studies: Polar Types

The next stage of our research strategy required an investigation into what has caused the firms to develop a set of flexible capabilities to adapt quickly when environmental change occurs. The case study method was selected as the most appropriate approach for exploring the processual and contextual factors that have influenced a firm's organizational flexibility. Moreover, our case studies are accounts of the transformation process of the companies because this process sheds light on the determinants of organizational flexibility (Volberda, 1999).

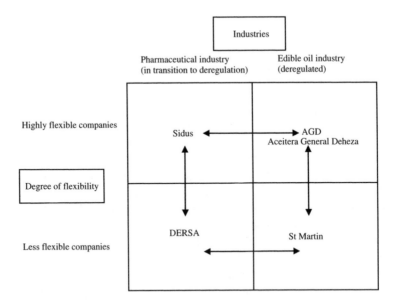

Note: The arrows indicate the comparisons undertaken in this research.

Figure A2   Highly flexible and less flexible companies in the pharmaceutical and edible oil industries

Table A4   Companies' profile[a]

Company	Industry	Related businesses	Employees (1999)	Turnover (1999) in US$ millions
AGD	Edible oils	Farming Crushing Transport (Railways/Port) Branding Distribution	1500	1042
St Martin	Edible oils	Crushing Port Branding Cotton ginning	1000	N/D
Sidus	Pharmaceuticals	Biotechnology Pharmaceutical products Retail (Pharmacies) Intermediary companies Distribution	950	232
DERSA	Pharmaceuticals	Pharmaceutical products (mainly dermatological products)	500	N/D

Note: Companies' data.

In line with Pettigrew's (1990) and Eisenhardt's (1989a) advice, in this study we chose to conduct longitudinal and comparative case studies of polar types. Due to the limited number of cases – four in total – it makes sense to choose polar types as case studies as they reflect opposite extremes of the phenomena to be studied (Eisenhardt, 1989a; Pettigrew, 1990).

Sidus (pharmaceuticals) and AGD (edible oils) emerged as the most flexible companies. DERSA (pharmaceuticals) and St Martin (edible oils) on the other hand turned out to be the least flexible firms.

Data Collection

Time frame of the study

When did the process of transformation begin in the firms under study? What time frame is the most appropriate to understand the way flexible capabilities developed? Given that there is not an absolute answer, the researcher must be guided by pragmatic considerations in order to clarify the beginning and the end of the analysis. Our time frame focused on major social breakpoints (Pettigrew, 1990; Tushman and Romanelli, 1985). As the national business environment shows, 1991 was a period of major social and economic transformation.

Longitudinal data about the transformation process in the four companies was collected covering the firms' activities over the period 1989–1999. While 1991 represents the opening up of the Argentinian economy and the starting point of market liberalization in Argentina, 1989 is a critical year for the whole economy – the peak of the 1980s economic crisis.

Interviews in the fieldwork

A total of 59 interviews were held in the companies. Pluralism in the selection of the interviewees was considered important because people from different levels of the organization's hierarchy can offer accounts of the transformation in their companies from different perspectives (Pettigrew, 1990). Accordingly, people affected by the transformation process – managers and employees, family and non-family members – and those initiators of strategic initiatives that entailed a shift in the core activities of the companies were interviewed.

Interview pro-forma

An interview pro-forma was developed following the analysis carried out in the literature review. A set of triggering questions were grouped by themes and used as a guide in the interview process.

The questions were grouped according to nine topics that sought to unravel issues about the historical background of the companies and industries (that is, the importance of the industry and economy, and the antecedents and history of the firms) and issues related to the transformation of the companies from a holistic point of view (that is, by means of an understanding of the strategy of the companies before the transformation process; changes throughout the 1990s; structure of the organization; market and products; management; governance; and, finally, values and culture). All the questions sought to understand the context, content and process of transformation of the firms (Pettigrew, 1985, 1997; Pettigrew *et al.*, 1989). The pro-forma was also useful in that it provided a consistent format for the interviews, thus conferring a certain coherence on the different interviews.

Data Analysis

So far, the research design and data collection have been explained. But what are the most appropriate methods of analysing the determinants of

Table A5   Data analysis: an interactive model

Main aspects	Main activities	Operationalization of the activity through . . .	Aims
Data reduction	• Coding and storage of data.	• Storage of data in broad categories of analysis. • Data storage on own database.	• Try to avoid 'death through data asphyxiation' (Pettigrew, 1990: 81).
Data display	• Writing up analytical chronologies.	• Analytical chronologies using suitable categories for the different companies (Pettigrew, 1990). These chronologies bear the seeds of the analysis.	• Understand the backdrop and key transformational changes in the organizations' development • Shaping the determinants of organizational flexibility.
Cross case analysis	• Comparison between the four companies using the five determinants of organizational flexibility found.	• Comparative analysis between flexible and less firms and also highlighting the differences between highly flexible firms, and between less flexible firms. • A series of methods pinned down in different literatures supporting the determinants used.	• Understanding how companies built organizational flexibility. • To find common patterns between flexible and non-flexible firms.

organizational flexibility? Huberman and Miles (1994) indicate that analysing data is an interactive operation that starts from the moment of data collection and includes also data reduction, data display, and drawing and verifying conclusions. Table A5 shows our framework for analysing the data.

The use of case studies and the analysis we undertook of them helped us to go deeper in the understanding of the determinants of organizational flexibility. This analysis, however, is far from being comprehensive and generalized to all situations. This book is a contribution to the understanding of the phenomena.

Bibliography

Aaker, D.A. and B. Mascarenhas (1984), 'The need for strategic flexibility', *Journal of Business Strategy*, **5**(2), 74–82.

Abrahamson, E. and C.J. Fombrun (1994), 'Macrocultures: determinants and consequences', *Academy of Management Review*, **19**(4), 728–55.

Ackoff, R.L. (1977), 'Towards flexible organizations: a multidimensional design', *OMEGA*, **5**(6), 649–62.

Adler, P.S. (1988), 'Managing flexible automation', *California Management Review*, **30**(3), 34–56.

Adler, P.S. (1996), 'Two types of bureaucracy: enabling and coercive', *Administrative Science Quarterly*, **41**(1), 61–89.

Adler, P.S. (1999), 'Building better bureaucracies', *Academy of Management Executive*, **13**(4), 36–49.

Albert, S. and D.A. Whetten (1985), 'Organizational identity', in L.L. Cummings and B.M. Staw *Research in Organizational Behaviour*, vol. 7, Greenwich, CI: JAI Press Inc., pp. 263–95.

Alvesson, M. (1987), 'Organizations, culture, and ideology', *International Studies of Management and Organization*, **17**(3), 4–18.

Anand, G. and P.T. Ward (2004), 'Fit, flexibility and performance in manufacturing: coping with dynamic environments', *Production and Operation Management*, **13** (4), 369–85.

Anderson, P. and M.L. Tushman (1990), 'Technological discontinuities and dominant designs: a cyclical model of technological change', *Administrative Science Quarterly*, **35**, 604–33.

Ang, S. and L.L. Cummings (1997), 'Strategic response to institutional influences on information systems outsourcing', *Organization Science*, **8**(3), 235–51.

Ansoff, I.H. (1988), *Corporate Strategy* (revised edn), London: Penguin Books.

Argyris, C. (1992), *On Organizational Learning*, Cambridge, MA: Blackwell.

Aronoff, C.E. and J.L. Ward (1997), *Preparing Your Family Business for Strategic Change*, Georgia,USA: Business Owner Resources.

Astley, G.W. and A. Van de Ven (1983), 'Central perspectives and debates in organization theory', *Administrative Science Quarterly*, **28**, 245–73.

Aswicahyono, H., K. Bird and H. Hill (1995), 'What happens to industrial structure when countries liberalize? Indonesia since the mid-1980s', *Journal of Development Studies*, **32**(3), 340–63.

Atkinson, J. and N. Meager (1986), 'Is flexibility just a flash in the pan?', *Personnel Management*, **18**(9), 26–9.

Bahrami, H. (1992), 'The emerging flexible organization: perspectives from Silicon Valley', *California Management Review*, **34**(4), 33–52.

Bahrami, H. and S. Evans (1995), 'Flexible re-cycling and high-technology entrepreneurship', *California Management Review*, **37**(3), 62–88.

Bantel, K.A. and S.E. Jackson (1989), 'Top management and innovations in banking: does the composition of the top team make a difference?', *Strategic Management Journal*, **10**, 107–24.

Barney, J.B., J.S. Bunderson, P. Foreman, L.T. Gustafson, A.S. Huff, L.L. Martins, R.K. Reger, Y. Sarason and J.L. Stimpert (1998), 'A strategy conversation on the topic of organization identity', in D.A Whetten and P.C. Godfrey (eds), *Identity in Organizations*, Thousand Oaks, CA: Sage Publications Inc., pp. 99–168.

Barr, P.S. and A.S. Huff (1997), 'Seeing isn't believing: understanding diversity in the timing of strategic response', *Journal of Management Studies*, **34**(3), 337–70.

Batley, R. (2000), 'The role of government in adjusting economies', unpublished paper prepared for the School of Public Policy, University of Birmingham, UK.

Beal, R.M. (2000), 'Competing effectively: environmental scanning, competitive strategy, and organizational performance in small manufacturing firms', *Journal of Small Business Management*, **38**(1), 24–47.

Benechi, M. (1999), 'Aceites Argentinos: como conquistar el mundo', *Revista Mercado*, January, 88–90.

Benner, M.J. and M.L. Tushman (2001), 'Process management and technological innovation: a longitudinal study of the photography and paint industries', *Business Policy and Strategy Division: Best Paper Proceedings*, Washington, DC: Academy of Management.

Bercovich, N. and J.M. Katz (1990), *Biotecnología y economía política: Estudios del caso Argentino*, Buenos Aires: Centro Editor de America Latina/CEPAL.

Biggadike, E.R. (1998), 'How CEOs, top teams, and Boards make successful transformations', in D.C. Hambrick, D.A. Nadler and M.L. Tushman (eds), *Navigating Change*, Boston, MA: Harvard Business School Press, pp. 369–94.

Birkinshaw, J. (2000), 'Network relationship inside and outside the firm, and the development of capabilities', in J. Birkinshaw and J. Hagedoom (eds), *The Flexible Firm*, Oxford: Oxford University Press, pp. 4–17.

Bisang, R. (2000), 'The responses of national holding companies', in B. Kosacoff (ed.), *Corporate Strategies Under Structural Adjustment in Argentina*, London: Macmillan Press, pp. 136–69.

Blau, P.M. (1956), *Bureaucracy in Modern Society*, New York: Random House.

Blomstrom, M. (1986), 'Multinationals and market structure in Mexico', *World Development*, **14**(4), 523–30.

Boynton, A.C. and B. Victor (1991), 'Beyond flexibility: building and managing the dynamically stable organization', *California Management Review*, **34**(1), 53–66.

Brown, S.L. and K.M. Eisenhardt (1997), 'The art of continuous change: linking complexity theory and time-paced evolution in relentlessly shifting organizations', *Administrative Science Quarterly*, **42**, 1–34.

Buckley, P.J. and M. Casson (1985), *The Economic Theory of the Multinational Enterprise*, London: Macmillan Press.

Burgelman, R.A. (1983), 'A process model of internal corporate venturing in the diversified major firm', *Administrative Science Quarterly*, **28**, 223–44.

Burgelman, R.A. (1994), 'Fading memories: a process theory of strategic business exit in dynamic environments', *Administrative Science Quarterly*, **39**, 24–56.

Burns, T. and G.M. Stalker (1961), *The Management of Innovation*, London: Tavistock Publications.

Calori, R., C. Baden-Fuller and B. Hunt (2000), 'Managing change at Novotel: back to the future', *Long Range Planning*, **33**, 779–804.

Carney, M. and E. Gedajlovic (2002), 'The co-evolution of institutional environments and organizational strategies: the rise of family business groups in the ASEAN region', *Organization Studies*, **23**(1), 1–29.

Carrera, A., E. Fracchia, H. Rocha and A. Vilaseca (2000), 'Strategic response from Argentine economic groups to the competitive shock of the 1990s', Strategic Management Society, Canada.

Carroll, G.R. (1988), 'Organizational ecology in theoretical perspective', in G.R. Carroll (ed.), *Ecological Models of Organizations*, Cambridge, MA: Ballinger Publishing Company, pp. 1–6.

CEP (Centro de Estudios para la Produccion) (1998), 'La inversion extranjera en la Argentina de los años 90, Tendencia y perspectivas', Buenos Aires: CEP.

Child, J. (1972), 'Organizational structure, environment and performance: the role of strategic choice', *Sociology*, **6**, 1–22.

Child, J. (1984), *Organization: A guide to problems and practice*, 2nd edn, London: Harper & Row.

Child, J. (1997), 'Strategic choice in the analysis of action, structure , organizations and environment: retrospect and prospect', *Organization Studies*, **18**(1), 43–76.

Child, J. (2005), *Organization. Contemporary Principles and Practice*, London: Blackwell.

Ching, H.Y. and T.T. Hsu (2006), 'The impact of dynamic capabilities with market orientation and resource-based approaches on NPD project performance', *Journal of American Academy of Business*, **8**(1), 215–29.

Cho, K.R. (1989), 'Foreign banking presence and banking market concentration: the case of Indonesia', *Journal of Development Studies*, **27**, 98–110.

Choo, C.W. (1999), 'The art of scanning the environment', *American Society for Information Science*, **25**(3), 21–4.

Clark, J. (1995), *Managing Innovation and Change*, London: Sage Publications.

Clark, P. (2000), *Organisations in Action: Competition Between Contexts*. London: Routledge.

Clark, P. and F. Muller (1996), Organizations and nations: from universalism to institutionalism, *British Journal of Management*, **7**, 125–39.

Collins, J.C. and J.I. Porras (1991), 'Organizational vision and visionary organizations', *California Management Review*, **34**(1), 30–53.

Collins, J.C. and J.I. Porras (2000), *Built to Last*, London: Random House Business Books.

Combe, I.A. and G.E. Greenley (2004), 'Capabilities for strategic flexibility: a cognitive content framework', *European Journal of Marketing*, **38**(11/12), 1456–80.

Contractor, F. (1998), 'A review of critical issues in the transformation of emerging countries', in F. Contractor *Economic Transformation in Emerging Countries*, Oxford: Elsevier Science, pp. 1–9.

Craig, T. (1996), 'The Japanese beer wars: initiating and responding to hypercompetition in new product development', *Organization Science*, **7**(3), 302–21.

Cyert, R.M. and J.G. March (1963), *A Behavioral Theory of the Firm*, Englewood Cliffs, NJ: Prentice Hall.

D'Aveni, R.A. (1994), *Hyper-Competition*, New York: The Free Press.

Dacin, T.M., J. Goodstein and R.W. Scott (2002), 'Institutional theory and institutional change: introduction to the special research forum', *Academy of Management Journal*, **45**(1), 45–56.

Dacin, T.M., M.J. Ventresca and B.D. Beal (1999), 'The embeddedness of organizations: dialogue and directions', *Journal of Management*, **25**(3), 317–56.

Daft, R. and K.E. Weick (1984), 'Toward a model of organizations as interpretation systems', *Academy of Management Review*, **9**(2), 284–95.

Daft, R. (1978), 'A dual-core model of organizational innovation', *Academy of Management Journal*, **21**(2), 193–210.

Daft, R., J. Sormunen and D. Parks (1988), 'Chief executive scanning, environmental characteristics, and company performance: an empirical study', *Strategic Management Journal*, **9**, 123–39.

Dal Bo, E. and B. Kosacoff (2000), 'Theoretical approaches to the micro-economic evidence about structural change', in B. Kosacoff (ed.), *Corporate Strategies under Structural Adjustment in Argentina*, London: Macmillan Press Ltd., pp. 7–35.

Damanpour, F. (1991), 'Organizational innovation: A meta-analysis of effects of determinants and moderators', *Academy of Management Journal*, **34**(3), 555–90.

Damanpour, F. (1992), 'Organizational size and innovation', *Organization Studies*, **13**(3), 375–402.

Damanpour, F. (1996), 'Organizational complexity and innovation: developing and testing multiple contingency models', *Management Science*, **42**(5), 693–716.

Daniel, E. and H.N. Wilson (2003), 'The role of dynamic capabilities in e-business transformation', *European Journal of Information System*, **20**, 282–96.

Dastmalchian, A. (2001), 'Workplace flexibility and the changing nature of work: an introduction', *Revue Canadienne De Sciences De L'Administration*, **18**(1), 1–4.

Delacroix, J. and A. Swaminathan (1991), 'Cosmetic, speculative, and adaptive organizational change in the wine industry: a longitudinal study', *Administrative Science Quarterly*, **36**, 631–61.

Di Tella, G. and M. Zimelman (1977), 'Período de preacondicionamiento 1876–1913', *Las etapas del desarrollo económico Argentino*, Buenos Aires-Argentina: Eudeba, pp. 37–102.

Diaz, A. (1993), 'Development of the biopharmaceutical market in Argentina and the need for innovative companies like BioSidus', in *Issues in the Commercialization of Biotechnology*, Vienna: UNIDO.

DiMaggio, P.J. and W.W. Powell (1983), 'The iron cage revisited: institutional isomorphism and collective rationality in organizational fields', *American Sociological Review*, **48**, 147–60.

Djelic, M.-L. and A. Ainamo (1999), 'The coevolution of new organizational forms in the fashion industry: a historical and comparative study of France, Italy and United States', *Organization Science*, **10**(5), 622–37.

Dreyer, B. and K. Grønhaug (2004), 'Uncertainty, flexibility, and sustained competitive advantage', *Journal of Business Research*, **57**(5), 484–94.

Dunning, J.H. (1993), *Multinational Enterprises and the Global Economy*. Reading, MA: Addison-Wesley.

Dunning, J.H. (1997), *Alliance Capitalism and Global Business*, London: Routledge.

Dutton, J.E. and J.M. Dukerich (1991), 'Keeping an eye on the mirror: image and identity in organizational adaptation', *Academy of Management Journal*, **34**(3), 517–54.

Dyer Gibb W. Jr. (1996), 'Integrating professional management into a family owned business', *Family Business Review*, (special issue), 44–50.

Dyer Gibb W. Jr. and M. Sanchez (1998), 'Current state of family business theory and practice as reflected in family business review 1988–1997', *Family Business Review*, **11**(4), 287–95.

Eisenhardt, K.M. (1989a), 'Building theories from case study research', *Academy of Management Review*, **14**(4), 532–50.

Eisenhardt, K.M. (1989b), 'Making fast strategic decisions in high-velocity environments', *Academy of Management Journal*, **32**(3), 543–76.

Eisenhardt, K.M., J.L. Kahwajy and L.J. Bourgeois III (1998), 'Conflict and strategic choice: how top management teams disagree', in D.C. Hambrick, D.A. Nadler and M.L. Tushman (eds), *Navigating Change*, Boston, MA: Harvard Business School Press, pp. 141–69.

Eisenhardt, K.M. and J.A. Martin (2000), 'Dynamic capabilities: What are they?' *Strategic Management Journal*, **21**(special issue), 1105–21.

Eisenhardt, K.M. and C.B. Schoonhoven (1990), 'Organizational growth: linking founding team, strategy, environment, and growth among US semiconductor ventures, 1978–1988', *Administrative Science Quarterly*, **35**, 504–29.

Eisenhardt, K.M. and B.N. Tabrizi (1995), 'Accelerating adaptive processes: product innovation in the global computer industry', *Administrative Science Quarterly*, **40**, 84–110.

Emery, F.E. and E.L. Trist (1965), 'The causal texture of organizational environments', *Human Relations*, **18**, 21–32.

Englehardt, C.S. and P.R. Simmons (2002), 'Organizational flexibility for a challenging world', *Leadership Organization Development Journal*, **23**, 113–22.

Escribano, J.C. (2001), 'Los Argentinos confían poco en sus instituciones', *La Nación*, 14 November, 4.

Evans, P.B. (1976a), 'Direct investment and industrial concentration', *Journal of Development Studies*, **13**(4), 373–86.

Evans, P.B. (1976b), 'Foreign investment and industrial transformation – a Brazilian case study', *Journal of Development Studies*, **13**(4), 117–39.

Ferrer, A. (1971), *La economía Argentina*, Buenos Aires: Fondo de Cultura Economica.

Floria, C. and C. García Belsunce (1992), *Historia de los Argentinos*, Buenos Aires: Editorial Kapeluz.

Floyd, S.W. and P.J. Lane (2000), 'Strategizing throughout the organization: managing role conflict in strategic renewal', *Academy of Management Review*, **25**(1), 154–77.

Fodor, J. and A. O'Connell (1972), 'La Argentina y la economía atlántica en la primera mitad del siglo XX', *Desarrollo Económico*, **13**(49), 3–65.

Fox-Wolfgramm, S.J., K.B. Boal and J.B. Hunt (1998), 'Organizational adaptation to institutional change: a comparative study of first-order change in prospector and defender banks', *Administrative Science Quarterly*, **43**(1), 87–127.

Fracchia, E. and J.P. Spinetto (1998), 'El comercio exterior Argentino y la inversión directa en los 90', Buenos Aires: *IAE (Instituto de Altos Estudios Empresariales)*.

Fredrickson, J.W. (1986), 'The strategic decision process and organizational structure', *Academy of Management Review*, **11**(2), 280–97.

Friedrich, P., L. Mesquita and A. Hatum (2006), 'The meaning of the difference: beyond cultural and managerial homogeneity stereotypes in Latin America', *Management Research*, **4**(1), 53–71.

Gagliardi, P. (1986), 'The creation and change of organizational cultures: a conceptual framework', *Organisation Studies*, **7**(2), 117–34.

Galbraith, J.R. (1994), *Competing with Flexible Lateral Organizations*. Reading, MA: Addison-Wesley.

Garcia Vazquez, E. (1995), *La política económica Argentina en los últimos cincuenta años*, Buenos Aires: Ediciones Macchi.

Georgsdottir, A.S. and I. Getz (2004), 'How flexibility facilitates innovation and ways to manage it in organizations', *Creativity and Innovation Management*, **13**(3), 166–175.

Gerchunoff, P. and L. Llach (1998), *El ciclo de la ilusión y el desencanto. Un siglo de políticas económicas Argentinas*, Buenos Aires: Ariel Sociedad Economica.

Gersick, K.E., J.A. Davis, M. McCollom Hampton and I. Lansberg (1997), *Generation to Generation. Life Cycles of the Family Business*, Boston, MA: Harvard Business Press.

Gersick, C.J.G. (1991), 'Revolutionary change theories: a multilevel exploration of the punctuated equilibrium paradigm', *Academy of Management Review*, **16**(1), 10–36.

Ghemawat, P. and T. Khanna (1998), 'The nature of diversified business groups: a research design and two case studies', *Journal of Industrial Economics*, **46**(1), 35–61.

Gnyawali, D.R. and M. Ravindranath (2001), 'Cooperative networks and competitive dynamics: a structural embeddedness perspective', *Academy of Management Review*, **26**(3), 431–45.

Golden, W. and P. Powell (2000), 'Towards a definition of flexibility: in search of the Holy Grail?' *OMEGA*, **28**, 373–84.

Goldman, S.L., R.N. Nagel and K. Preiss (1995), *Agile Competitors and Virtual Organizations*, New York: Van Nostrand Reinhold.

González Garcia, G., F. Tobar, R. Bisang, M. Limeres, C. Madies, M. Sellaues, G. Veniteram, C. Vasallo, R. Falbo and L.G. Garraza (1999), 'El mercado de medicamentos en la Argentina', Buenos Aires: CEP.

Goranson, H.T. (1999), *The Agile Virtual Enterprise*, Westport, CT: Quorum Books.

Guillén, M.F. and O.N. Toulán (1997), 'New organizational forms of internationalization in Latin America: the experience of Argentine firms', *Organization*, **4**, 552–63.

Grabowsky, H.G., J.M. Vernon and L.G. Thomas (1978), 'Estimating the effects of regulation on innovation: an international comparative analysis of the pharmaceutical industry', *Journal of Law and Economics*, **21**, 133–63.

Granell, E., D. Garaway and C. Malpica (1997), *Managing Culture for Success: Challenges and Opportunities in Venezuela*, Caracas: IESA.

Grant, R.M. (1996), 'Prospering in dynamically-competitive environments: Organizational capability as knowledge integration', *Organization Science*, **7**(4), 375–87.

Greenwood, R. and C.R. Hinings (1988), 'Organizational design types, tracks and the dynamics of strategic change', *Organization Science*, **9**(3), 293–316.

Greenwood, R. and C.R. Hinings (1996), 'Understanding radical organizational change: bringing together the old and the new institutionalism', *Academy of Management Review*, **21**(October), 1022–54.

Greenwood, R., R. Suddaby and C.R. Hinings (2002), 'Theorizing change: the role of professional associations in the transformation of institutionalized fields', *Academy of Management Journal*, **45**(1), 58–80.

Grinyer, P.H., D.G. Mayes and P. McKieran (1988), *Sharpbenders: The Secrets of Unleashing Corporate Potential*, Oxford: Basil Blackwell.

Guba, E.G. and S. Lincoln Yvonna (1994), 'Competing paradigms in qualitative research', in K. Denzin Norman and S. Lincoln Yvonna, *Handbook of Qualitative Research*, Thousand Oaks, CA: Sage Publications, Inc., pp. 105–17.

Gustafson, L.T. and R.K. Reger (1995), 'Using organizational identity to achieve stability and change in high velocity environments', *Academy of Management Journal*, best papers proceedings.

Haeckel, S.H. (1999), *Adaptive Enterprise*, Boston, MA: Harvard Business School Press.

Hage, J.T. (1999), 'Organizational innovation and organizational change', *Annual Review of Sociology*, **25**, 597–622.

Hage, J. and R. Dewar (1973), 'Elite values versus organizational structure in predicting innovation', *Administrative Science Quarterly*, **18**, 279–90.

Hambrick, D.C. (1989), 'Putting top managers back in the strategy picture', *Strategic Management Journal*, **10**, 5–15.

Hambrick, D.C. and P.A. Mason (1984), 'Upper echelons: the organization as a reflection of its top managers', *Academy of Management Review*, **9**(2), 193–206.

Hamed, K. and P. Miconnet (1999), 'Global diffusion of best practices: an analysis of the impact of national cultures at Ericson Radio Systems AB', unpublished doctoral dissertation prepared for Chalmers University of Technology, Goteborg, Sweden.

Hannan, M.T. and J. Freeman (1977), 'The population ecology of organizations', *American Journal of Sociology*, **82**(5), 929–64.

Hannan, M.T. and J. Freeman (1984), 'Structural inertia and organizational change', *American Sociological Review*, **49**(April), 149–64.

Hardy, C. (2001), 'Researching organizational discourse', *International Studies of Management & Organization*, **31**(3), 25–47.

Hargadon, A.B. and Y. Douglas (2001), 'When innovation meet institutions: Edison and the design of the electric bulb', *Administrative Science Quarterly*, **46**(3), 476–501.

Hatum, A. and A.M. Pettigrew (2006), 'Determinants of organizational flexibility: a study in an emerging economy', *British Journal of Management*, **17**, 115–37.

Haveman, H.A. (1993), 'Follow the leader: mimetic isomorphism and entry into new markets', *Administrative Science Quarterly*, **38**, 593–627.

Haynes, G.W., R. Walker, B.S. Rowe and G.S. Hong (1999), 'The intermingling of business and family finance in family-owned businesses', *Family Business Review*, **12**(3), 225–39.

Hedlund, G. (1994), 'A model of knowledge management and the N-form corporation', *Strategic Management Journal*, **15**, 73–90.

Heijltjes, M.G. (2000), 'Advanced manufacturing technologies and HRM policies. Findings from chemical and food and drink companies in the Netherlands and Great Britain', *Organization Studies*, **21**(4), 775–805.

Helfat, C.E. (1997), 'Know-how and asset complementarity and dynamic capability accumulation: the case of R&D', *Strategic Management Journal*, **18**(5), 339–60.

Helfat, C.E. (2000), 'The evolution of firm capabilities', *Strategic Management Journal*, **21**(special issue), 955–9.

Helleiner, G.K. (1990), *The New Global Economy and the Developing Countries*, Aldershot, UK and Brookfield, US: Edward Elgar.

Hickson, D.J., R.J. Butler, D. Cray, G.R. Mallory and D. Wilson (1986),

Top Decisions: Strategic Decision-making in Organizations, Oxford: Basil Blackwell.

Hofstede, G. (1980), *Culture's Consequences: International Differences in Work-related Values*, London: Sage Publications.

Hofstede, G. (1985), 'The interaction between national and organizational value system', *Journal of Management Studies*, **22**(4), 347–57.

Hofstede, G. (1991), *Cultures and Organizations: Software of the Mind*, London: McGraw-Hill Book Company Europe.

Hood, N. and S. Young (1979), *The Economies of Multinational Enterprise*, London: Longman.

Hoskisson, R.E., L. Eden, C.M. Lau and M. Wright (2000), 'Strategy in emerging economies', *Academy of Management Journal*, **43**(3), 249–67.

Hrebiniak, L.G. and W.F. Joyce (1985), 'Organizational adaptation: strategic choice and environmental determinism', *Administrative Science Quarterly*, **30**, 336–49.

Huberman, A.M. and M.B. Miles (1994), 'Data management and analysis methods', in K.N. Denzin and S.Y. Lincoln (eds), *Handbook of Qualitative Research*, Thousand Oaks, CA: Sage, pp. 428–44.

Huygens, M., C. Baden-Fuller, F.A.J. van den Bosch and H.W. Volberda (2001), 'Co-evolution of firm capabilities and industry competition: investigating the music industry, 1977–1997', Organization Studies, special issue on multilevel analysis and co-evolution, **22**(6), 971–1011.

International Family Enterprise Research Academy (IFERA) (2003), 'Family businesses dominate', *Family Business Review*, **16**(4), 235–9.

Ilinitch, A.Y., R.A. D'Aveni and A.Y. Lewin (1996), 'New organizational forms and strategies form managing in hypercompetitive environments', *Organizational Science*, **7**(3), 211–20.

IMS Health (1999), *Ranking principales laboratorios*, Buenos Aires: IMS Health.

Instituto Nacional de Estadisticas y Censos (INDEC) (1998), *Statistical Yearbook of the Argentine Republic 1998*, Buenos Aires: INDEC.

Jenkins, R. (1991), 'The impact of foreign investment on less developed countries: cross-section analysis versus industry studies', in P.J. Buckley and J. Clegg (eds), *Multinational Enterprises in Less Developed Countries*, London: Macmillan Academic and Professional, pp. 111–30.

Jones, G. (1996), *The Evolution of International Business: An Introduction*, London: Routledge.

Jonsson, S. (2000), 'Innovation in the networked firm: the need to develop new types of interface competence', in J. Birkinshaw and P. Hagstrom (eds), *The Flexible Firm*, Oxford: Oxford University Press.

Kanter, R.M. (1983), *The Change Masters*, London: International Thomson Business Press.

Katz, J.M. (1992), 'La industria farmacéutica Argentina en los años noventa', *Jornadas Internacionales de Economía de la Salud*, Insalud.

Kessler, E.H. and A.K. Chakrabarti (1996), 'Innovation speed: a conceptual model of context, antecedents, and outcomes', *Academy of Management Review*, **21**(4), 1143–91.

Ketelhohn, W., M. Moncayo and B. Allen (1998), 'Competitividad en la industria oleaginosa de America Latina', *INCAE-Centro Latinoamericano para la competitividad y el desarrollo sostenible*, Costa Rica.

Khandwalla, P.N. (1977), *The Design of Organizations*, New York: Harcourt Brace Jovanovich, Inc.

Khanna, T. and K. Palepu (2000), 'The future of business groups in emerging markets: Long-run evidence from Chile', *Academy of Management Journal*, **43**(3), 268–85.

Khanna, T. and K. Palepu (1997), 'Why focused strategies may be wrong for emerging markets', *Harvard Business Review*, **75**(July-August), 41–51.

Kimberly, J.R. (1979), 'Issues in the creation of organizations: initiation, innovation, and institutionalization', *Academy of Management Journal*, **22**(3), 437–57.

Kimberly, J.R. and M.J. Evanisko (1981), 'Organizational innovation: the influence of individual organizational, and contextual factors on hospital adoption of technological and administrative innovations', *Academy of Management Journal*, **24**(4), 689–713.

Kirkpatrick, C. (1987), 'Trade policy and industrialization in LDCs', in N. Gemmell *Surveys in Development Economics*, Oxford: Blackwell, pp. 56–89.

Kosacoff, B. (2000), *Corporate Strategies under Structural Adjustment in Argentina*, London: Macmillan Press.

Krijnen, H.C. (1979), 'The flexible firm', *Long Range Planning*, **12**, 63–75.

La Nación (various issues 1989–2000), Buenos Aires, *La Nación Newspaper*.

Lal, D. (1975), *Appraising Foreign Investment in Developing Countries*, London: Heinemann Educational Books.

Laurent, A. (1986), 'The cross-cultural puzzle of international human resource management', *Human Resource Management*, **25**(1), 91–102.

Leavy, B. and D. Wilson (1994), *Strategy and Leadership*, London: Routledge.

Lee, R.M. (2000), *Unobstrusive Methods in Social Research*, Buckingham: Open University Press.

Leonard-Barton, D. (1992), 'Core capabilities and core rigidities: a paradox in managing new product development', *Strategic Management Journal*, **13**, 111–25.

Lewin, A.Y. and M.P. Koza (2001), 'Empirical research in co-evolutionary processes of strategic adaptation and change: the promise and the challenge', *Organization Studies, Special Issue on multi-level analysis and co-evolution*, **22**(6), v–xi.

Lewin, A.Y. and H.W. Volberda (1999), 'Prolegomena on coevolution: a framework for research on strategy and new organizational forms', *Organization Science*, **10**(5), 519–34.

Lewin, A.Y., C.P. Long and T.N. Carrol (1999), 'The coevolution of new organizational forms', *Organization Science*, **10**(5), 535–50.

Lewin, A.Y., S. Massini, W. Ruigrok and T. Numagami (2002), 'Convergence and divergence of organizing: moderating effect of nation state', presentation to the AIB meeting Sydney, Australia.

Lewin, A.Y. and H. Volberda (2003), 'Co-evolutionary dynamics within and between firms: from evolution to co-evolution', *Journal of Management Studies*, **40**(8), 2111–36.

Liebeskind, J.P., A.L. Oliver, L.G. Zucker and M. Brewer (1996), 'Social networks, learning, and flexibility: sourcing scientific knowledge in new biotechnology firms', *Organization Science*, **7**(4), 428–43.

Llach, J. (1997), *Otro siglo, otra Argentina*, Buenos Aires: Ariel Sociedad Economica.

Mahérault, L. (2000), 'The influence of going public on investment policy: an empirical study of French family-owned businesses', *Family Business Review*, **13**(1), 71–9.

Mahon, J.F. and E.A. Murray Jr. (1981), 'Strategic planning for regulated companies', *Strategic Management Journal*, **2**, 251–62.

Manzone, A. (2000), 'Informe sectorial de la revista Mercado sobre distribución de productos medicinales', Buenos Aires: Revista Mercado.

March, J.G. (1995), 'The future, disposable organizations and the rigidities of imagination', *Organization*, **2**(3/4), 427–40.

March, J.G. and H.A. Simon (1958), *Organizations*, New York and London: Wiley.

Marshak, R.J. (2004), 'Morphing: the leading edge of organizational change in the twenty first century', *Organization Development Journal*, **22**(3), 8–22.

McGahan, A.M. and M. Porter (1997), 'How much does industry matter, really?' *Strategic Management Journal*, **18** (Summer special issue), 15–30.

McKinley, W. and A.G. Scherer (2000), 'Some unanticipated consequences of organizational restructuring', *Academy of Management Review*, **25**(4), 735–52.

Meyer, A.D., G. Brooks and J.B. Goes (1990), 'Environmental jolts and industry revolutions: organizational responses to discontinuous change', *Strategic Management Journal*, **11**, 93–110.

Miles, M.P., J.G. Covin and M.B. Heeley (2000), 'The relationship between environmental dynamism and small firm structure, strategy, and performance', *Journal of Marketing Theory and Practice*, **8**(2), 63–78.

Miller, D. and M.-J. Chen (1994), 'Sources and consequences of competitive inertia: a study of the US airline industry', *Administrative Science Quarterly*, **39**, 1–23.

Miller, D. and P.H. Friesen (1980), 'Momentum and revolution in organizational adaptation', *Academy of Management Journal*, **23**(4), 591–614.

Miller, D. and P.H. Friesen (1982), 'Innovation in conservative and entrepreneurial firms: Two modes of strategic momentum', *Strategic Management Journal*, **3**(1), 1–25.

Mintzberg, H., D. Raisinghani and A. Theoret (1976), 'The structure of "unstructured" decision processes', *Administrative Science Quarterly*, **21**, 246–75.

Moch, M.K. and E.V. Morse (1977), 'Size, centralization and organizational adoption of innovations', *American Sociological Review*, **42**, 716–25.

Moores, K. and J. Mula (2000), 'The salience of market, bureaucratic, and clan controls in the management of family firm transitions: some tentative Australian evidence', *Family Business Review*, **13**(2), 91–106.

Murray, A.I. (1989), 'Top management group heterogeneity and firm performance', *Strategic Management Journal*, **10**, 125–41.

Nault, B.R. and M.B. Vandenbosch (1996), 'Eating your own lunch: protection through preemption', *Organization Science*, **7**(3), 342–55.

Neubauer, F. and A.G. Lank (1998), *The Family Business*, London: Macmillan Press.

Newman, K.L. and S.D. Nollen (1998), *Managing Radical Organizational Change*, Thousand Oaks, CA: Sage Publications, Inc.

Ng, I. and A. Dastmalchian (2001), 'Organizational flexibility in Western and Asian firms: an examination of control and safeguard rules in five countries', *Revue Canadienne De Sciences De L'Administration*, **18**(1), 17–24.

Nicholson, N., A. Rees and A. Brooks-Rooney (1990), 'Strategy, innovation and performance', *Journal of Management Studies*, **27**(5), 511–34.

Noda, T. and J.L. Bower (1996), 'Strategy making as iterated process of resource allocation', *Strategic Management Journal*, **17**(special issue), 159–192.

Normann, R. (1971), 'Organizational innovativeness: product variation and reorientation', *Administrative Science Quarterly*, **16**, 203–15.

Oliver, C. (1991), Strategic responses to institutional processes, *Academy of Management Review*, **16**(1), 145–79.

Oliver, C. (1992), 'The antecedents of deinstitutionalization', *Organization Studies*, **13**(4), 563–88.

Ouchi, W.G. (1981), *Theory Z: How American Business can Meet the Japanese Challenge*, Reading, MA: Addison-Wesley.

Overholt, M.H. (1997), 'Flexible organizations: using organizational design as a competitive advantage', *Human Resources Planning*, **20**(1), 22–32.

Pettigrew, A.M. (1972), Information control as a power resource, *Sociology*, **6**, 187–92.

Pettigrew, A.M. (1979), 'On studying organizational cultures', *Administrative Science Quarterly*, **24**, 570–81.

Pettigrew, A.M. (1985), *The Awakening Giant*, Oxford: Basil Blackwell.

Pettigrew, A.M. (1987), 'Context and action in the transformation of the firm', *Journal of Management Studies*, **24**(6), 649–70.

Pettigrew, A.M. (1990), 'Longitudinal field research on change: theory and practice', *Organization Science*, **1**(3), 267–92.

Pettigrew, A.M. (1992), *Managing Change for Competitive Success*, Accounting Association of Australia and New Zealand.

Pettigrew, A.M. (1997), 'What is a processual analysis?', *Scandinavian Journal of Management*, **13**(4), 337–48.

Pettigrew, A.M. (1999), 'Organising to improve company performance', Warwick Business School, University of Warwick hot topics briefing papers.

Pettigrew, A.M. and E.M. Fenton (2000), *The Innovating Organization*, London: Sage Publications.

Pettigrew, A.M., E. Ferlie and L. McKee (1992), *Shaping Strategic Change*, London: Sage Publications.

Pettigrew, A.M. and R. Whipp (1991), *Managing Change for Competitive Success*, Oxford: Blackwell.

Pettigrew, A.M., R. Whipp and R. Rosenfeld (1989), 'Competitiveness and the management of strategic change processes', in A. Francis and P.K.M. Tharakan (eds), *The Competitiveness of European Industry*, London: Routledge, pp. 110–36.

Pettigrew, A.M., R. Whittington, L. Melin, C. Sánchez-Runde, F.A.J. van den Bosch, W. Ruigrok and T. Numagami (2003), *Innovative Forms of Organizing, International Perspectives*, London: Sage Publications.

Pettigrew, A.M., R.W. Woodman and K. Cameron (2001), 'Studying organizational change and development: challenges for future research', *Academy of Management Journal*, **44** (special research forum), 697–713.

Porter, M. (1981), 'The contributions of industrial organization to strategic management', *Academy of Management Journal*, **6**(4), 609–20.

Porter, M. (1990), *The Competitive Advantage of Nations*, London: Macmillan.

Poza, E.J. (1995), 'Global competition and the family-owned business in Latin America', *Family Business Review*, **8**(4), 301–11.

Pugh, D., R. Mansfield and M. Warner (1975), *Research in Organizational Behaviour: A British Survey*, London: Heinemann Educational.

Quinn, J.B. (1985), 'Managing innovation: controlled chaos', *Harvard Business Review*, (May-June), 73–84.

Raff, D.M.G. (2000), 'Superstores and the evolution of firm capabilities in American bookselling', *Strategic Management Journal*, **21**(special issue), 1043–59.

Ramamurti, R. (2000), 'A multilevel model of privatization in emerging countries', *Academy of Management Review*, **25**, 525–50.

Ramos, C.M. (2001), 'Empresas que progresan, pese a la crisis', *La Nación*, 8 June.

Reger, R.K., L.T. Gustafson, S.M. Demaried, J.V. Mullane (1994), 'Reframing the organization: why implementing total quality is easier said than done?' *Academy of Management Review*, **19**(3), 565–84.

Regner, P. (2000), 'Strategy in the periphery. The role of external linkages in strategy creation', in J. Birkinshaw and J. Hagedoom (eds), *The Flexible Firm*, Oxford: Oxford University Press, pp. 82–106.

Renzulli, L. (2005), 'Organizational environment and the emergence of charter schools in the United States', *Sociology of Education*, **78**(1), 1–26.

Revista Mercado (various issues 1989–1999), 'Ranking de las empresas Argentinas', Buenos Aires: Revista Mercado.

Rindova, V.P. and S. Kotha (2001), 'Continuous "morphing": competing through dynamic capabilities, form, and function', *Academy of Management Journal*, **44**(6), 1263–80.

Robertson, T.S. and Y. Wind (1983), 'Organizational cosmopolitanism and innovativeness', *Academy of Management Journal*, **26**(2), 332–8.

Rogers, E.M. (1983), *Diffusion of Innovations*, New York: Free Press.

Romanelli, E. and M.L. Tushman (1994), 'Organizational transformation as punctuated equilibrium: an empirical test', *Academy of Management Journal*, **37**(5), 1141–66.

Rosenbloom, R.S. (2000), 'Leadership, capabilities, and technological change: the transformation of NCR in the electronic era', *Strategic Management Journal*, **21**(special issue), 1083–103.

Scott, R.W. (1987), 'The adolescence of institutional theory', *Administrative Science Quarterly*, **32**, 493–511.

Sharma, S. (2000), 'Managerial interpretations and organizational context as predictors of corporate choice of environmental strategy', *Academy of Management Journal*, **43**(4), 681–97.

Singh, J.V., R.J. House and D.J. Tucker (1986), 'Organizational change and organizational mortality', *Administrative Science Quarterly*, **31**, 587–611.

Slappender, C. (1996), 'Perspectives on innovation in organizations', *Organization Studies*, **17**(1), 107–29.

Smith, K.G., C.M. Grimm, M.J. Gannon and M.-J. Chen (1991),

'Organizational information processing, competitive responses and performance in the US domestic airline industry', *Academy of Management Journal*, **34**(1), 60–85.

Smith, K.G. and C.M. Grimm (1987), 'Environmental variation, strategic change and firm performance: a study of railroad deregulation', *Strategic Management Journal*, **8**, 363–76.

Sondergaard, M. (2001), 'Organizational adaptation in the global business environment: the role of managerial intentionality in organizational adaptation in case of ABB 1988–1999', EGOS Conference. sub-theme 24: 'Mastering strategic renewal and organizational change in times of deconstruction', Lyon, France.

Stimpert, J.L., L.T. Gustafson and Y. Sarason (1998), 'Organizational identity within the strategic management conversation', in D.A. Whetten and P.C. Godfrey (eds), *Identity in Organizations*, Thousand Oaks, CA: Sage Publications, Inc., pp. 83–98.

Stinchombe, A.L. (1965), 'Social structure and organizations', in J.G. March (ed.), *Handbook of Organizations*, Chicago, IL: Rand McNally, pp. 142–93.

Sull, D.N. (1999a), 'Why good companies go bad', *Harvard Business Review*, **77**(4), 42–52.

Sull, D.N. (1999b), 'The dynamics of standing still: Firestone Tire & Rubber and the radial revolution', *Business History Review*, **73**, 430–64.

Sylla, R. and G. Toniolo (1991), *Patterns of European Industrialization. The Nineteenth Century*, London: Routledge.

Teece, D.J., G. Pisano and A. Shuen (1997), 'Dynamic capabilities and strategic management', *Strategic Management Journal*, **18**(7), 509–33.

The Economist (2001), 'Corruption index', 30 June (section: emerging market indicators).

The Economist (2002), 'Special report: Argentina's collapse', 2 March, 26–30.

Thomas, J.B., S.M. Clark and D.A. Gioia (1993), 'Strategic sensemaking and organizational performance: linkages among scanning, interpretation, action, and outcomes', *Academy of Management Journal*, **36**(2), 239–270.

Thompson, V.A. (1965), 'Bureaucracy and innovation', *Administrative Science Quarterly*, **10**, 1–20.

Thomson, N. and C.C.J.M. Millar (2001), 'The role of slack in transforming organizations', *International Studies of Management and Organization*, **21**(2), 65–83.

Tidd, J., J. Bessant and K. Pavit (1997), *Managing Innovation*, Chichester: Wiley.

Tomlinson, R.C. (1976), 'OR, Organizational design and adaptivity', *OMEGA*, **4**(5), 527–37.

Toulán, O. and M.F. Guillén (1997), 'Beneath the surface: the impact of radical economic reforms on the outward orientation of Argentine and Mendozan firms, 1989–1995', *Journal of Latin American Studies*, **29**, 395–418.

Trompenaars, F. (1992), *Riding the Wages of Cultures. Understanding Cultural Diversity in Business*, London: Nicholas Brealey Publishing.

Tushman, M.L. and W. Smith (2001), 'Technological change, ambidextrous organizations and organizational evolution', in J.A.C. Baum (ed.), *Companion to Organizations*, Maldon, MA: Blackwell Publishers.

Tushman, M.L., and P. Anderson, (1986), 'Technological discontinuities and organizational environments', *Administrative Science Quarterly*, **31**, 439–65.

Tushman, M.L. and E. Romanelli (1985), 'Organizational evolution: a metamorphosis model of convergence and reorientation', *Organizational Behavior*, **7**, 171–222.

Van de Ven, A. and M.S. Poole (1995), 'Explaining development and change in organizations', *Academy of Management Review*, **20**(3), 510–40.

Van de Ven, A., D.E. Polley, R. Garud and S. Venkataraman (1999), *The Innovation Journey*, Oxford: Oxford University Press.

van Eijnatten, F. and G.D. Putnik (2004), 'Chaos, complexity, learning, organization: towards a chaordic enterprise', *The Learning Organization*, **11**(6), 418–429.

Volberda, H.W. (1996), 'Toward the flexible form: how to remain vital in hypercompetitive environments', *Organization Science*, **7**(4), 359–74.

Volberda, H.W. (1997), 'Building flexible organizations for fast-moving markets', *Long Range Planning*, **2**, 169–83.

Volberda, H.W. (1999), *Building the Flexible Firm*, Oxford: Oxford University Press.

Volberda, H.W., C. Baden-Fuller and F.A.J. van den Bosch (2001), 'Mastering strategic renewal: mobilising renewal journeys in multi-unit firms', *Long Range Planning*, **34**, 159–78.

Ward, J.L. (1987), *Keeping Family Business Healthy: How to Plan for Continued Growth, Profitability, and Family Leadership.* San Francisco, CA: Jossey-Bass.

Webb, D.L. (1999), 'The temporal development of strategy: patterns in the UK insurance industry', Unpublished doctoral dissertation for the Warwick Business School, University of Warwick, UK.

Webb, D.L. and A.M. Pettigrew (1999), 'The temporal development of strategy: patterns in the U.K. insurance industry', *Organization Science*, **10**(5), 601–21.

Webb, E., D.T. Campbell, R.D. Schwartz and J. Sechrest (1966), *Unobtrusive Measures*, Chicago: Rand McNally & Company.

Weick, K.E. (1979), *The Social Psychology of Organizations* (2nd edn), Reading, MA: Addison-Wesley.

Westphal, J.D. and E.J. Zajac (2001), 'Decoupling policy from practice: the case of stock repurchase programs', *Administrative Science Quarterly*, **46**, 202–28.

Whipp, R. and P. Clark (1986), *Innovation and the Auto Industry*, London: Frances Pinter.

Whitley, R. (2000), *Divergent Capitalisms: The Social Structuring and Change of Business Systems*, Oxford: Oxford University Press.

Whitley, R. (1991), 'The social construction of business systems in East Asia', *Organization Studies*, **12/1**(001–028), 1–25.

Whittington, R. and A.M. Pettigrew (2003), 'Complementarities, change and performance', in A.M. Pettigrew, R. Whittington, L. Melin, C. Sanchez-Runde, F.A.J. van den Bosch, W. Ruigrock and T. Numagami (eds) *Innovative Forms of Organizations: International Perspectives*, London: Sage (Chapter 7).

Whittington, R. and M. Mayer (2000), *The European Corporation: Strategy, Structure and Social Science*, Oxford: Oxford University Press.

Wiersema, M.F. and K.A. Bantel (1992), 'Top management team demography and corporate strategic change', *Academy of Management Journal*, **35**(1), 91–121.

Wolfe, R.A. (1994), 'Organizational innovation: review, critique and suggested research directions', *Journal of Management Studies*, **31**, 405–31.

Woodward, J. (1965), *Industrial Organization: Theory and Practice*, London: Oxford University Press.

Yoguel, G. (2000), 'Responses of Small and medium-sized enterprises', in B. Kosacoff (ed.), *Corporate Strategies Under Structural Adjustment in Argentina*, London: Macmillan, pp. 100–135.

Yoguel, G. and D. Milesi (2001), '*Technological and organizational capabilities for the development of competitive advantages. The case of successful SME exporters in Argentina*', Buenos Aires: unpublished paper-Instituto de Industria- Universidad Nacional de General Sarmiento, accessed at www.druid.dk/conferences/nw/paper 1/Yougel_ milesi.pdft.

Zahra, S.A., and P. Sharma (2004), 'Family business research: a strategic reflection', *Family Business Review*, **17**(4), 331–46.

Zahra, S.A., R.D. Ireland, I. Gutierrez and M.A. Hitt (2000), 'Privatization and entrepreneurial transformation: emerging issues and a future research agenda', *Academy of Management Review*, **25**(3), 509–24.

Zaltman, G., R. Duncan and J. Holbek (1973), *Innovations and Organizations*, New York: Wiley.

Zammuto, R.F. and E.J. O'Connor (1992), 'Gaining advanced manufacturing technologies' benefits: The role of organization design and culture', *Academy of Management Review*, **14**(4), 701–28.

Zilber, T.B. (2002), 'Institutionalization as an interplay between actions, meanings, and actors: the case of a rape crisis center in Israel', *Academy of Management Journal*, **45**(1), 234–54.

Zondra, A.Z. and C.R. Hinings (1998), 'Organizational diversity and change in institutional theory', *Organization Studies*, **19**(5), 743–67.

Zysman, J. (1983), *Governments, Markets and Growth: Financial Systems and the Politics of Industrial Change*, New York: Cornell University Press.

Subject index

Name index